HURON COUNTY LIBRARY

W9-CKD-183

HURON COUNTY LIBRARY

HURON COUNTY LIBRARY
0030470224

When Cultures Clash

Case Studies in Multiculturalism

Second Edition

John W. Friesen

Detselig Enterprises Ltd.
Calgary, Alberta

DEC 24 1993

3286

John W. Friesen

The University of Calgary

Canadian Cataloguing in Publication Data

Friesen, John W.
   When cultures clash

   ISBN 1-55059-069-3

   1. Multiculturalism – Canada.*   2. Canada –
Population – Ethnic groups – Case studies.*
I. Title.
FC104.F74 1993   971'.004   C93-091478-3
F1035.A1F74 1993

© 1993 Detselig Enterprises Ltd.
210, 1220 Kensington Rd. N.W.
Calgary, Alberta T2N 3P5

All rights reserved. No part of this book may be reproduced in any form or by
any means without permission in writing from the publisher.

Printed in Canada   SAN 115-0324   ISBN 1-55059-069-3

To my wife, Virginia Agnes,

my caring companion and colleague

Other Books by John W. Friesen

Readings in Educational Philosophy, 1968

Cultural Change and Education (co-author), 1969

Religion for People: An Alternative, 1972

Profiles of Canadian Educators, (co-author), 1974

Canadian Education and Ideology: Readings, 1975

People, Culture & Learning, 1977

Teacher Participation: A Second Look (co-author) 1978

The Metis of Canada: An Annotated Bibliography (co-author), 1980

Schools as a Medium of Culture, 1981

The Helping Book, 1982

Strangled Roots, 1982

The Teacher's Voice, (co-author), 1983

Schools With a Purpose, 1983

A Multicultural Handbook for Teachers, 1984

When Cultures Clash: Case Studies in Multiculturalism, 1985

A Multicultural Handbook for Teachers, No. 2, 1986

Reforming the Schools – for Teachers, 1987

Rose of the North, 1987

The Evolution of Multiculturalism (co-author), 1988

The Community Doukhobors: A People in Transition (co-author), 1989

Introduction to Teaching: A Socio-cultural Approach (co-author), 1990

The Cultural Maze: Complex Questions on Native Destiny in Western Canada, 1991

Multiculturalism in Canada: Hope or Hoax? (1992).

Contents

Financial support provided by the Alberta Foundation for the Arts, a beneficiary of the Lottery Fund of the Government of Alberta.

Preface

By now it is almost old hat to speak of teaching university courses in multiculturalism or working in the area of multicultural education. At our institution, The University of Calgary, such courses have been offered since 1968. Like other universities such as Trent, Brandon, and Saskatchewan, Calgary's beginnings focussed primarily on the area of Native education, while the University of Alberta as early as early as 1970 made available a degree in "intercultural education." By now the phenomenon of multiculturalism has spread nation-wide and even American universities have taken up the challenge. Clearly the field has come of age.

It is encouraging to witness and be a part of the development of an exciting new field. Perhaps because of this close attachment it is also possible to point out the possible weaknesses of multiculturalism or to caution against over-optimistic illusions which usually accompany the rapid growth of any promising academic enterprise. Each time a new theory or methodology emerges in academia there are those who rally around as though the new thrust may represent a panacea for all pedagogical ills. While multiculturalism certainly holds its share of promise for producing a better-educated generation, it also has its share of pitfalls. Two such potential snares should be mentioned here.

Human beings are complex creatures. Almost any approach to the study of humankind will soon reveal that we exhibit many similarities and differences. This endeavor has produced a myriad of academic fields such as psychology, sociology, social psychology, anthropology and other social sciences, each of which is dedicated to the analysis of a "bit part" of the human enterprise. Because of the promise of the field, multiculturalists can easily become convinced of their having a fine edge in delineating how humans interact, but this may constitute a very limiting perspective. Cultural differences are important, but they do not singly comprise the telescope by which to view or explain all of human behavior. Besides, frequently humans will manifest greater individual differences as members of a given cultural configuration than may be apparent between individuals from *differing* cultural affiliations. In addition, there are many uniquenesses and differences among people which do not necessarily have a cultural explanation. These may derive from physiological, psychological or other human characteristics and may best be analyzed through other than multiculturally-related methods. Rather than a panacea, multiculturalism, at best, represents a partial explanation of human identities and lifestyles. Its conceptualizations and revelations must always be placed side-by-side with those of other disciplines which concern themselves with trying to understand the phenomenon of human functioning. In that sense, multiculturalism is not a leader, but a partner.

A second potential pitfall for students of multiculturalism has to do with the danger of inductive generalizing. It may be quite possible after some serious study to gain a good grasp of how another culture, different from one's own, may function. The insights gleaned from such study should be useful in explaining different patterns of human behavior, but they may have severe limitations in attempting to explain still another, or third, cultural configuration. In short, to understand how Hutterite society functions to some degree may be of limited use in trying to grasp the underpinnings of the French, Chinese or Sikh communities. While humans and human cultures share commonalties, they also possess uniquenesses or eccentricities, and it is not always easy to know when one or the other is in play. Thus multiculturalists need to tread unfamiliar cultural turf with some degree of caution.

It is always helpful when working in the context of the social sciences to set a particular study in the framework of related research and theory. This, the beginning chapters of his book are intended to provide. The discussion will include a look at the development of multiculturalism, provide an outline of its theoretical base (often rooted in what has become known as "ethnic studies,") and illustrate its more practical applications in the area of multicultural education. Some comparative observations between developments in the United States and Canada are also provided.

The case studies presented in this volume comprise ethnically-grounded examples set in an educational context, i.e., they show how five distinct ethnic communities have tried to deal with the challenge of cultural maintenance through the medium of schooling. The case studies include the so-called "charter nations of Canada," consisting of the French and English peoples, two Anabaptist groups (Hutterites and Mennonites), a specific Chinese community and the Sikh people in Canada. While each group has revealed a slightly varied approach to the challenge, there is consensus on the idea that the school is a principle vehicle for ensuring cultural identity and perpetuity.

In preparing a work of this magnitude one naturally build a series of obligations to individuals and institutions whose help has been invaluable in completing the work. I would therefore like to thank the various leaders who represent the ethnic communities which I have visited for the purpose of garnering information for this book. They have been helpful and kind in welcoming me and in sharing valuable information about their people. I would like to thank Kim Lan for providing the information for chapter nine which offers an intense look at schooling in her own community, the Chinese of Calgary. Martha Loeman of the Department of Educational Policy and Administrative Studies at the University of Calgary deserves special mention for secretarial assistance and my students need to be acknowledged and complimented for their patience and receptiveness to my trying out new ideas and teaching approaches through the years. I also want to thank my wife, Virginia Lyons Friesen, for her constant support and encouragement. I have grown to rely on her insight and assistance and I also want to acknowledge her ready collegiality in the field of multiculturalism.

Finally, though I hereby publicly render thanks to all of these people for their assistance, I must acknowledge that the ideas and interpretations (and mistakes) in this book are mine, and I am prepared to discuss and (I hope) defend them.

John W. Friesen
The University of Calgary

1

Multiculturalism as a Way of Life

The inherent complexities of Canada's multicultural make-up are usually overshadowed by the publicity which its attending slogans generate. In fact, it is only recently that formal recognition of the concept has been initiated. At first attention was focussed on the notion of a tri-part cultural make-up consisting of the Aboriginal peoples, the founding nations of French and English plus the many immigrate groups who chose Canada as their home at the turn of this century, particularly during the years 1890-1914. The beginning of this period marks the start of a major immigration movement which ends with the onslaught of World War One. Each of the three subsections of Canadian multiculturalism has a special history and through the years since Confederation has added a unique flavor to our multicultural mosaic. Add to this the impact of the steady stream of newcomers who continue to migrate here from various continents, and the result is a very culturally-rich and diverse society.

Towards Policy Formation

In the last two decades Canadian leaders have worked very hard to promote public awareness of and appreciation for the multicultural make-up of our national society. These efforts have been founded on a history of complex, albeit quite recent undertakings. Massive immigration to Canada essentially ceased with World War One, and it was not until the centennial year in 1967 that anyone thought much about formalizing any acknowledgment of the emerging Canadian multicultural identity. Thus Canadian multiculturalism is not exactly the result of long-term thinking (Friesen, 1977). Until a few decades ago the charter groups of French and English were satisfied to direct Canada's institutional life, and they were not too eager, nor did they see any advantage in sharing their power and wealth with incoming groups. In fact, some English groups still persist in viewing themselves as superior citizens and French Canadians have been loath to regard themselves as an ethnic group. Some English-Canadians do not want to recognize that anglo-dominance is a thing of the past while the French have concentrated their power-seeking in Quebec (McLeod, 1984). In the meantime, the strength of numbers and the enhanced quest for a voice in political policy-making on the part of incoming ethnic groups has afforded the notion of multiculturalism a sizable momentum. The text of the British North America Act acknowledged only the needs and institutional structures of the two dominant cultures, English and French. Aboriginal peoples were virtually ignored, and ethnocultural groups who migrated to Canada after 1867 ended up working in menial jobs, but they were often grateful for the opportunity to make a fresh start in a new land.

The first threat to British domination in the west came with the large influx of peoples at the turn of this century. The national plan was that all newcomers would simply bow to the establishment and gradually take on (assimilate) the values and trappings of dominant society. Within the period between 1901 and 1911, Canada's population rocketed by 43 percent, making the immigrant population rise to 22 percent of the nation's whole. In 1911, people of non-British and non-French origins formed 34 percent of the population of Manitoba, 40 percent of the population of Saskatchewan, and 33 percent of the population of Alberta (Palmer, 1984). There were early signs that the assimilationist philosophy was not completely effective in that arriving immigrants were *not* being absorbed into the dominant monoculture. National leaders could not understand why this was so, partially because their own ethnocentrism blinded them from appreciating any form of cultural diversity. A key factor in hindering assimilation was the nature of settlement patterns designed for immigrant groups, namely the bloc settlements. In effect, what was perceived as an excellent vehicle for incoming ethnic communities to retain their cultural ties with one another developed into secluded empires of alienation from the rest of society (Epp, 1974, Bagley, et al., 1988; Taylor, 1991).

By world war one, little had changed, and there were efforts to convince all new Canadians that loyalty to the Canadian nation and to the British Empire were synonymous and fundamental. The hyphenated Canadian was discriminated against and a series of negative ethnic stereotypes arose regarding Oriental and European groups who emphasized their peasant origins. In some circles it was even considered fashionable to be ethnically prejudiced. Although Canadians in the various regions reacted a bit differently, a general pattern could be identified in the west. As Palmer notes,

> In general, the differences among the western provinces in their pattern of ethnic relations are minor, the similarities among them more apparent. Belief in the superiority of Anglo-Saxons in particular and northern Europeans in general was deeply entrenched in all of the western provinces prior to World War II and all were dominated by a Protestant Anglo-Saxon elite. . . . the post-war period in each province saw the growth of greater tolerance generated by new social, economic and intellectual conditions (Palmer, 1982, 179-180).

Despite their negative regard, immigrants were actively recruited because of the need for cheap labor. The actual numbers of people admitted was reduced between the two major wars, affected no doubt by the economic depression which struck the nation. A restrictive immigration policy was put in place, showing a clear preference for immigrants from more "civilized countries." Also, now a different kind of human resource was being actively pursued, namely people with particular skills and experience appropriate to the emerging technological age. International competition for this kind of person had increased and thus the search had to be widened to nations not previously on the immigrant list (Scott, 1981).

The period after the Second World War is often considered to be one of adjustment to the devastation of international conflict. Even though this nation was drawn together after peace-making, many pre-war prejudices remained. Simultaneously, the arrival of many intellectuals among the postwar refugees from Eastern Europe, coupled with an enhanced motivation for upwardly mobility among many second and third generation resident non-angloCanadians, forced the issue of inequality out into the open. Increased intermarriage and residential dispersion also worked to break down traditional stereotypes and weaken previous rationalizations for discrimination. Though the period of the decade of the nineteen fifties is generally regarded as that of a "quiet revolution," the demand for greater government recognition on the part of "other ethnic groups" continued and gained momentum.

By the early nineteen sixties Canadian participation in various forums on human rights and fundamental freedoms was greatly increased. The American civil rights movement certainly influenced this nation, and forced attention on several neglected minorities, for example, Blacks in the U.S.A. and Canadian Native peoples. The central theme of the campaign was to provide opportunities to neglected minorities in an effort to "bring them up to par with the rest of society." Unfortunately, this implied that all responsibility to make emendations to motivation or lifestyle to fit the mainstream lay within the minority camp.Central to this position was the assumption that education would be *the* vehicle by which to accomplish the goal; good teaching and good education would serve to equalize opportunity and minimize differences (Friesen, 1985, 11).

On December 17, 1962 the federal government appointed the Royal Commission on Bilingualism and Biculturalism to "enquire into and report on the existing state of bilingualism and biculturalism in Canada and to recommend what steps should be taken to develop the Canadian Confederation on the basis of an equal partnership between the two founding races, taking into account the contributions made by the other ethnic groups to the cultural enrichment of Canada" (Friesen, 1991, 244). When the commission finally reported in 1970 it supported and encouraged the charter status of the French even though there was a great deal of opposition to the commission's conclusion about *charter* nations, as though the other nationalities did not matter. Many non-British and non-French groups, along with the Ukrainians in particular, disputed the notion that Canada was a *bicultural* nation. At least 25 percent of the nation's population was of other than British or French origins, over two hundred newspapers were being published in other than French or English, there were many fairly well-defined Italian, Jewish, Slavic and Chinese neighborhoods in larger Canadian cities, and there were visible concentrations of Ukrainians, Doukhobors, Mennonites and Hutterites, etc. scattered across the prairies. In fact, the only region in Canada that could truly be called bilingual and bicultural was the Province of New Brunswick, and it contained only about 2 or 3 percent of the total population of Canada. About one-fourth of the population of New Brunswick spoke French at home and two-thirds spoke English.Other languages were spoken less than 10 percent of the time (Driedger, 1978, 12).

An examination of the regions in Canada other than New Brunswick quickly establishes that Canada is indeed a regional mosaic. Prime Minister John G. Diefenbaker liked to compare Canada to a garden, rife with a wide variety of vegetables but with a unity of purpose. Still, the differences between the multilingual and multicultural northwest and the unilingual and unicultural east, for example, were then and still are significant. In addition, no one can ignore the presence and uniqueness of the French, least of which is their current political aspiration for separatism.

On October 8, 1971, Prime Minister Pierre Elliott Trudeau rose in the House of Commons to announce support for a policy of multiculturalism to complement the existing policy of official bilingualism. Though unrelenting on the question of official bilingualism, the government was now prepared to guarantee that every ethnic group would have the right to preserve and develop its own culture and values within the Canadian context. The government immediately set out to initiate programs to promote official multiculturalism in accordance with the following principles:

1. The Government of Canada will support all of Canada's cultures and will seek to assist, resources permitting, the development of those cultural groups which have demonstrated a desire and effort to continue to develop, a capacity to grow and contribute to Canada, as well as a clear need for assistance;
2. The Government will assist members of all cultural groups to overcome cultural barriers to full participation in Canadian society;
3. The Government will promote creative and interchange among all Canadian cultural groups in the interest of national unity; and
4. The Government will continue to assist immigrants to acquire at least one of Canada's official languages in order to become full participants in Canadian society (Canada, 1971, 8545-46; Remnant, 1976).

Many provinces quickly responded to the federal government's initiative by formulating multicultural programs of their own. A quick survey of provincial action, from west to east, shows their initial and more recent efforts in this regard.

Provincial Responses

British Columbia was slow to respond to the multicultural challenge, choosing to rely on an ad hoc committee on multiculturalism in education to define a policy and organize a colloquium on methods of implementation. The committee's recommendations were finally implemented in 1990 when a formal provincial policy on multiculturalism was announced through the office of the Provincial Secretary. Responsibilities of the policy are carried out through the Cabinet Committee on Multiculturalism. In announcing the policy the Premier made two somewhat quizzical demands of British Columbians: first, the elimination of the barriers which isolate individuals and groups from society as a whole, and a corresponding commitment by individuals to the central values which unite the country.

Alberta created the Alberta Cultural heritage Act in 1984 which was amended in 1987 to become the Alberta Multicultural Act. A Cabinet Committee on Cultural Diversity was established in 1983 and a Multicultural Advisory Council was identified in 1990. Other significant actions sponsored by the government include the Ghitter Commission on Tolerance and Understanding in 1984 and the ongoing Native Education Project. There is little question about the adequacy of appropriate legislation in effect in Alberta and there is no shortage of research pertaining thereto. As is undoubtedly the case in other provinces, and in the nation as a whole, public attitudes and actions will still determine the extent to which pluralism will be valued in Alberta.

Saskatchewan passed an Act on multiculturalism in 1984 to encourage multiculturalism in the province. Specifically, the Act would provide assistance to individuals and groups to increase opportunities available for them to learn about the nature of cultural heritages and the concomitant contributions of these communities to provincial culture. Initial services pertaining to the operational aspects of the policy had a distinct linguistic base. In 1989 the Minister of Saskatchewan Parks, Recreation and Culture released the Task Force Report on Multiculturalism in Saskatchewan and a great deal of controversy emanated from it. Startled by the results of the task force, in 1990 the government quickly responding by re-naming the department, Culture, Multiculturalism and Recreation. Its responsibilities were transferred to the Provincial Family Foundation the following year.

Manitoba offered the first response to federal action by formulating a provincial policy in 1972, designed with a view to redressing social and racial inequity. The anticipated goals of the policy were to: identify and remove barriers to equal participation; eradicate ethnic and racial discrimination; create a climate in which the principles of multiculturalism would be applied to all aspects of Manitoba life and society; and assure a proactive role in the protection of minority rights (Creamer and Sheridan, 1986). In 1990 the province established a Multicultural Secretariat to fulfill the mandate of the Manitoba Intercultural Act which was renewed in 1983. The government remains committed to guaranteeing for its citizens: the freedom and opportunity to express and foster their cultural heritage, the freedom and opportunity to participate in the broader life of society, and the responsibility to abide by and contribute to the laws and aspirations which unite society.

The Ontario Advisory Council on Multiculturalism was established in 1973 (and renewed in 1983) to monitor the delivery of programs and policies affecting cultural minorities, newly settled immigrants and Native peoples. A document issued in 1979 suggested that the goals of provincial policy were to a produce a bias-free curriculum, offer instruction in heritage languages and seek to improve Native education. In 1982 legislation was passed to incept the Ministry of Citizenship and Culture. In addition a variety of parallel activities have been undertaken by other departments and a series of useful publications have been made available. On June 24, 1987, the Minister of Citizenship and Culture announced a new strategy for multiculturalism in Ontario, and in 1990 outlined specific directions to be undertaken. The ministry mandate is to: promote the full participation of all the people of Ontario, regardless of culture or race in the development of the social, economic and cultural life of the provinces and to foster a shared identity which also respects the diversity of cultures and races in Ontario.

The Province of Quebec has consistently avoided any acknowledgement of the term "multiculturalism," premised on the belief that the nation has only *two* valid cultures, French and English. In 1981, however, the province initiated an *intercultural* policy designed for these express purposes: to preserve Quebec's French character; to promote respect for the principle of equality of individuals; to develop tolerance understanding and openness between ethnocultural communities, and the francophone communities; and to encourage full participation in Quebec society. A revised Act came into effect in 1985 and was renewed in 1990 through the Department of Cultural Communities and Immigration.

In 1986, the Province of New Brunswick tabled a Policy on Multiculturalism based on four principles: equality, appreciation, preservation of cultural heritages, and participation. The purpose of the document was to reduce ethnic and racial discrimination, help newcomers overcome cultural barriers, increase public understanding of the province's multicultural composition, encourage the retention of cultural heritage and provide access to one of the official languages. A Ministerial Advisory Committee was also established and reports annually to the Minister of Labour who is responsible for multiculturalism.

In 1979, the Nova Scotia Department of Education established an Ethnic Services Division with responsibilities for human rights education, multicultural education and education programs for visible minorities. Accordingly, the division has worked closely with the provincial teachers' union to develop in-services workshops. The union developed a broad policy on multiculturalism and within the next two years produced a handbook for teachers (McCreath, 1981). In 1989 the Department of Tourism and Culture passed an Act to Promote and Preserve Multiculturalism and set up a Cabinet Committee on Multiculturalism as well as an Advisory Committee.

Like Quebec, Prince Edward Island initially interpreted the bicultural and multicultural federal policies literally, arguing that they primarily have relevance for the national scene with the greatest value in urban settings. The province's leaders view island life as a uniculture, enriched by four main cultural groups: Scottish, Irish, Acadian and Native. From this perspective, federal policies have limited value in terms of promoting understanding about the Island's culture. However, in 1988 the Department of Community and Cultural Affairs established a formal policy on multiculturalism and set up a Ministerial Advisory Council which reports annually to Cabinet.

Newfoundland does not consider multiculturalism a major issue and has no formal policy, although support for all cultural groups is provided through the Newfoundland Multicultural and Folk Arts Council. For example, the Department of Education offers university courses in heritage languages and a special interest course in ethnic cooking, fiddle music and transitional theatre. Responsibility for multiculturalism currently rests with the Department of Municipal and Provincial Affairs, but it may be transferred to the Minister of Education.

Both Yukon and the Northwest Territories are currently without formal policies on multiculturalism though these responsibilities are delegated to the Departments of Education and Culture and Communications respectively.

While provincial governments were scurrying to meet the challenge of federal policy, Ottawa was continuing to expand its original vision to additional programming. Some critics argued that much of the activity was mere busywork and without substance (Lupul, 1982). Still, in an effort to maintain a high profile, in 1988, the House of Commons passed Bill C-93, an Act for the preservation and enhancement of multiculturalism in Canada. Opposition critics like M.P. Margaret Mitchell, for example, argued that the act was endangered by the failure of federal leaders to denounce hard-line threats against the policy. For example, Mitchell called on the Tory government to publicly denounce resolutions passed by the national Reform Party which campaigned vigorously to dismantle multiculturalism in favor of a melting-pot policy.

The federal government has defended its record of involvement in such areas as: race relations and cross-cultural understanding, heritage languages, community support, corporate activities, citizenship registration, national literacy program, voluntary action program and human rights. In light of the many other pressures currently on the government because of a shrinking economy it is doubtful that any significant actions will be undertaken on the multicultural scene in the immediate future.

A flurry of multicultural activity has been the trend in pretty well every sector of society in the last decades ranging from ethnic potluck dinners and festivals to international exchange programs. Generally speaking, these activities have been fostered without much substance, and have included three fairly superficial or negative objectives, namely: celebrations, curiosity and condescension. Multicultural *celebrations* have featured what might be called the "fun-food-festivals-and-finery" theme under the guise of fostering a substantial degree of intercultural understanding. At best these activities radiate a warm, albeit temporary feeling of fascination, but lack thoroughly in any dimension of meaningful intercultural exchange. The *curiosity* focus of multiculturalism is usually practiced as a lopsided form of interaction comprising an unhealthy attitude on the part of one party in relation to another. From this perspective others are viewed as objects of fascination because of their cultural affiliations – something out of the ordinary to be studied from afar or treated as unusual. The explanation for this stance emanates from an inadequate or erroneous concept of other cultures. Their validity is not appreciated; they are not seen as equal to one's own. A stronger form of this perspective results in a *condescending* demeanor towards other cultural perspectives, and the hope is expressed that "inferior" cultures can be helped to attain a degree of validity. Descriptions of viewpoints differing from one's own are frequently accompanied with expressions like, "it's too bad about those people." Clearly this approach leaves much to be desired in terms of fulfilling any kind of effective or sensitive mandate for multiculturalism.

There are at least four ways in which a more efficacious form of multiculturalism can be initiated in Canada. These include: case studies, consciousness-raising, confrontation and communication. To effectively undertake a *case study* requires a form of empathy when seeking to attain a measure of understanding about another way of life. It can hardly be achieved from reading a textbook, though this route is often attempted at the university level. For best results it involves meaningful inter-personal and inter-cultural contact and interaction. Such times require mutual respect and engagement in some form of activity which is non-threatening, pleasant, mutually-interdependent and long-term.

Public *consciousness-raising* programs about multicultural concerns have emphasized the extent to which prejudice and racism are rampant in our society (McKague, 1991). Proponents of public awareness programs have found that it is no longer sufficient simply to inform the public about intolerance and racism; effective programs need to be devised and marketed so that these negative forces can be abated if not completely eradicated. In the final analysis it will be a matter of basic societal values. The final word on the matter will be determined by the extent to which society is willing to make adjustments to alleviate inequity and other forms of what is essentially cruelty to others.

Confronting unpleasant situations is never an easy undertaking, but it is often essential if inequity is to be rectified. Multicultural educators have a prior obligation in this regard, however, and that is to confront their own feelings of ethnocentrism or intolerance before they can embark on any kind of public clean-up campaign. No one is raised without *some* element of cultural bias even though one might wish that this were not the case. Denial will not eliminate personal orientation or preference but some form of therapy might help with the process, even if primarily based on introspection. The act of confrontation, therefore, begins at home. When this agenda item has successfully been fulfilled, it may be quite appropriate to launch a more public campaign.

Communication experts advise that even the most rudimentary form of communication involves careful listening and responding with exactness to the communicated message. An effective response first implies checking out the exact nature of the message which the sender intended to communicate, and once the message has been confirmed by both parties, to offer a response. This process may appear somewhat simplistic at the outset, but once it is tested in an inter-cultural setting, involving quite different methods of sending and receiving messages, the complexities of such a situation become clearer – or do they?

What the Critics are Saying, and it's Not Always Nice

No one can deny the historical multicultural makeup of Canada even though it is only recently that any kind of serious attention has been paid to the feasibility of its operation. By "serious attention" is meant the legal-political kind of intent which specific legislation and other formal kinds of enactments imply.

One of the signs by which the legitimacy of a field of endeavor may be determined is by its becoming the target of severe analysis and criticism. Such writings can also serve as a kind of validation for a "discipline," indicating that its concerns and emphases have been taken seriously. Any field of endeavor which attracts a significant amount of attention indicates that its status has a firmer foundation than a fad, craze or fleeting interest. Against this background it can readily be substantiated that multiculturalism comprises a valid academic and practical educational enterprise.

Criticisms of multiculturalism tend to focus on both formal policy and practical function. Five major recurring criticisms will be examined here, each of which offers a logical and well-founded basis of objection, even though contrary arguments are also substantive. No celebration of the foundation of a field of inquiry is complete without a measure of self-examination and some heed to the concerns of the critics. At the very minimum the process can serve to clarify basic assumptions and thus, hopefully, to improve the field.

A Hindrance to National Unity

When the British North America Act was initiated in 1867 a two-nation culture was conceived based on the concept of "charter nations," meaning those peoples who "started the country." No acknowledgement was made of the Aboriginal peoples who were already here, and no one anticipated the subsequent cultural and political impact that immigrant groups would later have on the nation. During the 1960s, when Canadian participation in the "search for freedom and human rights" climaxed, the groundwork was laid to elaborate a working definitive explanation of Canada's nationhood. There were those who worried about *any* chance for a national identity to emerge, what with all the diverse groups searching for a unique niche in the nation's fabric. Thus when Prime Minister Lester B. Pearson announced the formation of a Royal Commission on Biculturalism and Bilingualism, the nation was poised to receive a definitive statement concerning the nation's cultural and linguistic composition.

The ink was barely dry on the Bi-and-Bi Report when the voices of those omitted in its contents argued that the composition of the nation was much more complex than the report indicated. Opponents to the pronouncements of the report quickly pointed out that the Canadian demographic profile revealed approximately 75 distinct ethnic or cultural distinctions across the land (Wood, 1980; Scott, 1981). In an effort to adjust to this reality, the federal government quickly reverted to a policy of multiculturalism to complement the existing policy of official bilingualism (Friesen, 1985).

The federal policy represented an attempt to rectify the error of the Bi-and-Bi Report and created a lifetime of work for writers dedicated to picking it apart. The media were particularly critical, arguing that the policy would feed splintering and separatism by making individual ethnic origin a matter for public debate. One writer blasted the government for spending millions of dollars in grants to "put the sheepskin back into ethnic coats" (Zolf, 1982). The government was accused of spending the money of the majority to appease the desires of a few. Instead of fostering a sense of nationhood, the government was accused of suggesting that Canadian citizens not just look back with affection on their heritage, but they were force-fed to do so at public expense (Gwyn, 1974). As one editorial questioned, "Do we want a common sense of citizenship based on shared values, despite our varied origins, or a more technical sense of citizenship based on the appreciation of how few values we do share, despite our passports?" (Globe and Mail, 1988). In this sense, multiculturalism should be seen as downright dangerous to the survival of the Canadian culture" (Zolf, 1982).

Early critics of multiculturalism liked to posit an "either-or" situation with regard to the question of national identity. Apparently, multiculturalism either fostered or hindered national identity; there was no middle road. Besides, it was argued, such reporting obviously made for more sensational "journalism." If proponents of multiculturalism did not participate in the parade to celebrate national identity, the critics argued, the nation would be splintered into a myriad of little islands of varying European cultures. It was one or the other; no man can serve two masters. The energies of these critics would perhaps have better been spent on defining just exactly what comprises Canadian culture, rather than blindly defending what might have been a non-entity at that point in time. A national study in the centennial year indicated that high school students knew very little about Canadian history and geography (Hodgetts, 1968). If national identity was at stake in the wake of the multicultural tidal wave, it would be well to know exactly what kind of culture the nation was losing. As Hodgetts put it, Canada's high school graduates "... are entering a society that does not yet possess the capacity to understand its position or maintain it with balance and charity..." (Hodgetts, 1968).

The Reply

Critics of the pluralist principle as a basis for societal operation often make the familiar error of believing that an assimilating society is a unified society. The example of the United States is frequently referred to in arguing for a more uniform way of life (Ehlers and Crawford, 1983), but there is evidence that the American melting-pot concept has not augured with equity for all ethnic groups in the U.S.A. Partially fuelled by the civil rights movement of the 1960s, which stressed for the need to maintain diversity and cultural pluralism in America, melting pot-theory was simply too totalitarian-oriented for the freedom seekers of the nineteen (Madaus, et al., 1989, 279).

Observers of the multicultural scene often erroneously assume that common bonds exist among members of the various ethnic groups resident in Canada, and they apparently speak with one voice as a community in terms of their cultural maintenance objectives (Burnet, 1984). Along with other myths about multiculturalism, the common error has been to gloss over the many differences inherent in any specific ethnocultural group, i.e., with respect to: region of concentration, time of arrival, occupation, income, education, physical characteristics, relations with homeland, degree of ethnic awareness and capacity for collective action (Burnet, 1984). With regard to homeland relations, for example, Canada sometimes attracts what have been called, "suitcase immigrants," that is, people who migrate here because of political unrest at home, but their dream is to return home when the conflict has abated. Some groups even send money home to help "finance the revolution." In this sense a distinction may be drawn between political refugees and immigrants, on the basis of their having different motivations for emigrating. For the most part we would *like* to think that when people migrate to Canada they will thank their lucky stars for the rest of their lives for being given such a wonderful opportunity to start life over again. Realistically, such is not always the case.

When seriously considering the complexities inherent in the melting-pot philosophy, cultural pluralism, by contrast, begins to take on a freshness of meaning. Since we are not all alike anyway, why not work out a formula that would be more functional in meeting the needs of a diverse community instead of aiming at total conformity? There are several difficulties to work out in this regard, of course, but the potential is appealing.

In the first place, theorists, educators and multicultural practitioners must rid themselves of the erroneous notion that conflict is necessarily adverse, or that paradoxes, differences, inconsistencies and inefficiency are dishonorable traits. Try raising a family of five children with exactly the same formula of expectations for each child! History shows that the various ethnocultural communities in Canada have negotiated a variety of "deals" with governments in power, many of which are inconsistent with the rights granted to other groups. For example, the Aboriginal Peoples use the "right of first arrival"; they consider themselves "citizens-plus" when it comes to rights, and they further support their argument with the observation that the treaty-making process was negotiated on a *nation-to-nation* basis. This was a unique happening and no other group resident in the country can make that claim.

On a different but familiar note, the French and English majorities like to refer to the BNA Act as affirmation of their "charter" status which somehow gives them a continuing right to pattern Canadian institutional operations after the style of their particular homeland. And there are other examples as well. Sometimes rights are given and taken away. When the railroad was finished in 1885, the Chinese were no longer wanted in the country and their right of entry was forbidden. When the Second World War broke out the Japanese were suddenly considered undesirables and their possessions were confiscated. Hutterites were welcomed to Alberta after World War One, but twenty-five years later, when citizens considered them a threat to the farming industry, the Social Credit Government virtually abolished their right to buy more land in Alberta. Finally, when the Mennonites arrived in Canada in 1874 they were given the right to buy land without taking an Oath of Allegiance to the Crown. Thirty years later, another incoming group, the Doukhobors, had their lands confiscated and placed on the public market because they refused to sign an Oath of Allegiance. No one bothered to tell them that, like the Mennonites, they might have kept their land by bypassing the taking of an oath and simply "solemnly affirming" that their word was reliable (Friesen, 1985).

Complexities and contradictions are part and parcel of the operations of a pluralist society. The notion that we should pursue as social goals a complete absence of conflict and strive for complete unanimity on all issues is both unworkable and unrealistic. It would be more fruitful if a workable method was found to accommodate individual and group differences and disparities, without a detriment to our nation-hood, since these appear to be an inevitable part of Canadian life. Moreover, there are numerous benefits to be gained from an enlarged perspective of society which cannot possibly be incorporated in a singular, conformist view of society.

Perhaps the most fundamental question that multiculturalists have to deal with is this: to what extent is it possible to have a viable social structure in which each of the parts affirms and asserts its own identity while paying *some* attention to the totality of the structure? (Bancroft, 1979). In this context multiculturalism cannot be isolated as a social policy without examining its political and economic dimensions as well Cole, 1989). In a pluralist society the question of where minorities fit into the larger mosaic is a wide-angled question. Discrimination and intolerance are not merely *social* happenings that can be isolated from other societal processes. The discriminated person will feel the most harsh effect of that practice in the political and economic domains. Intolerance and discrimination are applied to the job market, housing, education and in the lack of political clout with equal severity to those occurring in the social arena.

A Sop to the Ethnics

Critics have not minced words in condemning the selective basis on which multicultural funding has sometimes been done. Keith Spicer, who was appointed to head a national commission a few years ago to determine what Canadians want as a nation, called it a "sop to the ethnics" (Spicer, 1988; Macleod, 1989). Cynicism has developed because *some* ethnic leaders have allegedly discovered that multicultural dollars are available to fund private parties and pleasure trips for ethnic leaders (Fisher, 1987). The phrase, "the great Canadian mosaic" has become music to the ears of Canadian politicians vying for extra votes. Further, for a little expense the government has hindered the development of nationhood in Canada by promoting the hyphenated Canadian. "Centuries from now, the dictionary will offer this definition: 'HYPHEN – a horizontal dash from ancient writings, now used only in Canada to identify tribes'" (Macleod, 1989). In essence, then, the government is accused of paying *some* Canadians for having an ethnic background just to gain votes. They may also inadvertently have contributed to creating a new class of political power brokers within each ethnic group. . . (*Globe and Mail,* 1988). Maximized, government policy may also contribute toward disintegration within the ethnic community by encouraging inter-group fighting for funds or for a place in the country's political power class. Thus the potential clout of the country's third national force (besides English and French) will be rendered politically impotent (Spicer, 1988).

The ethnic ledger in Canada clearly shows that some Canadians are more equal than others. Most institutional life is patterned after British and French models, and Native peoples occupy the bottom rung on the nation's ladder of success. This can easily be borne out with statistics on income, for example. The rest of the country is the "ethnic third" which tries to climb higher on the ladder of economic success but is limited by a lack of familiarity with established institutional processes. By fostering multiculturalism, the third force is appeased into believing that some day, they will make it too (Zolf, 1982).

As Porter noted in the early stages of multicultural development, economic forces have created the inequalities of ethnic stratification. The advantage of such a system provides the building up of a labor force for a particular type of economy (Porter, 1972). Thus the system is maintained for a very practical purpose and safeguarded with inbuilt techniques such a limited degree of interaction, intimacy and social distance between classes.

The Reply

The bottom line for most institutional changes in Canada has to do with money. Funding for multiculturalism, while certainly not extensive, has increased since the policy was incepted in 1971. To suggest that its promotion is significant, however, is to exaggerate a very limited segment of government activity. A few spin-off industries may have developed as a result, but for the most part it is business as usual in Canada, with or without the trappings of multiculturalism.

Opponents of multiculturalism often defend the dominant anglo hold on society (French in Quebec), under the guise of wanting Canadians to develop an identity of a "single distinctive people" (Epp, 1988). Naturally, this identity will have familiar anglo markings and thus the future is predictable. The weakness of this contention is that it adheres to the established myth about British villainy and the unremitting oppression of other ethnic groups by those of British origin (Burnet, 1984). Once in place, the function of this myth is that it justifies any shortcoming by members of other ethnic groups since it limits their chances of success. Should success be achieved, however, it is the exception to the rule and probably due to happenstance. In actuality, many individuals with immigrant-sounding names *have* done well in economic-political terms, but not sufficiently to squelch the myth of anglo-saxon arrogance.

An objective appraisal of multicultural successes reveals that its original promulgation may have been based on benevolent albeit condescending terms. On the other hand, any attempt to bridge the gap between newcomers and established citizens is better than none. We must be prepared to admit, however, that any form of multiculturalism has its limitations. After all, perhaps the anglo middle-class lacks the ability to understand or teach about other cultures radically different from their own (Cole, 1989). Unless the various enthnocultural communities buy into the multicultural process by becoming equal partners in the giving and receiving of information, multiculturalism may indeed be only a sop. If so, it will be a sop to *all* participants in the enterprise.

Magnifying Differences

A common concern about multiculturalism is that it fosters separatism, cultural isolation and ethnocentrism (Bibby, 1990). The complaint goes, "If you encourage multiculturalism, you threaten national unity.... Measuring attitudes of school children can only provoke negative attitudes from them" (Kehoe, 1984). At first glance these concerns have a ring of sincerity about them, but a even a slightly deeper probe reveals that they are, in essence, quite ethnocentric. A further concern goes, "If different ethnic groups are encouraged to retain their distinctive cultures, they will ultimately be denied equality of opportunity in the larger society (Kehoe, 1984). While sounding like the pleas of a concerned citizen, it takes only a little analysis to identify the patronizing tone of this utterance.

The either-or nature of the above charges is simplistic, but clear. You can't have one without the other, it is argued. Either you promote multiculturalism, or you promote national unity. If you teach about differences, you foster conflict. If ethnocultural minorities keep their cultures, they will lose out economically. Of course no social process works out just the way it is perceived in a fluid democracy, and there is no reason why such a formula should dictate the exact results in a multicultural context. Life is simply much more complicated than that.

The Reply

Wood suggests that multiculturalism, or the encouragement of cultural pluralism *does* threaten democracy and well it should (Wood, 1980). Too much separateness can be harmful to a society just as too much togetherness can be. The educational process in a democracy values, above all else, the development of reasoning abilities, wisdom and morality in the individual. There is basically no other means by which the inevitable process of cultural evolution can be guided (Hutcheon, 1975). Democracy requires total input from all of its participants if the search for truth is taken seriously. Diversity and digression are valued commodities in such an enterprise. Without the free and continual juxtaposing of differing experiences and perceptions, the process may be severely limited. In this sense multiculturalism is a blessing, not a bane.

A corollary discussion to the argument about splintering Canadian society by encouraging cultural pluralism raises the question of affirmative action. Affirmative action is based on the principle that society should offer each individual an equal chance to experience "the good life." The primary tack of this approach is to arrange for extraordinary opportunities for disadvantaged groups so as to provide a path to equality for them. If this means that some people should be given an "extra" chance to catch up with the rest of society, so be it

(Friesen, 1989). Presumably the process is based on a form of natural law and reinforced in the well-known maxims of the great religions of the world – Christianity, Buddhism, Islam, Hinduism, etc. (Garcia, 1982). Opponents of affirmative action argue that it perpetuates invidious distinctions by attaching advantage to them (Moodley, 1984).

For the record, affirmative action is part and parcel of the Canadian past. Its framework may be extended back to the constitution itself. The BNA Act explicitly recognizes the legitimacy of groups – those of religion and of language – and accords rights or privileges to members of one group which do not exist for another, for example, the act guarantees educational rights for the use of both English or French in the federal parliament and the federal and Quebec courts. Thus there are both historical and legislative precedents for granting *some* Canadians, defined by ascription, special treatment (Weinfeld, 1981). To argue otherwise is to negate our country's history.

Charter Nation Objections

Fearful of losing its status as a charter nation, the French community has opposed Canada's multicultural policy from the beginning. The French see multiculturalism as a threat to be shunned, because any admission to the legitimacy of cultures in Canada other than English or their own, they feel, is an admission to equality which they do not prefer to make. In essence the French community has been uneasy about a possible loss of their rights since the 1960s (Lupul, 1978). The Royal Commission on Bilingualism and Biculturalism established English and French as official languages and cultures, and French-speaking citizens "thought they had it made." After all, for them this was an up-to-date interpretation and reaffirmation of the intents of the BNA Act.

Their peace of mind was short-lived, for with the passing of the Multicultural Act of 1971, their culture was relegated to the same status as that of immigrants, newcomers and the Aboriginal Peoples. Even today the Government of Quebec prefers use of the word "intercultural" when discussing multicultural matters, though considerable legislation about understanding other lifestyles has been passed.

The wording and possible intent of Quebec government decrees on "multi-cultural," however, are positive and generous (Wilson, 1984). Although there is no formal provincial educational policy on intercultural/multicultural education to date, citizens of Quebec have been encouraged to: (1) ensure the maintenance and development of cultural communities, other than French, in their midst; (2) sensitize themselves to the enrichment brought by other cultural communities; and (3) promote their integration into Quebec society (Zinman, 1988).

The results of a recent study indicate that the Quebecois believe more strongly than other Canadians that immigrants often bring discrimination upon themselves by their refusal to integrate with Canadian society. The responsibility of immigrants is to try harder to be like other Canadians. French Canadians are particularly opposed to further immigration from England, the United states and Italy. They are also strong in their belief that the cultural assimilation of immigrants is mandatory. They also have grave doubts about the value of immigrant contributions to this country (Lambert and Curtis, 1983).

The Reply

Undoubtedly many francophone concerns about possible cultural loss due to enhanced multiculturalism in Canada are well-founded. As the face of Canada's cultural makeup has changed, partially due to continued immigration, and partially due to the growth of the dominant monoculture, the Quebecois have witnessed a diminishing quality of French culture. With today's improved forms of communication, enhanced media role and greater ease of transportation, Canadians are being drawn closer together. We see the same television programs, watch the same movies and read the same books. Every Canadian can watch every act of government (in replay) every night on television. With common knowledge comes a common identity. Thus, Canada will "come to be."

Parallel to the concern about possible cultural loss is the germ of French nationalism, based in Quebec. It is not an isolated development, for its birth paralleled ethnic movements which were occurring everywhere in the world, and in many cases leading to the birth of new nations (Burnet, 1987). A variety of factors have fuelled this stance in the last two decades and there is uncertainty in the minds of many Canadians as to what effect possible Quebec independence will have on the rest of the country.

Inadequate Theoretical Base

Several decades ago academics would have been amused by the proposal that studies in the "discipline of multiculturalism" should be advanced by the institutions of higher learning. The first such course was offered on the campus of The University of Calgary in 1968 on Saturdays and without remuneration for the instructors, because the department administrator felt that such an offering lacked appropriate academic justification. The course went ahead, and was gradually endorsed as a legitimate involvement for a university. Three years later, when a graduate level course in multiculturalism was proposed to the Department of Educational Foundations, the majority of department faculty voted against the plan on the grounds that multiculturalism lacked a disciplinary base and was thus not qualified as a course offering at the graduate level. In retrospect, this view seems almost archaic now.

The charge of inadequacy of theory and disciplinary attachment is not new to academe. The fields of sociology and anthropology, among other social sciences have been made to "pay their dues" through the passage of time and through the accumulation of appropriate publications. They have had to earn their place in the hall of fame of legitimate academic pursuits. The study of education as a discipline was a concern of its critics in the 1960s and departments of educational foundations, for example, hardly dared to claim such a measure of legitimacy for themselves in that same time frame. As "fate" would have it, many of these departments have since been refurbished or transformed through rebirth in the name of "policy and/or administrative studies."

As the literature in multiculturalism has grown in the last two decades, its markings have been diverse, for example, under the guise of ethnic or intercultural studies, minority or ethnocultural studies, or studies of cultural pluralism and even racism. These writings have been produced by a variety of researchers with a respected credibility in the fields of sociology, anthropology, political science, ethnology, history, education and even policy and administration.

A twist in the road to identifying the parameters of multicultural studies reveals strong educational leanings when the practical aspects of the field are explored. For this pursuit the term, *"multicultural education"* is usually employed, and frequently incorporates the concerns of women, the rights of children and religious groups and the issues important to many other contemporary parties (Tiedt and Tiedt, 1990). Educators argue that the first goal of multicultural education is to develop competencies for functioning within the context of multiple cultures and to provide members of all cultural groups with equal educational opportunity (Bennett, 1990). Its mandate is to assist students in gaining understanding of and appreciation for alternative lifestyles and cultural options, including one's own background (Pasternak, 1979).

There are those who charge that multicultural studies were originated as a means of encouraging ethnocultural peoples to maintain their respective identities. Such research then comprises a method of condoning the transplanting of foreign cultures and languages to a new location. Of course there are legal and economic ramifications, as well as ideological concerns and those pertaining to social structure (Burnet, 1981; Anderson and Frideres, 1981). In effect, these are corollary problems to the whole notion of cultural pluralism and thus render the pursuit of defining a theoretical base for multiculturalism that much more difficult.

The Reply

The multicultural reality of Canada's population necessitates the formulation of both a definition and the elaboration of a policy and lends an urgency to the entitlement of a needed field of study. Canadian governments have assisted in the attainment of these goals through a multiplicity of federal and provincial endeavors. As the academic literature continues to mount the validity of the enterprise gradually takes form, almost inadvertently because of the sheer pressure to find a rubric under which to classify it in library holdings. In time, the various dimensions of the *discipline,* (if we dare to use that word), will also be fleshed out and the question of legitimacy and validity will become as so many "scholarly" things are, "elementary, my dear Watson!"

References

Anderson, Alan B. & James S. Frideres. (1981). *Ethnicity in Canada: Theoretical perspectives.* Toronto: Butterworths.

Bagley, Christopher, Harold Coward & John W. Friesen. (1988). *The evolution of multiculturalism.* Calgary: The Calgary Institute for the Humanities.

Bancroft, George. (1979), A place to stand – What place for the minorities in multi-culturalism? *Multiculturalism,* 2(3), 17-21.

Bennett, Christine I. (1990). *Comprehensive multicultural education: Theory and prac-tice.* Second edition. Boston: Allyn and Bacon.

Bibby, Reginald W. (1990). *Mosaic madness: The poverty and potential of life in Canada.* Toronto: Stoddart.

Burnet, Jean. (1981). Multiculturalism as a state policy. *Ethnicity, power and politics.* Jorgen Dahlie and Tissa, eds. Toronto: Methuen.

Burnet, Jean. (1984). Myths and multiculturalism. *Multiculturalism in Canada: Social and educational perspectives.* Ronald J. Samuda, et al., eds. Toronto: Allyn and Bacon.

Burnet, Jean. (1987). Multiculturalism in Canada. *Ethnic Canada: Identities and ine-qualities.* Leo Driedger, ed. Toronto: Copp Clark Pitman, 65-81.

Canada, House of Commons. (1971). *Debates,* October 8.

Cole, Mike. (1989). Chance for a Change. *The Guardian* (London, U.K.), Tuesday, May 30.

Creamer, Brian & Sheridan. (1986). *Provincial multicultural agencies and policies.* (Prepared for the House of Commons Standing Committee on Multiculturalism). Ottawa: Minister of Supply and Services.

Driedger, Leo. (1978). *The Canadian ethnic mosaic: A quest for identity.* Toronto: McClelland and Stewart.

Ehlers, Henry & Dean Crawford. (1983). Multicultural education and national unity. *Educational Forum*, XLVII(3), Spring, 263-277.

Epp. Ernie. (1988). Multiculturalism should bring all Canadians closer. *Ottawa Citizen*, July 29.

Epp, Frank H. (1974). *Mennonites in Canada, Vol. 1, 1786-1920.* Toronto: Macmillan.

Fisher, Douglas. (1987). Multicult has peaked. *The Calgary Sun,* December 3.

Friesen, John W. (1977). *People, culture & learning.* Calgary: Detselig Enterprises.

Friesen, John W. (1985). *When cultures clash: Case studies in multiculturalism.* Calgary: Detselig Enterprises.

Friesen, John W. (1989). Institutional response to multicultural policy: A Pilot Study of the Business Sector. *Multicultural and intercultural education: Building Canada.* Sonia V. Morris, ed. Calgary: Detselig Enterprises. 13-24.

Friesen, John W. (1991). *The cultural maze: Complex questions on Native destiny in western Canada.* Calgary: Detselig Enterprises.

Garcia, Ricardo. (1982). *Teaching in a pluralistic society.* New York: Harper.

Globe and Mail. (1988). At the Cultural Crossroads. Saturday, June 4.

Gwyn, Sandra. (1974). Multiculturalism: A threat and a promise. *Saturday Night,* February, 15-18.

Hodgetts, A. B. (1968). *What culture? What heritage? A study of civic education in Canada.* Toronto: Ontario Institute for Studies in Education.

Hutcheon, Pat Duffy. (1975). *A sociology of Canadian education.* Toronto: Van Nostrand.

Kehoe, Jack. (1984). *A handbook for enhancing the multicultural climate of the school.* Vancouver: Western Development Group.

Kreutzweiser, Erwin. (1979). Canada, a Mosaic? *Chelsea Journal,* July/August.

Lambert, R. D. & J. E. Curtis. (1983). Opposition to multiculturalism among Quebecois and English Canadians. *Canadian Review of Sociology and Anthropology, 20*(2), May, 193-207.

Lupul, Manoly R. (1978). Multiculturalism and educational policies in Canada. *Multi-culturalism. 1*(4), 13-16.

Lupul, Manoly, R. (1982). The Political implementation of multiculturalism, *Journal of Canadian Studies,* 17(1) 93-102.

Macleod, Stewart. (1989). Subsidizing the hyphenated Canadian. *Maclean's.* January 9.

Madaus, George F., Thomas Kellaghan & Richard L. Schwab. (1989. *Teach them well: An introduction to education.* New York: Harper and Row.

McCreath, Peter L,. Ed. (1981). *Multiculturalism: A handbook for teachers.* Halifax: Nova Scotia Teachers' Union.

McKague, Ormond. (1991). *Racism in Canada.* Saskatoon: Fifth House Publishers.

McLeod, Keith A. (1984). Multiculturalism and multicultural education, in Ronald J. Samuda, et al., eds. *Multiculturalism in Canada: Social and educational perspectives.* Toronto: Allyn and Bacon, 30-49.

Moodley, Kogila A. (1984). The predicament of racial affirmative action: A critical review of equality now. *Queen's Quarterly. 94*(4), Winter, 795-806.

Multiculturalism and Citizenship Canada, (1991). *Operation of the Canadian multiculturalism act,* Annual report, 1989-90, Ottawa: Minister of Supply and Services.

Palmer, Howard. (1982). *Patterns of prejudice:A history of nativism in Alberta.* Toronto: McClelland and Stewart.

Palmer, Howard H. (1984). Reluctant hosts: Anglo Canadian views of multiculturalism in the twentieth century, in John R. Mallea & Jonathan C. Young, eds. *Cultural diversity and Canadian identity: Issues and innovations.* Ottawa: Carleton University Press, 21-40.

Pasternak, Michael G. (1979). *Helping kids learn multi-cultural concepts.* Champaign, Ill.: Research Press.

Porter, John. (1972). Dilemmas and contradictions of a multi-ethnic society. *Transactions of the royal society of Canada.* IV:X, 193-205.

Remnant, Robert. (1976). Our multicultural policy: Vive la difference, *Canada and the world,* 42:, October, 12-13.

Scott, Gil.(1981). Multiculturalism in Canada. *Multiculturalism: A handbook for teachers.* Peter L. McCreath, ed. Halifax: Nova Scotia Teachers' Union, 24-32.

Spicer, Keith. (1988). The best and worst of multiculturalism. *The Ottawa Citizen,* July 13.

Taylor, K.W. (1991). Racism in Canadian immigration policy, *Canadian Ethnic Studies,* XXIII (1) 1-20.

Tiedt, Pamela & Iris M. Tiedt. (1990). *Multicultural teaching: A handbook of activities, information, and resources. Third edition.* Boston: Allyn and Bacon.

Weinfeld, Morton (1981). The development of affirmative action in Canada. *Canadian Ethnic Studies.* XIII (2), 23-39.

Wilson, J. Donald. (1984). Multicultural programmes in Canadian education. *Multiculturalism in Canada: Social and educational perspectives.* Ronald J. Samuda, et al., eds. Toronto: Allyn and Bacon, 62-77.

Wood, Dean. (1980). Multiculturalism: Appreciating our diversity. *Accord,* November/December, 7.

Zinman, R. (1988). *A multicultural/multiracial approach to education in the schools of the protestant school board of greater Montreal.* Montreal: Report of the Task Force on Multicultural Education, The Protestant School Board of Montreal.

Zolf, Larry. (1982). How multiculturalism corrupts. *Maclean's,* November 15, 21.

2

Multiculturalism in Theory and Practice

As the field of multiculturalism in Canada has continued to expand, academics concerned about its theoretical validation have postulated suppositions which are often at variance but have raised serious questions about its theoretical base. Some scholars, in fact, take issue with the very suggestion that multiculturalism is a legitimate field, borrowing as it does from a multiplicity of disciplines without necessarily working the results into a theoretical whole. Undoubtedly, the only way to still the voices of the critics is to analyze the continually burgeoning literature and work towards some kind of solidification of inherent or created concepts and assumptions.

Building A Framework

Generally speaking, multiculturalism is an emerging social science, featuring a developmental frame-work that borrows heavily from a variety of related fields.

Basic Assumptions

In essence the foundation for the study of muliculturalism rests on four presuppositions enunciated by social scientists generally. These include:

a. Human nature is varied. In fact, there are often greater differences among individuals who are members of any particular racial or cultural group than they are among individuals with varying cultural origins or allegiances. This questions the concept that there are self-contained, pure groups which are readily distinguishable from one another and that the differences between these groups are unbridgeable.

b. The concept of "the good life" serves as a universal goal toward which most cultures strive and functions as a kind of universal binding force among people. It has been demonstrated that the characteristics of the good life find almost complete unanimity among peoples of almost any ethnic, racial or cultural background. These include such items as desiring decent living conditions, valuing respect for one's fellows, equality before the law, etc.

c. A new emphasis on the concept of individuality is emerging. This orientation de-emphasizs the particular background (cultural, physiological, familial, etc.), of the individual and suggests respect for the person. In a real sense the social sciences have already done much to overcome the mischievous tendency toward label thinking.

d. Generosity and goodwill are indicative of healthy personal adjustment. There is evidence to indicate that those who go through life striving to show that exclusiveness is an essential ingredient to cultural purity, are psychologically maladjusted. It has been shown, for example, that continuous excessive anger brings about illness, whereas kindness and goodwill promote a relatively well-balanced psychological and physical well-being (Overstreet, 1962).

In recent decades multiculturalism has emerged as a vital force dedicated towards promoting a more enlightened citizenry who will respect each other's cultures and languages (Mazurek and Kach, 1990). A brief examination of the growth and development of the field will illustrate the complexity of this undertaking.

Origins of Multicultural Education

Originally defined as "intercultural education," the field of multicultural education represents the working arm of Canadian multiculturalism. After all, if the practical implications of the area were to be properly attended, what better place than in the schools of the nation? To start with, the endeavor received some measure of validation by a first inclusion in the *Encyclopedia of Educational Research* as far back as 1960 when the idea was described as being in the stage of establishing a knowledge base (Van Til, 1960). Canadian endeavors initially manifested themselves in the form of spasmodic studies which recommended useful classroom methodologies for teachers specifically functioning in North American Indian communities. The work of a number of American anthropologists provided a loose disciplinary base for these recommendations, even though direct cultural applicability was not a primary concern (Henry, 1960; Kluckhohn, 1961; Mead, 1963; Spindler and Spindler, 1965). Minority case studies supplemented the vague theoretical underpinnings, notably in Black and Mexican-American communities, and a number of universities responded with appropriate centres, for example, the Mexican-American Studies Center at Claremont, California; Afro-American Studies at Columbia University; the Center for Migration Studies at Brooklyn College; and the Ethnic Studies Program at San Diego State College (Friesen, 1977).

Against these developments it would seem that a specific direction could be developed by multicultural promulgators, but this was not the case. As the last two decades have passed multiculturalism appears not to have rolled with the punches, but instead has followed a somewhat aimless path. A warning to educators, issued by American philosopher, John Dewey, some thirty years ago, is appropriate to the discussion. Dewey cautioned that any educational innovation should be accompanied by a well thought-out philosophy. Otherwise, it might be undertaken without a clear idea of the ends in way of ruling attitudes or desire or purpose that were to be created and the effort might end up being conducted blindly, in response to social pressures, or simply under the control or customs or traditions that had never been examined (Archambault, 1964, 17).

Undoubtedly, most social changes in our society occur without a great deal of philosophical deliberation, and it would be futile to try logically to validate some of the fads, booms or crazes that have comprised the themes of recent decades of change. There is also reason to believe that many of the newer educational emphases like cooperative learning, global and peace education, community schools and the effective schools movement have been incepted without an explicitly spelled-out philosophy of education. While even a cursory investigation will reveal that these themes primarily reflect the ideas of the progressivist education movement, for the most part their promoters appear unaware of or unconcerned about philosophical linkages (Friesen and Wieler, 1988). In the case of multicultural education, the development of specific social models has not yet reached any level of sophistication, perhaps because of the lack of a clear theoretical or disciplinary base for the endeavor or a failure to commit to the underlying goals.

False Starts

By the mid nineteen sixties a number of multicultural education programs were operationalized by the various levels of government grounded on the assumption that "we need to do something for our minorities." These efforts were encouraged by the "dogooder" sector of society because the cause was too demeaning for the community's upper echelons to undertake. Programs were primarily aimed at the lower socio-economic levels of society. Human welfare programs, particularly schooling, were the main target of multicultural efforts, and the accompanying objectives were remedial in nature. This translated to mean that if minorities were provided with an opportunity to access standardized programs they would integrate fully into dominant society (Bowd, 1977). Education was considered the key to minority success both in economic and professional terms and was aimed at helping minorities to access a dominant social identity. A supplemental thrust was to educate the public about minority cultures for the purpose of promoting tolerance and understanding while the processes of integration and assimilation were underway (Tiedt and Tiedt, 1990).

Measures which were alleged to have positive effects in culturally-interactive situations included curricular emphases on ethnic foods, festivities, dress and holidays. Other more generalized approaches used in group settings included role-playing and intergroup contact (Brookover, 1955; Sargent and Williamson, 1958). Clearly the implied patronism of these efforts showed their inappropriateness as meaningful curriculum content.

Some promoters of multiculturalism in the 1960s surmised that tolerance could be legislated, and their faith was at least partially rewarded when laws enacted to affect public accommodations produced positive results. It was found that laws, in fact, did make a difference, but always the emphasis was to fit the culturally-different to the strictures of dominant society. This orientation lasted for more than a decade until ethnic minorities gathered sufficient spirit to react with indignation to being the target of patronizing programs. In general they were part of the larger movement to gain equity for neglected sectors of society which included civil rights, women's rights and, in the United States at least, opposition to involvement in the Vietnam War.

Methodological Alternatives

Gibson's groundbreaking analysis of the objectives of multicultural teaching has become a much-quoted work (Gibson, 1976). According to Gibson, four approaches to this kind of teaching could be detailed, i.e. (i) education of the culturally different; (ii) education *about* cultural differences; (iii) teaching *for* cultural pluralism; and, (iv) bicultural education. Recognizing that the four could overlap to some extent, Gibson tried to clarify the distinctions among these approaches. The first, educating the culturally different, represents an attempt to equalize educational opportunities for the "culturally different" student. The approach aims at providing a solution to the difficulties of the lower achieving student, the drop-out, and those who graduate with restricted career aspirations. It rejects cultural or genetic deficit models which claim to explain these characteristics. The intent of this approach is to reduce home/school discord and improve students' self-image and consequently their motivation and academic success. A defect in this approach is its subtle assimilationist bent which aims at manipulating equality of educational opportunity in order to ensure that a significant degree of conformity to established societal norms will prevail (Young, 1979).

Gibson's second approach identifies teaching *about* cultural differences in order to promote multicultural understanding. This approach is aimed at all students in a school in an attempt to motivate them towards an appreciation of the value of ethnic and cultural diversity and the right of others to be different. Realistically this is a task which schools have traditionally failed to accomplish, partly because it has only recently become part of their mandate, and partly based on the premises and content implicit in a white, Anglo-Saxon Protestant orientation (Hodgetts, 1968). The approach has been accompanied by shortcomings in the areas of teacher training as well (Henley and Young, 1981).

Gibson's third approach concentrates on education for cultural pluralism with the primary objective of maintaining and extending ethnic and cultural diversity within society. Implied is a structural recognition of cultural differences as a way to increase the influence of minority groups within the school system, thus creating a climate for educational success. One of the ways in which this goal has been realized is through the establishment of heritage language schools operated by various ethnocultural groups. In the regular school curriculum the promotion of diversity is limited since it follows the traditional mandate identified though not necessarily universally endorsed. In a very real sense the nature of the school's only legitimate social task is to establish a single, present cultural relationship among the children served by the system (Lawson, 1982).

The final approach identified by Gibson promotes the idea of enabling learners who belong two different cultural configurations, heritage culture and dominant society, to cope adequately within them. The concept was originally interpreted to imply an incorporation of loyalty to the dominant culture (if different from the heritage culture), while maintaining an allegiance to the second cultural identity in a meaningful but subservient way. The argument that an individual can be equally comfortable in two different cultural contexts requires serious analysis because of the reality that cultural schizophrenia could result. There is also reason to believe that individuals may at best formulate a functional framework of values which represents one or the other of the two cultural alternatives. Their personally-concocted admixture of cultures may even be out of sinc with the rest of society. It would be difficult to perceive that such a predicament would foster an attitude of understanding and tolerance toward other value systems thereby limiting the value of this approach as a worthy pedagogical objective.

Some leaders of ethnocultural communities postulate that their children *should* be able to maintain their heritage culture and identity while simultaneously learning how to function effectively in the dominant Canadian society. This approach has an inbuilt consolation for those who might not experience success in the national monoculture. By keeping their fingers in the "home pie," they will have some place in which to hang their "cultural hat." This kind of deliberation has given rise to a new interpretation of the concept of "biculturalism." The central notion is that individuals caught between two different cultural worlds can actually gain a measure of satisfaction from both, provided they remain loyal to their heritage culture and simply borrow elements from the dominant culture to add to their personal cultural repertoire. Ethnocultural leaders sometimes urge their young people to follow this course of action. Two examples would include recommendations in this regard from a popular Doukhobor leader in the 1930s, Peter Petrovich Verigin (Friesen and Verigin,

1989) and a recent recommendation from an Indian chief of the Stoney Tribe near Calgary, Alberta (Snow, 1977). The central idea is that minority children can remain anchored to their heritage culture and still undergo some degree of assimilation." Using this approach, minority leaders hope to avoid the issue of divided loyalties brought about by cultural marginality.

A second schematic outlining four options for multicultural teaching is targeted at dealing with the problems of conflicting ideologies and relativism which are composite in a culturally-plural society (Ouellet, 1992). Assimilation-ists often object to any plan which they fear may fragment the system. They resent any action on the part of state officials to promote other than a "systems" approach to education. Cultural pluralists, on the other hand, opt for a more flexible and perhaps less efficient approach that would recognize and perhaps foster more divergent lifestyles. The diversity of envisaged goals can possibly be reduced to four options:

a. the monocultural option, in which the state tries to socialize all citizens to an appreciation of the "national culture;"

b. the multicultural option, in which the state has the responsibility to help all ethnic groups to preserve their language and heritage;

c. the intercultural option, in which the state is to enhance harmonious relations among its various ethnocultural sectors by means of exchange and collaboration; and

d. the transcultural option, in which the state must encourage the members of the various ethnic groups to go beyond the borders of their group and face with creativity and dynamism the new challenges raised by the acceleration of change in the world economy.

Heritage Language Schools

By the nineteen seventies, minority leaders took issue with being targets of "special" albeit condescending betterment programs, and began to attack what they saw as a program of empty slogans. Citing the pluralist principle so often given lip service in politics and in the public service they became outspoken in their campaign for equality. New Canadian immigrants, for example, prepared briefs which petitioned for funding to support heritage cultural programs. In luring them to this continent, immigration officials led them to believe that they could become part of the Canadian scene without sacrificing any elements of their past. Translated, this meant support for immigrant cultural heritage pro-grams. Within a decade there were nearly 130 000 minority children enrolled in newly established heritage language schools which offered classes in nearly 60 different languages other than the two official languages, French and English (Pelech, 1988). Although seen as attractive programs for cultural maintenance by many incoming groups, grants to support these schools in Alberta, for example, have not increased in more than ten years.

Educators charged with the responsibility of teaching the two national languages to immigrants have always relied on the remedial model of instruction (Bowd, 1977). Few have paid any attention to the possible ramifications of cultural background in learning language since it is commonly believed by ESL educators that students' heritage culture is of little consequence in their attaining any measure of success in the Canadian workplace. Educators also gloss over the concept that a strong first language competence is necessary for children to do well in a second language. In addition, minority children who lack educational support for their first language often develop a subtractive form of bilingualism in which first language skills are not replaced by second language skills. (Cummins, 1989). In other words, heritage language programs are merely token measures of accommodation rather than effective multicultural policy. Educators will have to look elsewhere if they want to find a multicultural program worthy of the objective of enhancing appreciation for cultural differences.

Affirmative Action

The phenomenon of affirmative action has stimulated a great deal of discussion in policy circles. Essentially the concept elaborates the principle that minorities need to be treated "unequally" so that they may experience equity. Two kinds of unintended consequences of these programs have arisen, affecting both participants and "bystanders." Participants have suffered because they never clearly know whether their subsequent successes are due to their own merits or because of institutional tokenism. A second consequence emanates from outsiders' perceptions of what affirmative action programs do to stymie their own chances of success (Roberts, 1979). A common complaint arises, "why should newcomers have all the advantages?"

Minority objections to being treated unequally even if for a "noble cause" are twofold. Some have argued that inequity implies a lower status of citizenship and ascribes minorities a charity status which perpetuates their unequal position. Others have pressed hard on the pluralist principle, which implies that a truly diverse nation inherently fosters a multiplicity of systems, standards and philosophies. Pluralism decrees that no one way of doing anything is justifiable in any area, whether in economics, education, human welfare, culture or politics. National leaders and multiculturalists who buy into these objections quickly surmise that there must be inherent differences among cultures to account for the unusual request to be "excused from joining the Canadian monoculture." The bottom line is that they find it hard to understand why anyone would not want to be a "mainline" Canadian?

The Learning Styles Debate

A gratifying turn of events for those on the firing line of having to accommodate minority differences originally came from research targeting the American Indian (Friesen, 1991). Initial discoveries posited that there were distinct differences in learning styles between Indian and non-Indian children and different teaching methodologies were therefore required. This work was reminiscent of the work of anthropologists who were interested in the cranial capacities of difference races, and theorized that the larger the cranial cavity, the larger the brain (Gossett, 1970; Chrisjohn and Peters, 1986). Others postulated differences in right-brain and left-brain functioning between Indians and non-Indians and rendered the conclusion that Indians, whose "left brain is symmetrical to the right results in a lack of verbal facility." These findings explained why Indian children did poorly on WISC-R and other standardized tests and, in the eyes of the researchers at least, voided the need to investigate societal/cultural reasons for inadequate performance (Ross, 1982; Chrisjohn and Peters; 1986). The joy of the left-brain, right-brain researchers was short-lived when it was pointed out that their studies were not "blind" studies; in other words, the researchers were aware of the ethnic origins of the brains under investigation and thus produced biased reports (Chrisjohn and Peters, 1986).

More (1987) contends that there are certain degrees of similarity between learning styles and methods among members of a given cultural milieu, even though individual differences will still emerge. Educators should be careful not to expect that all members of a particular cultural group will have the same learning style any more than they will have a common personality. This does not negate the fact that certain teachers will be more comfortable with some students than with others (Kleinfeld, 1975), but it offers no valid ground for explaining away the lack of school achievement by inventing a fresh set of labels to explain the lack of success on the part of a particular minority child (Browne, 1990).

Developments in Multicultural Studies

The phenomenon of multicultural and ethnic studies has spawned a series of university responses in the areas of course instruction and research, and in the case of professional faculties such as education, in teacher training. These trends are continuing, thereby furnishing ample evidence that what was once considered a fad or short-term emphasis is now a legitimate component of North American higher education. As this maturity of studies continues into the future no doubt a more composite theoretical base will also emerge. A brief review of university developments will help to illustrate the force of the continuing trend.

American Beginnings

The primary focus of university programs in the 1960s was on minorities per se, i.e., ethnic groups, racial minorities, religious groups, women's groups, civil rights groups, etc. Still, a variety of themes soon emerged from the formalization of the various aspects of American life related to the ethnic factor. For example, in the mid-sixties a Mexican American Studies Centre was established at Claremont, California, designed to develop a multiethnic resources library and laboratory to meet the needs of students with that particular background. A total of fifteen courses was initiated, and within a few years the Centre enrolled over 200 students, 20% of whom had Mexican American background *(Intercultural Education,* 1970).

A similar effort occurred at Columbia university in 1968 featuring a program of ethnic studies with an Afro-American theme. The program offered on both an undergraduate and graduate basis, and incorporated a field-work component. University faculty were encouraged to participate on the assumption that their off-campus travel would comprise a source of enrichment for them *(Intercultural education,* 1970).

In 1965 the Center for Migration Studies was established at Brooklyn College of the City University of New York, and designed to procure and make available information regarding immigration and acculturation about various incoming American subcultures. One objective of the centre was to gain the assistance of scholars in the social sciences, education, humanities and related fields in the collection, preservation and analysis of data related to migration and the process of assimilation. The centre hoped to shed light on the everyday challenges faced by incoming groups, and sought to accomplish its goals through a series of conferences, workshops, courses and research projects *(Intercultural Education,* 1970).

San Diego State College began conducting intensive summer programs in 1968, offering graduate courses to acquaint administrators, teachers and community college students with the concept of ethnic relations. Sponsored workshops dealt with controversial themes such as intercultural relations, bilingualism, dropping out due to intercultural frustration, and the idea that "only Chicanos can teach Chicanos" *(Intercultural Education,* 1970).

As these groundbreaking programs gained momentum similar efforts were initiated across the United States. For the most part, the directions adopted by the new centres included the study of prejudice and discrimination, the relative deprivation of distinct minority groups, and how to gain greater cooperation among the various sectors of American society in an effort to achieve better equity.

Native American Studies

Initially a great deal of effort in ethnic or multicultural studies was focussed on Indian peoples. Concerned about such factors as absenteeism and dropouts, a number of universities sought to devise special teacher training programs to alleviate these realities. The University of North Dakota formulated such a program combining course work in the social sciences with psychology and English. Where possible the curriculum offered in Native schools took on a job-related orientation, thereby allowing the university to play a practical role in training.

In the 1960s the University of Arizona became the first state university of higher education in the United States to initiate a centre devoted to Aboriginal studies. The centre sponsored an annual conference and developed the *Journal of American Indian Education* which is a leading publication in its field. A variety of research and practice topics are featured in both the annual conference and the journal covering all aspects of Indian education and related matters such as economic development, leadership training, etc. In many ways the Arizona centre has served as a model for similar institutionalized service depots in universities across North America.

University developments in Native education in Canada parallelled those in the United States. For example, motivated by requests from the Indian community, in the 1960s the St. Lawrence University developed a course in the Department of Anthropology based on explaining the various facets of Indian culture. Lavel University began its Centre for Northern Studies, the University of Montreal established the Northern Research Group in their Department of Anthropology, and McGill University established a Committee on Northern Research. Native Studies was the theme of an Institute at Trent University, and the University of Saskatchewan which offered a graduate degree in the field in 1970.

Although the University of Calgary offered a first course in intercultural education in 1968, the University of Alberta formalized a full degree program at the same time. Then, in cooperation with the University of Lethbridge, the three institutions established a joint committee to encourage research in intercultural education and share the results of their work (Kirman, 1969; Friesen, 1972). In addition the University of Alberta sponsored related northern research through the Boreal Institute and the University of Calgary established a Native Outreach Program designed to provide degree programs on Indian reserves. The University of Lethbridge initiated a similar effort among Indian tribes in southern Alberta.

Indian Education and Teacher Education

One of the first research discoveries in Native education pertained to the lack of appropriate teacher training. Most teachers who ventured into Native communities found themselves unequipped to deal with cultural variations to the degree they found in reserve communities, both in terms of knowledge content and methodology. To that end, with attending Native encouragement, a number of universities responded by initiating more relevant courses and field experiences. The University of Saskatchewan was a pioneer in this area and sought to develop relevancy in a number of fronts including curriculum and methodology and familiarity with Native cultural configurations. By the 1970s similar efforts had been launched across the nation by such institutions as the University of British Columbia, The University of Calgary, Brandon University, the University of Manitoba, Laurentian University, Trent University, the University of Western Ontario, etc. A number of institutions, like the University of Calgary, began course offerings on site so that Native students did not have to relocate to urban centers to get their university education started. Many practical concerns were targeted in these on-site ventures including selection of a degree program, the development of effective study habits, and how to cope with the complexities of bussing and parenting while engaged in fulltime studies.

Some Projections

The Perpetuity of Ethnicity

There is little doubt that the study of multiculturalism will prevail long into the future because of a series of factors which contribute towards and assure its perpetuity. So long as Canadians continue to make something of visible differences, these differences will effect some degree of atypical social interaction. For example, a student recently complained that people were too concerned with who she was in terms of her ethnic heritage. "Who are you, *really,*" they would ask, obviously perplexed by her appearance which has resulted from the admixture of her heritage cultures – Anglo-Saxon, West Indies, East Indian and Black. Clearly some degree of education in the form of sensitizing people towards others is justified on these grounds.

Canada's cultural makeup is a mosaic, and within this unique milieu ethnocultural communities are encouraged to maintain and develop their own values and lifestyles. As a result many such communities have developed a high degree of institutional completeness whereby they manage to provide a full socialization catalogue for their children – educationally, religiously, socially, and even economically. It will be difficult, however, to develop a strong national identity in light of these assumed privileges, but that is the reality of a pluralist society (Anderson and Frideres, 1981). As it is there are many factors which make it difficult for Canadians to know and respect one another, and thus assist in the maintenance of our mosaic. Further, Canadians tend to resist the American penchant for a melting-pot society, and much of this resistance emanates from the quarters of the charter nations. These groups pride themselves on maintaining their own historical leadership structures to the extent of resisting an effective pluralism. Were a truly multicultural society created, it would make available equal privileges of governance opportunity to incoming cultural groups. There is some indication that the cultures-in-charge believe that such an arrangement should be avoided.

Implications for Schooling

During the two decades since the formal announcement of a federal policy in Canada, much energy has been directed towards developing workable teacher training programs and providing relevant, accurate school curricula. A recent encouraging trend has been for members of ethnocultural communities themselves to produce materials, often in an effort "to set the record straight." Unfortunately, much of the new material comprises a bit of oversell in that heritage cultures are unrealistically portrayed in the sense of being almost perfect peoples. A case in point is a book penned by an unbaptized Hutterite called *Born Hutterite,* which contains humorous and folksy stories about being raised on a Hutterite colony (Hofer, 1991). At no time does the author allow that Hutterites engage in normal human dysfunctional behaviors or experience personal or group conflicts which cause traumatic crises in individual lives or even damage human personalities. Essentially the book paints a picture of Hutterite life as idyllic, poetic and unbelievable. Thus to conclude that materials produced by ethnocultural community members themselves will be void of antithetical content is unrealistic. In this arena, as in many others, cultural sensitivity and peaceful, meaningful ethnic co-existence can only come about through *inter-cultural* cooperation.

There are a number of very promising educational fronts which offer valuable potential multicultural insights and practice. Hopefully it will also be possible to formulate appropriate theoretical underpinnings for these efforts. In a few instances these will be familiar themes, but their multicultural implications have not sufficiently been harvested.

Promoting Self-Esteem

For some years educators have emphasized the importance of a feeling of well-being in relation to learning success and personal achievement. Stress on the importance of classroom discipline per se has given way to the realization that a misbehaving child may be an unhealthy child, and the encouragement of a positive self-esteem may also be viewed as one approach to discipline (Charles, 1985). Teachers who themselves possess a healthy sense of well-being exhibit such useful characteristics as emotional stability, buoyancy, attractiveness and cooperativeness (Ornstein, 1990, 547). Naturally this sense of well-being is passed on to students who in turn feel better about themselves and hence achieve better.

One of the components of a healthy self-esteem has to do with cultural background, and if the picture is to be complete, students should be encouraged to accept themselves as they really are – socially, culturally, spiritually, etc. They should even be encouraged to come to grips with who they are in all of these areas, and the school curriculum and environment should be conducive towards such a goal. Further, students should be encouraged to accept their peers as *they* are, and to see their own uniquenesses and those of their peers as assets, not liabilities (Tiedt and Tiedt, 1990). In this way it may be possible to achieve two simultaneous goals: (i) to enhance personal self-esteem, and (ii) to bring students to a fuller appreciation of the pluralistic nature of Canadian society and be better prepared to contribute towards it from their own unique value orientation and personality.

Community Sensitivity

It is difficult for a teacher to locate to a new occupational setting when such factors as ethnicity, culture or religion are involved in a pronounced way, or even if the new situation requires a rural-to-urban re-orientation. Regardless of one's professional mandate, it is often perplexing to know if doing one's job is effective or if one's interpretation of the professional role sometimes interferes with local community goals. Too often this has been the case, for example, when educational systems seek to deliver an urban anglo-saxon, middle class school program in a northern Native setting. Sometimes teachers who locate to such communities come with an air of reform about them. After all, they have been hired to promote literacy, and they are quite prepared to do that. Listening to the locals and perhaps learning about their ways are merely corollary objectives. As a result of this attitude several unfortunate results may occur. Teachers may become alienated, the school may be viewed as an interloper and community cooperation may be eliminated. It behooves the outsider teacher in such situations to see education as a two-way process; teachers in such communities may actually learn just as much as they teach (Friesen, 1987). In addition, teachers functioning in cross-cultural situations should in no way abdicate their own value system under the guise of trying to fit it. Living out one's own cultural values can afford the local community the richness of learning about an alternative, outside way of life (Wolcott, 1967).

Two Canadian studies that have helped set the stage for improving Native education are Harry Wolcott's, *A Kwakiutl Village and School* (1967), and Richard King's, *The School at Mopass* (1967). King acknowledged the dichotomy expected of Native students, pointing out that where the Indian and non-Indian worlds overlapped there was a minimal congruence of purposes, values and perceptions. He lamented that residential school staff were ignorant of Indian ways and called them ". . . the end men of huge bureaucratic organizations . . . that are so organized as to provide no reflection of the local communities." He recommended that sectarianism be eliminated from Indian education and that the legal designation of the Native as a "status person" be discarded. Obviously King did not suspect the nature of the forthcoming White-Paper/Red-Paper dispute which followed shortly. One recommendation of his study which did see immediate fruition was the closing of residential schools. However, King also recognized that it might be expedient for these schools to continue functioning for a few years in isolated areas. Today, his vision for Indian-operated schools is finally a reality.

Wolcott's recommendations were more specific, demonstrating a remarkable contemporary relevance, despite their having been written a quarter of a century ago. This is particularly true in the area of potential value conflicts for Native children. Wolcott suggested that the educational needs of Native people should be determined, by Native people themselves, before the introduction of new schemes. He also emphasized that school programs to meet certain needs should only be developed in schools equipped to handle these, and these programs should be geared specifically to meet local needs. The latter would necessitate amending standardized curricula to include areas of local interest and relevance. Wolcott warned teachers to tread carefully in the realm of cultural values; to avoid denying their personal values or asserting the superiority of Native values. He also cautioned teachers against becoming community reformers, tempting as the latter role may be. He revealed an interest in purely local conditions when he made his final recommendations. He stated that young Native children need to be helped to: (i) develop the ability to communicate in English; (ii) learn at least a smattering of the "stuff" you learn in school, i.e. Canadian content, etc.; (iii) become acquainted with knowledge on how to conduct a business meeting, and to do so democratically; (iv) accumulate knowledge about how to handle leisure time; (v) gain knowledge of how to use public transportation and communication facilities; and (vi) obtain helpful health information. Critics later suggested an element of cultural bias in some of Wolcott's observations, particularly with regard to items that implied an assimilative or patronizing stance, i.e. a need for knowledge about democracy or having to learn those things which are common to all Canadian children.

One of Wolcott's more foresighted statements concerned teacher-pupil interactions in a multicultural context:

For any child attending the school the contact with the teacher provides on of the earliest extended opportunities for ... encounters with cultural agents. ... Except for a fleeting glimpse of the Indian agent ... his relationship with his teachers may be among the first and among the very few opportunities the village child will ever have for prolonged contact with Whites of a middle class orientation Wolcott, 1967, 131).

The rub of the situation is clearly demonstrated in the case of an adventurous urban teacher who went to a northern Native community and tried to ride the fence between reform and community absorption by taking a non-judgmental, yet helpful stance. His position threw the community off-guard, since they were used to either would-be reformers or potential cultural converts. Thus a local chief made this comment about the newcomer. He is ... "the biggest threat to Indian people that we have seen in the north for a long time" (Robinson, 1981). The statement reveals a pleasant surprise at this prospect and could perhaps be translated to say, "What a nice change; imagine someone who wants to work with us without promoting a secret agenda."

Too often the urban, middle-class format of schooling in our society is taken for granted as an essential component of life. In some cultural settings, however, it can be quite a disruptive institution, particularly when that lifestyle operates according to a different time schedule than is typical of modern schooling. Consider, for example, the case of the trapping culture in northern Canadian regions where the family relocates to the bush during the wintertime and returns to the settlement when the ice breaks in the spring. Usually it is the family's preference to be accompanied by their children when they retreat to the bush, but this means that the children are removed from the local settlement school. If the children are left in the settlement to further their education it may mean months of time lapse with no parental contact. Another alternative is for the mother to remain at home with the children while the father migrates to the trapline alone to make his living.

The Northland School Division recently inaugurated a split-year program of schooling geared to the trapline year instead of going by the urban calendar. Thus school for trapline families is in session during the summer months, offering a winter solstice instead. Another significant move has involved the restructuring of school curriculum content to take greater cognizance of local culture (Murdoch, 1984). Now the child of the trapline family can learn about hunting and trapping and ice-fishing in school instead of reading stories about city kids taking a trip to the country to see their grandparents.

English as a Second Language (ESL)

As the Canadian government continues to encourage immigration there will be newcomers who do not speak either of the official languages. Naturally the responsibility for offering appropriate instruction will fall to the schools. The related field is commonly known as E.S.L., and although a strong disciplinary base has not yet been developed for the field, there are many organizations, such as the TESL Canada Council which have shown a real interest in examining the relationship between language and culture. Their studies have shown the need for teachers to become knowledgeable about the heritage cultures of their ESL students as well as to develop special skills and techniques for teaching English-as-a-second language. A related educational concern has been the development of studies in the inner city since most immigrants locate there on their arrival in Canada (Bates and Vernon, 1979). As schools continue to adjust to these realities they become more relevant in the sense of offering instruction and training in areas that relate to the local community.

Toward a Philosophy of Multicultural Education

John Dewey's warning about the importance of direction in determining educational objectives was alluded to earlier in this discussion. Dewey was concerned that without first clarifying where they are headed, educators might find themselves designing educational programs that do not reflect their own views of life. A similar concern applies to multicultural education which may not be effective if it is merely fashioned on the tenets of the general philosophy of education which supports common schooling. Perhaps some additional premises or presuppositions need to be spelled out in relation to such phenomena as the structure of ethnicity in Canada, basic societal constraints on its expression, the support of basic human rights, the practical demands placed on education and the ideological objectives of Canadian society generally (Buchignani, 1980).

The practical test of philosophy is the nature of its translation into practice. How do educators perceive the personal/educational development of the immigrant child or the Native child? To what extent does culture play a part in this development, and what is required of teachers if they want to function effectively in such situations? These questions can only be answered when a well thought-out statement of basic assumptions and school objectives is articulated. Otherwise the derived activities may be based on little more than personal or professional guess-work.

The framework of early multicultural efforts tended to reflect the times, but more recent analysis has revealed the bent of the underlying assumptions on which educators of those times operated. In the 1960s it was envisaged that assimilation of enthnocultural communities into the mainstream was a valued goal, and the sooner it was accomplished the better. It was also believed that people who were not part of the mainstream basically wanted to be assimilated. After all, such a choice would assure them of equality of opportunity. Schooling, therefore, operated on the premise that minority children should be provided with the tools they would need to be successful in dominant society.

Obviously, the platform of the above program to absorb ethnocultural communities into the mainstream is deficient in light of more recent developments. As it turns out the process of assimilation is *not* always desirable, either by mainstream citizens nor by minority members. If multiculturalism is to be effective in the future it will be necessary to keep one ear to the ground in order to determine what might turn out to be workable in a given situation. If a philosophy is then formed, logically, consistently and clearly, it should reflect an interplay of assessment with need and purpose, and it will necessarily have to have the principle of flexibility built into it.

Law, Policy and Practice

The formulation of legislation aimed at guaranteeing citizen rights or, conversely, alleviating an unequal situation is a good starting point. Laws reflect philosophy, or minimally, whatever the public will settle for. Laws are *supposed* to be an entrenchment of basic social values and when passed they become a more or less permanent manifestation of a society's basic framework. In order to be effective, laws must be translated into policy. It is all very well for laws to be passed that guarantee certain rights and privileges, but unless these are spelled out in specific policies for given situations, little by way of the implicit objectives may result. For example, laws pertaining to fair hiring practices or guaranteeing equal access to public accommodations will do little good unless the circumstances pertaining thereto are specified. A Bill of Rights does little good as a statement of principle until the various institutions specify what those principles mean in operational terms within their jurisdictions.

Finally, there is the practice of multiculturalism – both good and bad. This brings the question into the personal arena and raises the question of how to "create" multicultural persons. Such an individual is someone who is intellectually and emotionally committed to the unity of all human beings, while at the same time recognizing, accepting and appreciating the uniquenesses of individuals regardless of their cultural origins (Adler, 1981). These convictions may be derived from one's personal outlook and world-view, by an understanding of the universe as a dynamically unfolding process, by the way one reflects the interconnectedness of life in one's thoughts and actions, and by the way one remains open to the eminences of experience. At first glance this would appear to be a lifetime agenda, but it would almost certainly be a rewarding life.

References

Adler, Peter. Beyond cultural identity: Reflections on cultural and multicultural man. *Multiculturalism,* IV(3), 18-22.

Anderson, Alan B. & James S. Frideres. (1981). *Ethnicity in Canada: Theoretical perspectives.* Toronto: Butterworths.

Archambault, Reginald, ed. (1964). *John Dewey on education.* New York: Modern Library.

Bates, John H. & Jill Vernon. (1979). The inner city's characteristics and implications for policy and programs. *Multiculturalism,* 3(2), 27-29.

Bowd, Alan D. (1977). Ten years after the Hawthorn report: Changing psychological implications for the education of Canadian Native peoples. *Canadian Psychological Review,* 18(1), October, 332-345.

Brookover, William B. (1955). *A sociology of education.* New York: American Book Company.

Browne, Bell Browne. (1990). Learning styles and Native Americans. *Canadian Journal of Native Education,* 17(1), 23-35.

Buchignani, Norman. (1980). Culture or identity? Addressing ethnicity in Canadian education. *McGill Journal of Education.* XV(1), Winter, 79-93.

Charles, C. M. (1985). *Building classroom discipline: From models to practice.* Second edition. New York: Longmans.

Chrisjohn, R. & M. Peters. (1986). The right brain Indian: Fact or fiction? *Canadian Journal of Indian Education,* 13(1), 62-71.

Cummins, Jim. (1989). *Empowering minority students.* Sacramento, Calif: Califonia Association for Bilingual Education.

Friesen, John W. (1972). Intercultural education in Alberta universities. *The Northian,* 8(4), March, 25-26.

Friesen, John W. (1977). *People, culture & learning.* Calgary: Detselig Enterprises.

Friesen, John W. (1987). *Rose of the north.* Ottawa: Borealis.

Friesen, John W. (1991). *The cultural maze: Complex questions on Native destiny in western Canada.* Calgary: Detselig Enterprises.

Friesen, John W. & Michael M. Verigin. (1989). *The community Doukhobors: A people in transition.* Ottawa: Borealis.

Friesen, John W. & E. E. Wieler. (1988). New robes for an old order: Multicultural education, peace education, cooperative learning and progressive education. *Journal of Educational Thought.* 22(1), 46-56.

Gibson, Margaret. (1976). Approaches to multicultural education in the U.S.A.: Some concepts and assumptions. *Anthropology and* Education Quarterly, 7(4), 7-18.

Gossett, Thomas F. (1970). *Race: The history of an idea in America.* New York: Schocken.

Henley, Richard & Jonathan C. Young. (1981). Multicultural education: Contemporary variations on a historical theme. *The History and Social Science Teacher,* 17(1), Fall, 7-16.

Henry, Jules. (1960). A cross-cultural outline of education. *Current Anthropology,* 1, July, 267-306.

Hodgetts, A. (1968). *What culture? What heritage? A study of civic education in Canada.* Toronto: Ontario Institute for Studies in Education.

Hofer, Samuel. (1991). *Born Hutterite.* Saskatoon: Hofer Publishing.

Intercultural education. (1970). An information service of education and world affairs. 522 Fifth Avenue, New York: 1, January.

King, A. Richard. (1967). *The school at Mopass: A problem of identity.* New York: Holt, Rinehart and Winston.

Kirman, J. K. (1969). The University of Alberta's Intercultural Education Program. *Peabody Journal of Education,* 47, July, 15-19.

Kleinfeld, J. (1975). Effective teachers of Eskimo and Indian students. *School Review,* February, 301-343.

Kluckhohn, Florence & Fred L. Strodbeck. (1961). *Variations in value-orientations.* New York: Row Peterson.

Lawson, Robert F. (1982). A view from the Ivory Tower: On cultural, bicultural and multicultural questions. *Challenge in Educational Administration,* 21(2), 36.

Mazurek, Kaz & Nick Kach. (1990). Multiculturalism, society and education. *Canadian education: Historical themes and contemporary issues.* Brian Titley, ed. Calgary: Detselig Enterprises, 133-160.

Mead, Margaret, ed. (1963). *Cultural patterns and technological changes.* New York: Mentor.

More, A. (1987). Native Indian learning styles: A review for researchers and teachers. *Journal of American Indian Education,* 27(3), October, 17-29.

Murdoch, John. (1984). Ethno-Relativism in Cree curriculum development. *Multiculturalism in Canada.* Ronald J. Samuda, et al. eds. Toronto: Allyn and Bacon, 292-300.

Ornstein, Allan C. (1990). *Strategies for effective teaching.* New York: Harper and Row.

Pelech, Fiona, ed. (1988). *Proceedings of the tenth conference of the northern Alberta heritage languages association.* Edmonton: Alberta Cultural Heritage Foundation.

Quelett, Fernand. (1992). Education in a pluralistic society: Proposal for an enrichment of teacher education, *Beyond multicultural education: International perspectives.* Kogila A. Moodley, ed. Calgary: Detselig Enterprises, 281-302.

Overstreet, Harry A. (1962). Some contributions to the easing of group tensions. *American minorities: A textbook of readings in intergroup relations.* Milton L. Barron, ed. New York: Alfred A. Knopf, 26: 513-518.

Roberts, Lance W. (1979). Some unintended consequences of affirmative action: A critical review of 'Equality Now.' *Canadian public policy,* 5, Winter, 90-96.

Robinson, Paul. (1981). Multiculturalism – The curriculum, the community and the school. *Multiculturalism: A handbook for teachers.* Peter L.

McCreath, ed. Halifax: Nova Scotia Teachers' Association, 9-12.

Ross, A. C. (1982). Brain Hemispheric Functions and the Native American. *Journal of American Indian Education,* 21(2), May, 2-5.

Sargeant, S. Stansfeld & Robert C. Williamson. (1958). *Social psychology. Second edition. New York: Ronald Press.*

Snow, Chief John. (1977). *These mountains are our sacred places: The story of the Stoney Indians.* Toronto: Samuel Stevens.

Spindler, George & Louise Spindler. (1965). Researching the perception of cultural alternatives: The instrumnt activities inventory. *Context and meaning in cultural anthropology.* Melford E. Spiro, ed. New York: Free Press, 312-337.,

Tiedt, Iris L. & Pamela M. Tiedt. (1990). *Multicultural teaching: A handbook of activities, information and resources.* Third edition. Boston: Allyn and Bacon.

Van Til, William. (1960). Intercultural education. *Encyclopedia of educational research.* New York: Macmillan, 718-728.

Wolcott, Harry F. (1967). *A Kwakiutl village and school.* New York: Holt, Rinehart and Winston

Young, Jonathan C. (1979). Education in a multicultural society: What sort of education? *Canadian Journal of Education,* 4(3), 5-21.

3

Understanding Ethnicity

The study of ethnic cultural configurations as a professional concern is scarcely two decades old in Canada, hardly long enough to establish an academic discipline. Still, the production of related research studies and the teaching of appropriate subject matter in schools and universities has burgeoned. In 1989, the Canadian Ethnic Studies Association held its twentieth anniversary celebration by hosting a conference at The University of Calgary with the appropriately valuative theme, "Canadian Ethnic Studies: The State of the Art." The organizers planned for an appraisal of progress in the study of ethnicity from an interdisciplinary perspective, and the theme and the conference papers reflected this. Represented in the sessions were the perspectives of anthropology, sociology, history, geography, psychology, history, education and folklore. evident in the various conference discussions were such concepts as: multiculturalism, intercultural education, minority studies, cross-cultural studies, culturally-unique, biculturalism, etc. In evaluating the event, analysts worried that while the field of ethnic studies is still in its early growth stages, its future will largely be dependent upon a wide variety of interrelated factors: changing ideological currents and fashions in academia; changing public opinions on immigration, multiculturalism and ethnic relations; government funding and the availability of jobs in universities. An element of consolation was evident in the fact that ethnic themes and concerns have been integrated into a variety of disciplines and subject matters, and it is hard to tell exactly how effective this arrangement will be. As conferences continue to feature a high degree of interdisciplinary interaction and a cross-fertilization of ideas, there is every reason to believe that the thrust of ethnic studies will be sizable in the future (Burnet and Palmer, 1990).

Defining Ethnicity

The definition framed by Louis Wirth may help to give direction to a meaningful discussion of ethnicity. Wirth suggested that

> We may define a minority as a group of people who, because of their physical or cultural characteristics, are singled out from the others in the society in which

47

they live for differential and unequal treatment, and who regard themselves as objects of collective discrimination (Barron, 1962, 6).

Sociologists subsequent to Wirth have endeavored to refine and improve on his work. Kallen, for example, characterized minorities as groups who are set apart by society on grounds of being different, distinct or even "suspect" for some reason. They are restricted in some way, treated as objects of discrimination and often made to suffer economic and political inequities. As a result they are forced to occupy a subordinate, disadvantaged and stigmatized social position (Kallen, 1982). An additional element of the definition, not noted by Kallen, is the centrality of *awareness of identity* originated by Francis (1947), and elaborated in Gordon's classic work on assimilation (1960). Driedger's criteria for defining ethnicity include this concept, i.e., (i) identification with an ecological territory; (ii) ethnic institutional identification to the extent of institutional completeness; (iii) identification with ethnic culture through language usage, choice of friends and participation in cultural religious and educational organizations; (iv) identification with historical symbols; (v) identification with an ideology which can rally followers around a goal beyond cultural and institutional values; and, (vi) charismatic leadership and identification (Driedger, 1978).

Strictly speaking, "ethnicity" refers to "an involuntary group of people who share the same culture, or descendants of such people who identify themselves and/or are identified by others as belonging to the same involuntary group (Isajiw, 1985, 16). Abu-Laban and Mottershead (1981) propose that the criteria for delineating ethnic minorities should be regarded as variables rather than fixed categories. They hold to the primacy of two variables, namely, (i) a cultural tradition centering around one or more foci of ethnicity (norms, values, language, religion, race, or national origin) and a communal institutional structure; and (ii) a dominant feeling in the group of group consciousness which represents the psychological dimension and involves attraction and loyalty to the ethnic group and identification with it. The result of this discussion is that ethnicity or its synonym, multiculturalism, describe a state of being, and do not amply provide for the fact of cultural change, growth or flexibility. In that sense, one *could* say that the *operational* word for ethnic studies is "inter-culturalism" in the sense that the term conveys some form of interplay or interaction among the various sectors of a multicultural reality. It has even been suggested that the popular rendition of this reality, "multiculturalism" is a purely Canadian invention (Cummins and Danesi, 1990, 99), and is supplemented by a series of national accomplishments which amount to *inter-culturalism.* These include what might be called a very generous immigration policy (compared to other countries), Canada being the first country to pass a national multicultural act (in 1988), and the first to establish a federal Department of Multiculturalism and Citizenship.

The Canadian Reality

Canadian society has often been referred to as a "salad-bowl" society, a pluralistic whole in which the various elements, including subcultures are still identifiable. Naturally there are ethnocultural communities whose leaders are more vociferous in demanding official recognition for their group's status, rights and requests, and thus the identity of the less outspoken groups in Canada may be less visible. Majority and minority identities in Canada may also vary from one community to another and may change over time, depending on a variety of circumstances. Essentially, those who can claim British ancestry, are an exception because they have always enjoyed a higher status than the Aboriginal peoples, the French or people of immigrant status. After Confederation, most Canadian institutions were patterned after the British model and anyone who wanted to be successful had to learn how to function within those imported cultural strictures (Elliott, 1971). Not to do so meant occupying a lower rung on the Canadian ladder of success.

The acknowledgement that British groups have always fared better in Canadian society is sometimes paralleled by the corollary assertion that they have also been responsible for inflicting unfortunate circumstances on less privileged minorities. Burnet suggests that racial and ethnic prejudice are not unique to any one ethnocultural community, and suggests that the British have been unfairly blamed. Given the unique set of circumstances in which they found themselves, they probably acted no differently than any other group would have in the same situation (Burnet, 1979).

At present, a wide variety of cultural backgrounds are represented in Canada with origins in a multiplicity of countries. About two-thirds of today's immigrants arrive from Asian countries, but it would not be accurate by any means to suggest that they represent a single cultural configuration. In fact, there has always been a great cultural diversity among peoples who have migrated to Canada, regardless of their land of origin, because few countries in the world can be described as a uniculture. Thus to conceive of cultural groups who arrive in Canada as being distinct by virtue of the country from which they originated is not sufficient. In addition, sometimes cultural conflicts in the homeland are also transferred to the adopted homeland (Jaenen, 1979).

The Immigration Factor

The roots of Canada's cultural pluralism are at least three centuries old if one begins with the invasion of the two dominant incoming European groups – English and French. Aboriginal peoples naturally take issue with this assumption since the diversity of Native cultures which existed here prior to the coming of the Europeans was at least equally diverse. They similarly object to the dating of the nation to 1867, implying that no nation existed prior to that time. It appears that the flavor of the recent constitutional talks has been such that Aboriginal contentions are finally being heard. Perhaps in the near future all talk about the very recent origins of this nation will be amended by the Aboriginal correction of written history.

Clearly the most significant period of immigration in Canada, at least in terms of numbers, occurred between 1896 and 1914. During that time, because of the massive influx of peoples from so many different cultural backgrounds, ethnicity in Canada came to be. Contrary to what this somewhat generous attitude might imply on the part of Canadians, the truth of the matter is that we were, at best, reluctant hosts to incoming groups. Throughout this period of immigration, anglo-conformity was the predominant ideology, based on the philosophy of the dominant culture. It was expected that newcomers would adopt the values and institutions of anglophone Canadian society. There was virtually no thought given to the possibility that WASPish values might not be the apex of civilization which all citizens should strive for (Palmer, 1984, 23).

The intrigue of Canada's massive immigration period arises from the fact that while people of many different cultural backgrounds were being lured here, little consideration was given to the matter of their adjustment to Canadian life. The "brains" behind the immigration move, was, of course, Clifford Sifton, Minister of the Interior from 1896 to 1905. Sifton viewed immigration as a business proposition and a long-term investment for the country, and his actions showed the extent to which a single individual can influence national policy (Friesen, 1984). Sifton was clearly a businessman, not a social scientist. He believed that settlers from many different countries in the world should be encouraged to immigrate, they should settle on the prairies, and this would ensure maximum national productivity. His goal was to get the job done as quickly as possible, with as many people as possible. Thus he simplified federal legislation to promote home-steading, freed many of the encumbered lands, and conducted large-scale promotion of immigration in the United states and overseas (Hall, 1977).

The ethnic factor was pronounced in the immigration period supervised by Clifford Sifton. At this time the British Empire was at its height and the concomitant immigration policies reflected this. In fact, a preferential list for potential immigrants was drawn up featuring anglo British and Americans at the top. Next came northern and western Europeans as the most desirable, followed by central and eastern Europeans who had a slight edge over Jews and southern Europeans. These groups were followed in the pecking order by "strange" groups such as Mennonites, Hutterites and Doukhobors, with no thought as to the possible cultural and philosophical differences among them. Last were the "Asian hordes," including the Chinese, Japanese, East Indians and Blacks (Palmer, 1984). This "official" attitude undoubtedly set the tone for the reception these groups were later to enjoy or endure at the hands of their future neighbors.

If it was not enough to act with discrimination in group selection with regard to immigration, a search of past records also reveals ample evidence of misleading advertising in order to lure Immigrants to this "land of plenty." The west was advertised as the land of opportunity, a land virtually flowing with milk and honey, where anyone exerting only minimal effort would grow rich. As one government pamphlet put it: "It is no Utopian dream to look forward and see the endless plains thickly populated with millions to whom western Canada has given happy homes, larger opportunities in life, and the assurance of a prosperous future (Francis, 1989, 109). It is plausible that a correlation may be drawn between the later disillusionment which many of the "less desirable" groups felt and the treatment they received in their invitation to make Canada their home (Fleras and Elliott, 1992, 6).

The status of ethnic groups in Canada is such that they frequently encounter complex, albeit problematic situations in trying to attain their objectives for a satisfactory lifestyle. The very existence of a minority implies a majority which is usually in charge of things. Thus cultural groups are subordinate entities in a complex societal configuration. They may also possess special traits which are perceived as undesirable by the majority group. For example, their leadership may work very hard to maintain membership lines or to transmit identity through endogamous marriages to the disdain of the majority. Such exclusivity or social isolation may in fact perpetuate the identity of the group, but it may also serve to arouse suspicion or scorn on the part of society at large.

The establishment of a multicultural policy to promote equity through diversity is itself a commendable act, but even the *best* laws cannot guarantee their fulfillment on the street. In the first place, a multicultural policy should reflect a certain relevance and be designed with a specific population in mind. According to some critics, such a policy would nearly have to achieve the impossible in light of the magnitude of Canada's cultural diversity. Driedger, for example, suggests that Canada may geographically be divided into six ethnic and linguistic regions, only one of which represents the original intent of the notion of bilingualism and biculturalism which predated the formation of Canada's multicultural policy.

a. The northlands, which are really unilingual in the sense that sixty-nine percent of the population of the territories in question – Yukon, The Northwest Territories and roughly two-thirds of the six most westerly provinces, are of Native origin and 56 percent of them speak a Native tongue. This area accounts for virtually four-fifths of Canada's landscape.

b. The west, which includes the southern portions of the four westerly provinces, and although they were once the domain of various Native peoples, they were settled most recently by a diversity of European immigrants. Although these groups originally spoke English, German, French and Ukrainian, today they mainly employ the English language.

c. Upper Canada, which consists of southern Ontario, and which until very recently could be considered the domain of the British in linguistic and cultural terms. Many different ethnocultural immigrants have flocked to the province in recent decades, but Driedger estimates that 75 percent of the residents still employ English as their major language.

d. Lower Canada, which has historically been referred to as a French territory, and which includes most of the southern portion of Quebec. In fact, the use of English in the home is probably declining as much of the nation's financial and industrial base relocates to Ontario in reaction to Quebec's move toward independence. This shift also makes room for the development of Quebec's French culture.

e. The Maritime region, which includes Newfoundland, Prince Edward Island and Nova Scotia, and represents unilingualism and uniculturalism. Ninety-five percent of the province's residents speak English at home, and since very few immigrants enter these provinces, their ethnic and linguistic identity will remain strong.

f. New Brunswick alone represents the notion of biculturalism and bilingualism even though its population is only two or three percent of the nation's total. About one-fourth of the residents speak French at home and two-thirds speak English. Less than 10 percent of the rest of the population speak other languages at home (Driedger, 1978).

The accommodation of cultural differences and the promise of equitable treatment are not easy commodities to deliver. For example, when the Canadian Charter of Rights and Freedoms was passed a few years ago, many believed that racism and intolerance were now outlawed in Canada. In reality the Charter has made little difference on either count, and even its goal of encouraging national unity has been "fragile and often threatened by intolerance" (Trudeau, 1990, 336). The bottom line is that the implementation of the spirit and letter of the Charter are dependent upon the will and spirit of the people (Ray, 1985, 10). The Charter does not have authority to override other laws that violate human rights. This is because the Charter, like much other "human interest" legislation is interpretive and does not confer rights. It is intended only as suggesting behavior which is consistent with "the preservation and enhancement of the multicultural heritage of Canada" (Leal, 1983, 25). The Charter prohibits racial discrimination in law but it cannot require governments (nor citizens) to promote racial or cultural equality. It is, at best, indicative of a long-range social goal or ideology (Matas, 1991).

The Quandary of Minority Status

The challenge of seeking to accommodate cultural pluralism is very complex because at any given time there are groups who express unhappiness with their lot. For government leaders, the administration of jurisdictions marked by diversity and variety is no small task. When laws are passed in the interests of "the common good" they may actually function against the wishes and very survival of smaller ethnocultural communities. On a practical level, there is often the expectation that governments are responsible for ensuring equality for all citizens, even for groups that are considered undesirable by the majority of the population. The most logical stance, from a democratic perspective, is for governments to cater to the majority, even though they run the risk of becoming a tool of powerful political lobbyists. Majority-dominated governments may frequently justify what they do on the basis that smaller communities prefer to be left alone because they are culturally eccentric, unusual or isolationist, or they do not fit into the mainstream. Traditionally, ruling parties have selected one of a list of six approaches to determining the limitations or destiny of atypical communities within their boundaries. These have included : (i) forced or permitted assimilation; (ii) pluralism; (iii) legal protection of minorities; (iv) peaceful or forced population transfer; (v) continued subjugation; and, (vi) extermination (Simpson and Yinger, 1958).

In analyzing the above model, numerous Canadian examples come to mind. While we give ample lip service to the notion of cultural pluralism, there are many minorities, cultural and otherwise, who can lay claim to being the targets or even victims of any of the above "adjustment" routes. The Aboriginal peoples, for example, have a long history of being the target of mainstream assimilation, particularly through schooling (Brookes, 1990). The history of the Japanese in Canada during the second world war brings to mind the confiscation of property and the eradication of their rights. Promises have been made to minority members and not kept. Wilful destruction of atypical communities, such as the Doukhobors, has been eliminated through special, harmful legislation (Friesen and Verigin, 1989).

It is sometimes argued by spokespersons for dominant society that minorities do not "pull their weight" when they choose alternative ways of functioning. The pacifist stance of religious communities like Anabaptists, Quakers, Jehovah's Witnesses and Doukhobors has sometimes brought members of the Canadian Legion to their feet complaining about the cowardly failure of these groups to do their duty for their country. Retreatist groups like Hutterites, Amish, Back-to-the-Landers and those who prefer to live in Chinatowns are sometimes depreciated for withdrawing to ghetto life. Four classic complaints can be identified in this regard. They are:

a. Minorities do not maximize their potential by refusing to participate in dominant society. Their children are cheated out of realizing their potential when the parents choose to seclude theme from full participation in the institutional life of the dominant monoculture.

b. Groups who elect a different and "less productive" lifestyle do not contribute their share to the national economy. A related underlying assumption is that if minorities became more assimilated, and therefore less vulnerable to discrimination, the country would be better off financially. For some minorities, this double-edged assumption poses a very serious threat.

c. A community which elects a lifestyle that differs from the majority is sometimes labelled a deviant community. The attending implication is that their population is somehow associated with undesirable social behavior which may result (it is hinted) in various forms of crime and violence. As a result, *any* deviation is perceived as irregular and, hence, undesirable. For example, a few years ago an Indian youth was picked up in Calgary for allegedly loitering outside a warehouse building during the lunch-hour. When asked by the police as to his business, he replied that he was doing nothing. Not until the Native court-worker later explained the situation on behalf of the young man did the arresting officer understand that he had been given a culturally-appropriate response by the Indian youth. The young man was, in fact, on his lunch hour, and was waiting for the doors to re-open so he could resume work. At the time of the incident, from his perspective, he *was* doing nothing!

d. Too many ethnocultural communities foster values which conflict with the Canadian mainstream and may, in fact, demean the Canadian way of life. It would be difficult to define the "Canadian way of life" in this or perhaps *any* context, particularly in light of the pluralist principle which Canadian leaders are fond of espousing, and the difficulties national leaders have experienced in trying to formulate a national constitution bear this out. Still, some citizens are allegedly in possession of knowledge about the *traditional* Canadian way, and they mince no words in expressing unhappiness with people who do not share their views. A few years ago a furor was created when the Royal Canadian Mounted Police elected to allow for special head-gear for one of their members who adhered to the Sikh faith. Immediately a hue and cry went out about preserving a vital Canadian tradition (a gift from the British, by the way, via the *Northwest Mounted Police*). Finally, someone pointed out that RCMP head-gear had gone through several significant changes over the years and it would be difficult to identity the form most representative of "the Canadian way." In the meantime, in some circles the debate still continues.

Prejudice and Discrimination

Both prejudice and discrimination can be manifested in various ways, most of them quite harmful. Prejudice simply means to pre-judge a person, object or event on the basis previous sometimes partial information, without examining the evidence pertaining to the immediate situation. Thus to prejudge a person is to function with respect to a predetermined label regardless of how that person may actually behave. To discriminate, on the other hand, is to engage in a neutral form of behavior in the sense of choosing between options, i.e. choosing to use one's left hand rather than the right in performing a simple action. Discrimination enters the realm of the unfair only when individuals or groups are regarded as less than equal because of a given characteristic which is unrelated to the matter at hand. The most obvious example of unfair discrimination probably has to do with mistreatment of persons because of physical features or skin color.

There is some indication that cultural security is related to the practice of discrimination. When individuals perceive that their own way of life may be threatened by the recognition of any divergence they may begin to discriminate negatively as a means of self-protection. Discrimination is classically studied in terms of one's tolerance for other ethnic groups vis-a-vis the concept of cultural diversity, but it may be affected or even motivated by other attitudes. It may involve an objective appraisal of one's cultural milieu, including a recognition of both the faults and virtues of one's own group and this may affect positively one's level of tolerance for the cultural distinctiveness of others. Individuals who are more at ease with their own cultural identity are more likely to practice tolerance toward other cultural configurations (Friesen, 1983).

The practice of regarding individuals unfairly is not a sign of personal well-being. Frequently such behavior is a symptom of other factors – limited exposure to other cultures and lifestyles, unhappy personal experiences, inappropriate socialization, lack of self-esteem, etc. In truth, all human are members of a single species, and "race" is a social construct which corresponds to no biological reality. Differences between human populations are smaller than those within them, and such differences as *do* exist, for example, those resulting from an I.Q. test, are largely, if not entirely, the product of social environment. Racism and ethnocentrism are irrational, dysfunctional attitudes, if not downright aberrations, and it is largely rigid, authoritarian types of personalities who are prone to them. These attitudes must be combated through social therapy based on equal status contact between groups (van den Berghe, 1981).

Minority Inconveniences

Discrimination can take various forms, and it is often subtle and even unintended when ignorance of differences is the cause. It is often difficult to relate to a person of a unique cultural identity, especially if such individuals evince the kind of peculiarity which makes it easy to patronize or even to pity. Unless these persons can relate to one another in a way so that racial, cultural, credal and religious differences are minimized, there is always a danger that condescension will occur. For example, if one person admits to another that he or she has particular ethnic or religious allegiances, the uninformed listener might respond with just a little too much enthusiasm, "So you belong to that group. My, how nice!" There may be nothing *nice* about the linkage, and the unwarranted degree of enthusiasm revealed by the exclamation may simply be evidence of prejudice, albeit minimal or unintended. An example may help to illustrate this point.

Some time ago a magazine published by the Indian Affairs Branch of the federal government included a story about a Native man who had been appointed special assistant to the Minister of Indian Affairs. The publication carried a picture of the individual with a byline that said, "Mr. _____, British Columbia born and educated, is proving that Indian can and will take their proper place in the Canadian mosaic" *(Indian News,* 1969). The implication of the story was that Indian people had not yet taken their *proper place* in the Canadian mosaic, but they apparently *should* do so.

A more difficult condition of minority status is having one's lifestyle managed by the majority group who may sometimes be quite unsympathetic to the minority situation. Promoters of the democratic set-up are fond of saying that the "majority rules and the minority opposes." Politically, this has some advantages in that the minority frequently plays the role of watch-dog – keeping the legislature on its toes. In the area of minority relations, however, there are many intervening variables. It is not always only a matter of dealing with prospective decisions simply because cultural beliefs, patterns of behavior and religious convictions weigh heavily in such deliberations. In this sense the position of the dominant group is a difficult one, for while the members may act in what they perceive to be the best interests of all citizenry, they may actually be sponsoring programs deemed unfavorable by the minority. The repercussions of this arrangement are not always minimal.

It must be accepted as inevitable in a democracy that majority groups will pass legislation and establish codes of behavior that negatively affect certain minorities. However, these groups can also voice dissatisfaction and agitate to have the rules changed. In a democratic system, that is both their privilege and responsibility. Obviously this is much easier said than done, as in the case of the Aboriginal peoples who for many decades unsuccessfully opposed educational programs aimed at deliberately assimilating their children. It was only in 1970, after a month-long sit-in by 300 people at the Blue Quills Native Education Centre in St. Paul, Alberta, that the Federal Government of Canada took seriously the Native demand for local control of education (Bashford and Heinzerling, 1987).

Inter-ethnic Co-existence

Ethnocultural communities are not uniform in terms of the degree to which they wish to integrate with dominant society, and one factor which affects this is the attitude of the majority towards such groups. Often there is a relationship between values espoused and what participants may see as "survival crisis" and the latter may significantly alter the former. In times of stress brought on by war, for example, where the life of a nation is seen to be at stake, a degree of social harmony and mutual cooperation may evolve which rarely prevails in times of peace. On the other hand, survival crises such as strikes and economic depressions frequently provide the occasion for a breakdown of traditional values and the violation of minority rights, notwithstanding all the liberal sentiments inculcated in the schools and professed by the majority in times of prosperity (Bidney, 1968).

The maintenance of ethnic identity in the above circumstances is a complicated undertaking, and part of the problem lies in the conceptualization of future destiny on the part of each particular community. A classic schematic incorporates four envisioned paths: (i) cultural pluralism; (ii) assimilation; (iii) secession; and, (iv) militancy (Overstreet, 1962). In Canada, Chinatowns throughout their century of history have survived through periods of budding, blooming and withering, only to be revived in the last decade as an expression of realized cultural pluralism (Lai, 1988). Political observers have realized that Chinatown provides a social, cultural and recreational development which enriches the community, the city, the province and indeed the whole country (*Calgary Herald,* April 9, 1969).

It is doubtful that any cultural group in Canada has specifically set for itself the goal of obliterating its identity through assimilation, but there is often a tendency for the younger members of immigrant groups to downplay their cultural heritage and opt for life in the Canadian mainstream. This is probably true of many groups who migrated to Canada during the height of the immigration period at the turn of this century, but by the same token, there are also later generations of immigrants who have rediscovered their heritage cultures and have renewed their allegiances towards them, perhaps through a form of modified assimilation (Driedger, 1989, 163).

About five million Canadians speak French as their first language and live in what they like to think of as French culture. Since the Commission on Bilingualism and Biculturalism reported on the status of the two charter nations in 1969 there has arisen a strong concern among the French in Quebec about losing their cultural heritage and language. The commission stressed the importance of recognizing both charter nations on an equal basis, but some Canadians, particularly immigrant groups, were not quite prepared to project a continuance
This reaction drew the French community closer
d for independence for the Province of
have indicated that they will remain in
egarding governance and taxation are
st have objected to French demands
lling out of the union. In light of

developments in 1992, one could say that Canadian nationhood, such as it is, has no long-term guarantees.

To a certain extent, in a cultural pluralism, groups should be able to function with some degree of isolation depending on the attitudes of the majority toward that orientation. An isolationists stance can imply a number of subtle alternatives, i.e. (i) those who want to be left alone to work out their own lifestyles which they see as superior to others, e.g. Hutterites; (ii) those with a distinct and visible racial identity who participate fully in the educational and economic mainstream but tend to maintain a separate social life, e.g. Chinatowns; (iii) those who by law hold special status or recognition, e.g. Native peoples; and (iv) those who prefer a separate lifestyle as a temporary means of building group strength and identity after which the group may be ready to move into a pluralist situation with power and confidence. An example would be newly-arrived newcomer groups who seek the assurance of a measure of political power before fully integrating into the dominant society (Havighurst and Levine, 1979). Their position may also be motivated by a lack of familiarity with the operations of national institutions, a fear of the unknown and a less than enthusiastic welcome on the part of their newly-adopted neighbors.

The history of most nations contains at least a short chapter dealing with the results of hard feelings resulting in some form of conflict among the citizenry, arising from a myriad of sources. The Canadian record is no exception and it is easy to ferret out examples such as the Winnipeg labor strike in 1919, the Indian "Red Power" movement in the 1960s, the FLQ crisis of the following decade and the struggle of Ontario Indians at Oka, P.Q., only a few years ago. Militancy is no stranger in Canada, and Canadian history is full of rural protest movements and other forms of confrontation (Lower, 1977, 505). To date, most such verbal (and physical?) skirmishes have not necessarily been ethnic-related.

The continued existence of particular minority life patterns is frequently complicated by a variety of factors such as government policy, personal platforms of community functionaries (and sometimes reactionaries), and public pressure or opposition (Friesen, 1984). When and if minorities *do* choose to agitate for change, there are several options open to them depending on the degree to which they choose to work from within or without basic societal institutions. These include institutional integration, secession or social assimilation (Himes, 1974). Institutional integration refers to the legitimate right of minorities to participate in all sectors and every rank of society's bureaucratic apparatus. This includes occupational roles in the economy and positions of power in political and governmental structures. Secession refers to the collective struggle for ecological separation and local political autonomy. In this case the minority perceives society as oppressive and concludes that it cannot achieve its legitimate aims within the oppressive system. Its solution is to withdraw and retreat to a private ecological and political subsystem. Finally, social assimilation, which is favored by the democratic tradition, involves striving for inclusion within the dominant society, both informally, in terms of friendship and cliques, and formally, at the political and economic levels. In essence, the third option is a surrender to majority rule and rarely involves a struggle.

Inter-ethnic misunderstandings and conflict sometimes arise without warning. Such situations may occur when a group aspires to draw more political attention that is currently awarded it. One of the difficulties in achieving this goal might simply be the lack of political clout, perhaps due to a lack of information or knowledge about how to access given agencies. Cultural misunderstandings can also contribute to possible conflicts, particularly in such sensitive areas as funding, for example, when grants are applied for and awarded it may not always be a clear case of "first come, first served" (Glazer, 1980). Another complex area involves what might be called, "homeland concern." This occurs when an incoming group seeks to maintain strong ties with their land of origin, perhaps even to the extent of sending money back home, perhaps to "help finance the revolution."

Ultimately, in an integrated society, the dilemma of belonging to an ethnocultural community becomes a personal challenge. This scenario is classically known as a bicultural situation and may lead to marginality in the sense that the individual involved may feel part of two different cultures but be truly at home in neither. Current interpretations of biculturalism are more positive, however, and some proponents argue that it may be possible for someone to feel a part of and function effectively in two different cultural configurations with equal ease (Snow, 1977). This is accomplished by operating within one's heritage cultural configuration and selecting from dominant society whatever they choose, then adding it to their personal cultural inventory as a meaningful addition.

The condition of marginality is not always avoidable despite the best efforts of individuals to do so. This is brought out well in a novel by James Mitchener who described such an individual living in the Orient. Hugh Channing, the character in question, was of Native and non-Native parentage and was thus labelled a "Eurasian." His dilemma was that Caucasians would not recognize him as a European because of his mixed parentage, and since he was not a *true* Asian, he was not allowed to pull a rickshaw or to clean gutters. He was expected to be a clerk in a shop, nothing more. Socially he could go neither up nor down. As he put it, "What am I? I am a Eurasian. I can never be a European as long as Englishmen despise anyone with even a drop of color. I can never be an Asian as long as my parents bring me up to imitate the white man" (Landis, 1958, 118).

Too often the dilemma of marginality is not a theoretical construct, but a reality. It is a condition forced upon individuals when they are negatively regarded because of an accident of birth. The society which Canada allegedly aspires to is one in which one may make such statements as the following with equal pride and without internal uneasiness at the juxtaposition, "I am a Jew or a Catholic, or a Protestant, a Black or an Indian or an Oriental; I am a Canadian, I am a person" (Gordon, 1964, 265).

Special Rights and Minority Status

There are many instances in Canadian history which reveal mistreatment of minority groups, cultural or otherwise, but there are also instances where such groups have successfully sought and gained special rights or status. The procurement of special rights in the current context of democracy is difficult because no individual or group can have any rights except those granted by the majority. In the legal context the rights and duties of minorities are also recognized as acting as a safeguard for minority rights. One might even go so far as to suggest that when decisions are made by the majority the opposition may have to go along with them, but they do not have to like them. Moreover, they have the democratic right and responsibility to work against such decisions in an effort to eventually overthrow them through the appropriate process. This assumes that due process is accessible by the minority in question, but this is not necessarily the case when certain ethnic groups do not know about or deliberately choose to disregard the recognized political process.

Perhaps if the democratic notion of consensus, which emphasizes the pursuit of consensus on as many matters as possible, was altered and focussed instead on granting as many concessions and rights as possible we may arrive at a truly multicultural society. If this were the case, perhaps the unique wishes of minorities could be better accommodated and the pluralist principle which Canada promotes would be better served. Several avenues remain open for a defence of this concept of democracy which would place primary emphasis on the rights of individuals and groups as opposed to the notion of "the greatest good for the greatest number." In fact, honoring unique and even controversial agreements with specific groups is in keeping with the fundamental notion of a multicultural reality. Individual rights can easily be ignored or even violated if every major national policy is formulated simply on the basis of majority rule. Can there be a "common good" if it does not apply to the average citizen? The following examples illustrate the complexity and sometimes contradictory components of this challenge. These examples also illustrate that rights are too often temporary allotments; they can be given and they can be taken away.

Bilingualism in Manitoba

The Province of Manitoba's current debate over language is rooted in the 'iar legal history of the province whose French-speaking Metis population but within two decades the English language was made the language of the majority. A bill passed in 1890 made it official; English was now to be the language of the people. Periodically, the issue flared up, but it was only a few years ago that it received any serious legal attention. In 1979, the Supreme Court of Canada ruled that the Bill of 1890 was in violation of federal jurisdiction. A traffic ticket issued in English to a French-speaking Manitoban, was fought in the courts – all the way to the Supreme Court of Canada. Suddenly thousands of provincial statutes were in jeopardy, and the province's premier, Howard Pawley of the NDP, quickly introduced legislation that would again extend equal language rights to the francophones who, incidently, make up only five percent of the province's population. Successful maneuvers by the opposition Conservatives forced the legislation to a crawl, but the matter was eventually resolved in favor of equal language rights.

Language rights were an issue in the 1984 federal leadership race in the liberal party and prime minister hopeful, John Turner, suggested that there be no federal interference in a provincial matter. Later, due to pressure from all sides, he reversed his position and admitted that parliament *should* play a role in protecting the rights of minorities. Another leadership contender, John Chretien, took a different position than Turner and argued that constitutionally-protected minority language rights were the proud heritage of the liberal party. Because the two leading liberal candidates took a stand on the issue, other candidates were forced to voice their opinions as well. Eventually the Manitoba provincial government *did* endorse official bilingualism and obtained the court's permission to have five years in which to translate all of Manitoba's laws into the French language.

The issue of langauge rights in Manitoba is closely aligned with the concept of two founding nations, which was elaborated in the BNA Act of 1867. The act recognized the legal status of both English and French but subsequent practice permitted the limitation of both languages in the various provinces. Quebec placed limitations on the English language and other provinces did the same for French. Until the Supreme Court ruling regarding Manitoba, French-speaking people outside Quebec had little hope of gaining any recognition for their mother tongue. A little research into the Alberta and Saskatchewan histories will reveal the extent to which this has similarly been the case in those provinces. There is little evidence in either case that the rights of a minority have been, at best, anything more than the recipient of reluctant tolerance. Apparently Canada's cultural pluralism still has severe limitations when it comes to language.

Indian Land Claims

The current situation with regard to Native land claims in Canada is such that some people have visions of non-Natives being run off their lands, out of their homes and businesses, and even out of the country. After all, there are currently 310 outstanding Native land claims covering 53 percent of the surface of Canada. What Native people are asking for includes all of Labrador, two-thirds of British Columbia, including downtown Vancouver, and one-third of Quebec. In light of these claims it would seem that a great deal of negotiation will need to occur in the decade ahead. This seems to be a desirable course of action even though negotiators will initially be overwhelmed by the size of Native land claims. It would be wise to keep in mind that Native land claims have as valid a legal base as any Canadian legislation. The treaties they signed with the federal government were negotiated on a nation-to-nation basis, and the promises made were enunciated in these terms: "as long as the rivers run, the sun shines and the grass grows." No one can easily dismiss the legitimacy of the documents on which Native claims are based (Friesen, 1971).

A perusal of Indian claims reveals that they are not inordinate demands, nor is it impossible to translate them into 20th century terms. The basis of Native land claims is the assumption that their people deserve as high a standard of living as that of other Canadians. Other than that, there is some variation in Native demands, for example, with respect to the "provision of a medicine chest" mentioned in Treaty number Six, but not in Treaty Seven. Native leaders interpret the provision of the medicine chest, which was to be located at the office of the Indian agent on the reserve, to be the equivalent of free medicare today. Naturally, *that* suggestion has met with some resistance in government circles because of feared excessive costs.

There are two fundamental issues emanating from a discussion of Native land claims, the first having to do with the value of Canadian legislation in the form of the treaties. If negotiated treaties, which constitute legislation, are not honored, how can any valid and trusting basis for future negotiation be effected? Second, is the issue of trying to update the meaning of the treaties an inherent intent of the treaties. Does the provision of a medicine chest a century ago translate literally into a medicine chest or is the *intent* of that provision to be provided in an updated form?

The subject of Native land claims on the basis of the treaties clearly reveals that Native people have not been able to count on legislation to achieve what is rightfully theirs. Ongoing negotiations continue to underscore this reality but a true cultural pluralism, based on mutual respect to the extent of recognizing and respecting equal rights, will not be possible if legal obligations are not met.

Hutterite Land Purchases

The differences between Anabaptist groups such as Amish, Mennonites and Hutterites are not immediately clear to the casual observer, but it is an important distinction to recognize that only the Hutterites are a communal group. They have maintained this form of lifestyle for over four centuries, specifically since the year since 1530. Their form of communism has aroused considerable resistance from "rugged individualist-type" farmers in the west, so much that when some colonies have tried to expand they have experienced severe opposition. Their experience in Alberta is a case in point.

In 1942 the Government of Alberta passed the Land Sales Prohibition Act, which was amended in 1943 to include land leases as well as sales. A new Act was passed in 1944 that specifically referred to Hutterites and was to remain in effect until after the second world war. It was reviewed in 1947, and left on the books with the specific stipulation that colonies were permitted to buy up to 6 400 acres for a new colony. The new site could be no closer than forty miles to an existing colony. The law was amended in 1960 so that the forty mile clause was eliminated and the stipulation added that hearings before a community property board would have to be undergone and approval given by legislation before any new lands could be purchased (Hostetler and Huntingdon, 1967; Janzen, 1990). In 1972 the Select Committee of the Assembly (Communal Property of the Government of Alberta) recommended in its report that the Communal Property Act should be abolished since it contradicted the intent of the provincial Bill of Rights. The report recommended that the government establish a watchdog committee to study the impact of various aspects of Hutterite life on Alberta over a five year period. It also recommended that all future legislation apply equally to all citizens of the province. When the five year term of the watchdog committee was completed it was disbanded. Hutterites were again allowed to purchase farm lands according to the same rights as other Canadian citizens.

Mennonites and the Manitoba School Question

In 1874, several thousand German-speaking Mennonites migrated to Manitoba from Russia to escape military conscription. A century earlier they had been lured to Russia from Europe and promised such privileges as free land, exemption from military conscription and the right to maintain their own language, private schools and their own form of Anabaptist religious practice. Now, with the erosion of those freedoms they sought residence in Canada with the same list of demands. After negotiations with the Secretary of the Department of Agriculture, Government of Canada, they were granted a similar set of privileges. The agreement on education read:

> 10. The fullest privilege of exercising their religious principles is by law afforded to the Mennonites, without any kind of molestation or restriction whatsoever; and the same privilege extends to the education of their children in schools (Schmeiser, 1965, 168).

The agreement eventually reached the federal cabinet which, on recommendation of the Minister, amended the agreement to include the words, *as provided by law*. Mennonite leaders were not informed of the change, neither were they made aware that the federal government had no legal right to make agreements concerning schooling, and so they completed their settlement and built and operated their own schools. A generation later, when the Manitoba separate school system was evaluated, and according to a newly-passed provincial school act, it was closed down. Private schools were ordered shut down as well. After all, this was what the law provided.

In 1959, a compromise on private schooling was reached on the basis of recommendations by a Royal Commission on Education. It was concluded that minorities in Manitoba did have a right to dissent on matters not acceptable to them, but individual rights could not supercede the public interest. Ethno-religious minorities such as the Mennonites were thus allowed the privilege of adding a half hour to the public school day for the purpose of religious or language instruction. This compromise did little to appease members of the Old Colony Mennonite Church who saw the compromise as breach of promise. Their leaders managed to procure promises of freedom from the Mexican government similar to those originally offered in Canada and, in 1922, 5 000 people migrated there (Smith, 1957). Others took up residence in various South American countries, or in the states of Florida and Mississippi.

The issue of military conscription turned out in a similar way for Mennonite immigrants. Having been promised freedom from conscription in early negotiations with federal representatives, they were horrified to discover that their young men were to be conscripted for military service in World War One. Again, a similar pattern occurred; after forming an agreement for military exemption with Mennonite leaders, a secret Order-in-Council inserted the clause, *except in times of war*. Thus, when Canada officially became involved in the war, Mennonite men were conscripted. It was another case of promises made (in writing), but not kept. The federal government naturally justified its action in the name of the public good.

Practical Approaches

Any program to change public attitudes toward an appreciation of ethnicity will be successful only if it goes beyond providing knowledge of other cultures. What is needed is information that will raise awareness levels of appreciating intercultural similarities and provide an understanding of the roots of cultural diversity. Recent findings indicate that such efforts can be successful in an educational context provided that a combination of cognitive and highly experimental techniques are employed and evaluation is undertaken commensurate with specified behavioral objectives (Ijaz and Ijaz, 1981). To that extent Ornstein has articulated a number of helpful principles:

(i) we need to move away from the premise that problems of identity and diversity are only or even primarily related to ethnic minorities;

(ii) there is a danger that ethnic studies can easily be transformed into an ideology and lead to an ethnocentrism that rejects meaningful interaction with or appreciation of other cultural lifestyles. As ethnic group members discover themselves they may develop a disdain for North American values, construing them as WASPish or patronizing. Ethnic studies can produce quite unfortunate results if the new pluralism is pushed too far;

(iii) the mobility factor of North American society demands that the citizenry be educated toward a broader concept of "neighbor" since the average North American, for example, geographically relocates every five to seven years;

(iv) teacher training in multiculturalism is not a simplistic task and should be oriented toward a wide spectrum of activities, including in-service education, and not limited to the specific offerings of an established institute, program or department; and,

(v) Political questions will arise when implementing programs designed to meet specific needs. Programs that work with a given minority may not auger well for any other. Similarly, cooperation with the leadership of one ethnic group may work in a manner that proves completely impractical under other circumstances. In an economic context, when jobs are created, for example, the creation of pressure groups brings to fruition what some groups may label as equality of opportunity. On a larger scale there is no doubt that multiculturalism has significant implications for all levels of government and administration (Ornstein, 1981).

Problems connected with the development of workable approaches to multicultural education will no doubt emerge as the variations of a fluctuating and changing society. Still, a few "established observations based in past literature appear to have some validity. These are:

a. The need to eliminate spurious generalizing and stereotyping.

A stereotype is a category of "truth" that singles out individuals as sharing assumed characteristics on the basis of their group membership. This means that individuals may be judged, positively or negatively, on the basis of ethnic background or another characteristic or affiliation. Stereotypes sometimes have a measure of truth to them because they do not originate in a vacuum. However, to assume that *everyone* who belongs to a particular group exhibits only group characteristics is erroneous. This practice originated several decades ago in the work of anthropologist, Ruth Benedict, who depicted Native cultures in terms of "modal personality." For example, she depicted southwest pueblo Indians as Apollonian in personality, meaning they were all peace-loving, gentle individuals, while the Pacific Westcoast tribe, the Kwakiutl, were Dionyesian or aggressive in personality (Benedict, 1934).

The truth about stereotypes is that some of them are false or even harmful. Eradicating them is a task not necessarily limited to the classroom. The media, for example, thrive on the familiarity of expected roles portrayed in books, movies or television. Stereotypes furnish short-cuts to serious thinking about matters concerning human interaction, and allow for the conceptualization of easy solutions to everyday problems. Naturally stereotypes that are similar to our own way of thinking are less offensive than those that differ and they do not become targets of disdain or hostility. When the content of two stereotypes overlap, however, like those of a favored group and a disfavored one, extremely negative attitudes toward the disfavored group are less likely (Cauthen, et al., 1971). If it is true that accurate or at least a fair portrayal of information can even partially resolve potential conflict situations, then surely the dissemination of accurate information devoid of a particular slant, ought to be a major thrust of any institution with a social conscience.

b. The employment of reliable and experimental educational measures.

A persistent popular notion about solving social dilemmas is to relegate some aspect of the solution to the school. Thus it comes as no surprise that one of the most enterprising components of a program to eradicate prejudice and discrimination should fall to the school. In a sense, this mandate is antithetical to schooling since that institution has traditionally fostered a measure of exclusivity and promoted the status quo. Now the emphasis has changed and educators are being challenged to teach a respect for cultural differences and to help preserve ethnicity (Buchignani, 1980). It would be naive to assume that the school can sufficiently bring about an attitude change that will have both an influential as well as a lasting effect. As Kehoe points out, although there is a positive correlation between the level of education and open-mindedness, one cannot be said to cause the other. At worst, it may be that those with more education are better at hiding prejudice. At best, higher education leads to higher self-concepts and we do not know that there is an inverse relationship between the self-concepts of students and their levels of prejudice (Kehoe, 1981).

c. Developing an atmosphere of acceptance.

Any attempt to shift the emphasis toward enhanced tolerance of differences in the Canadian mainstream will need to be a multi-dimensional undertaking involving all major societal institutions. Governments may set the stage by developing appropriate legislation and even policies, but the final test will be in the marketplace of commerce, education, religion and other forms of institutional life. Another factor involves the attitudes of ethnocultural communities members themselves – how sensitive will they be towards the well-meaning but inappropriate actions of dominant society's actions towards them? How much will they be willing to give and take in situations which will inevitably occur and which will involve an interplay of human rights? To what extent will their leaders seek to provide avenues of intercultural understanding instead of merely demanding attention to their special needs? In the final analysis, the intercultural process is a two-way process implying shared responsibility for all involved. One cannot learn about another lifestyle unless one is taught. In such situations it would also be desirable to have willing students.

Ethnicity as a National Challenge

Although most political leaders in English-speaking Canada have accepted and supported the desirability of Canada's ethnic diversity, the Canadian public has sometimes been slow in endorsing the policy. Legitimate questions that arise in this regard have to do with the possibility of formulating a workable pluralist society, e.g. what possible effect will the encouragement of pluralism have on the vertical mosaic in which socio-economic class lines coincide with ethnic lines? How can one hope to establish government policies that are mutually compatible with a myriad of subcultural goals and lifestyles? Finally, there is the question of how much the encouragement of ethnic group solidarity threatens the freedom of individuals who are members of such communities? In reality there can be a great gulf between multicultural policy and practice. Originally the problem of synthesizing the two entities developed when incoming groups objected to being assimilated into the mainstream. The bloc settlements which immigrant groups were encouraged to establish in the west, at the turn of this century, further hindered the social interaction necessary to unified nation-building. Each of the groups occupying bloc settlements developed their own institutions, and maintained their own separate lifestyles quite apart from the rest of the country. In some instances their neighbors resented their isolation and treated them with suspicion. The bloc settlements developed neighborhood "walls" and inadvertently fostered exclusivity, thereby contributing to the racism that developed in that period and which persisted in modified form in the decades that followed (Friesen and Verigin, 1989).

Incidents of racism in Canadian history are easily documented, (McKague, 1991), even though there are those who claim that racism has virtually been eliminated. In essence there are two theories of racism in Canada, particularly with regard to immigration policy and practice. One theory holds that racism has disappeared while the others see racism persisting in changed form (Taylor, 1991, 3). Brown argues that racism and discrimination cease only when the victims of these practices, alone or in solidarity with others, muster the power to force the aggressor to stop. Until this happens, the option is dialogue between aggressor and victim with the latter creating sufficient pressure on the power of the dominant group so that it decides that the dialogue is either in its best interest, or at least superior to the alternative (Brown, 1991, 163). Appeals to government as a means of combatting racism are quite ineffective since the ultimate resolution of their situation is found in political organization and political action. This will require community support or at least some measure of tolerance on the part of dominant society. Generally speaking, "white ethnics" or anglophones are by no means a natural support group. As one observer put it, "Indeed it would undoubtedly be easier to muster support for Canadian seals than Canadian racial minorities" (Buchignani, 1991, 204).

As the twentieth century has unfolded, there is evidence that at least one social institution has picked up more than its share of responsibilities in seeking to resolve social ills such as racism. This overworked institution is the school which has continually undertaken an increasingly heavy workload ranging from becoming a glorified babysitting agency to dealing with a myriad of other social "obligations" such as the provision of driver education, consumer education, family life and sex education, substance abuse education, etc. All of this is to be accomplished while effectively carrying out the traditional mandate of instilling the 3 "R's" (Friesen and Boberg, 1990, 2). Naturally, when the subject of multicultural education came up, with its attending challenges of combatting discrimination and racism, the public made a "quick trip the school to lengthen the school day" (Friesen, 1987, vii).

References

Abu-laban, Baha & Donald Mottershead. (1981). Cultural pluralism and varieties of ethnic politics. *Canadian Ethnic Studies,* XIII(3), 44-63.

Barron, Milton L. ed. (1962). *A textbook of readings in intergroup relations.* New York: Alfred A. Knopf.

Bashford, Lucy & Hans Heinzerling. (1987). Blue Quills Native Education Centre. *Indian education in Canada, Volume 2: The challenge.* Jean Barman, Yvonne Hebert & Don McCaskill, eds. Vancouver: University of British Columbia Press, 126-141.

Benedict, Ruth. (1934). *Patterns of culture.* New York: Mentor.

Bidney, David. (1968). *Theoretical anthropology.* New York: Columbia University Press.

Brookes, Sonia. (1990). An analysis of Indian education policy, 1960-1989. Unpublished M.A. Thesis, The University of Calgary.

Brown, Rosemary. (1991). Overcoming sexism and racism – How? *Racism in Canada.* Orville McKague, ed. Saskatoon: Fifth House, 163-178.

Buchignani, Norman. (1980). Culture or identity? Addressing ethnicity in Canadian education. *McGill Journal of Education,* XV(1), Winter, 79-93.

Burnet, Jean. (1979). Myths and multiculturalism. *Canadian Journal of Education,* 4(4), 43-58.

Burnet, Jean & Howard Palmer. (1990). State of the art. *Canadian Ethnic Studies,* XXII(1), 1-7.

Cauthen, Nelson R. (1971). Stereotypes: A review of the literature: 1926-1968. *The Journal of Social Psychology,* 84: 103-125.

Cummins, Jim & Marcel Danesi, eds. (1990). *Heritage languages: The development and denial or Canada's linguistic resources.* Toronto: McGraw-Hill.

Driedger, Leo. (1978). *The Canadian ethnic mosaic.* Toronto: McClelland and Stewart.

Driedger, Leo. (1989). *The ethnic factor: Identity in diversity.* Toronto: McGraw-Hill Ryerson.

Elliott, Jean Leonard. (1971). *Immigrant groups.* Scarborough: Prentice-Hall.

Fleras, Augie & Jean Leonard Elliott. (1992). *Multiculturalism in Canada: The challenge of diversity.* Scarborough: Nelson Canada.

Francis, E. K. (1947). The Nature of the ethnic group. *American Journal of Sociology,* 52(5), March, 393-400.

Francis, R. Douglas. (1989). *Images of the west: Responses of the Canadian prairies.* Saskatoon: Western Producer Prairie Books.

Friesen, John W. (1971). Some philosophical bases of Indian educational wants. *Journal of Education,* Special edition, No. 17, April, 56-70.

Friesen, John W. (1983). *Schools with a purpose.* Calgary: Detselig Enterprises.

Friesen, John W. (1984). Factors affecting minority education: A rural perspective. *Multiculturalism in Canada: Social and educational perspectives.* Ronald J. Samuda, John W. Berry & Michel Laferriere, eds. Toronto: Allyn and Bacon, 282-291.

Friesen, John W. (1987). *Reforming the schools – for teachers.* Lanham, Md.: University Press of America.

Friesen, John W. & Michael M. Verigin. (1989). *The community Doukhobors: a people in transition.* Ottawa: Borealis Press.

Friesen, John W. & Alice L. Boberg. (1990). *Introduction to teaching: A socio-cultural approach.* Debuque, Iowa: Kendall-Hunt.

Glazer, Nathan. (1980). Towards a sociology of small ethnic groups. A discourse and discussion. *Canadian Ethnic Sudies,* XII(2), 1-16.

Gordon, Milton M. (1964). *Assimilation in American life: The role of race, religion and national origins.* New York: Oxford University Press.

Hall, D. J. (1977). Clifford Sifton: Immigration and settlement policy, 1896-1905. *The settlement of the west,* Howard Palmer, ed. Calgary: Comprint Publishing Co., 60-77.

Havighurst, Robert J. & Daniel Levine. (1975). *Society and education.* Fifth edition. Boston: Allyn and Bacon.

Himes. Joseph. (1974). *Racial and ethnic relations.* Dubuque, Iowa: William C. Brown.

Hostetler, John A. & Gertrude Enders Huntingdon. (1967). *The Hutterites in North America.* New York: Holt, Rinehart and Winston.

Ijaz, M. Ahmed & I. Helene Ijaz. (1981). A cultural program for changing racial attitudes. *The History and Social Science Teacher,* 17(1), Fall, 17-20.

Indian News. (1969). Ottawa: Indian Affairs Branch. 11:7, 5.

Isajiw, Wsevolod, W. (1985). Definitions of ethnicity. *Ethnicity and ethnic relations in Canada: A book of readings.* Rita M. Bienvenue & Jay E. Goldstein, eds. Toronto: Butterworths, 5-17.

Jaenen, Cornelius J. (1979). French roots in the prairies. *Two nations, many cultures.* Jean Leonard Elliott, ed. Scarborough: Prentice-Hall, 136-152.

Janzen, William. (1990). *Limits on liberty: the experience of Mennonite, Hutterite, and Doukhobor communities in Canada.* Toronto: University of Toronto Press.

Kallen, Evelyn. (1982). *Ethnicity and human rights in Canada.* Toronto: Gage.

Kehoe, John W. (1981). Effective tools for combatting racism in the school. *Multiculturalism,* 4(3), 3-9.

Lai, David Chuenyan. (1988). *Chinatowns: Towns within cities in Canada.* Vancouver: University of British Columbia Press.

Landis, Paul H. (1958). *Introductory sociology.* New York: Ronald Press.

Leal, H. Allan. (1983). Multiculturalism and the Charter of Rights and Freedoms. *Multiculturalism,* VII(1), 24-28.

Lower, Arthur, R. M. (1977). *Colony to nation: A history of Canada.* Toronto: McClelland and Stewart.

Martin, James G. & Clyde W. Franklin. (1973). *Minority group relations.* Columbus, Ohio.: Charles E. Merrill.

Matas. David. (1991). The Charter and racism. *Currents,* 7(1), 14-15.

McKague, O. (1991). *Racism in Canada.* Saskatoon: Fifth House.

Ornstein, Allan. (1981). The ethnic factor in education. *The High Sshool Journal,* 65: December, 74-81.

Overstreet, Harry A. (1962). Some contributions to the easing of group tensions. *American minorities: A textbook of readings in intergroup relations.* Milton L. Barron, ed. New York: Alfred A. Knopf, 513-518.

Palmer, Howard. (1984). Reluctant hosts: Anglo-Canadian views of multiculturalism in the twentieth century. *Cultural diversity and Canadian education: Issues and innovations.* John R. Mallea & Jonathan C. Young eds. Ottawa: Carleton University Press, 21-40.

Ray, Douglas. (1985). Human rights and multicultural perspective. *Multiculturalism,* IX(1), 10-12.

Schmeiser, D. A. (1965). *Civil liberties in Canada.* London: Oxford University Press.

Simpson, George Eaton & J. Milton Yinger. (1958). *Racial and cultural minorities: An analysis of prejudice and discrimination.* New York: Harper and Row.

Smith, C. Henry. (1957). *The story of the Mennonites.* Fourth edition. Newton, Ks.: Mennonite Publication House.

Snow, Chief John. (1977). *These mountains are our sacred places: The story of the Stoney Indians.* Toronto: Samuel Stevens.

Taylor, K. W. (1991). Racism in Canadian immigration policy. *Canadian Ethnic Studies,* 23(1), 1-20.

Trudeau, Pierre Elliott. (1990). The values of a just society. *Towards a just society.* Thomas S. Axworthy & Pierre Elliott Trudeau, eds. Markham: Penguin, 357-385.

van den Berghe, Pierre L. (1981). Science publishers. *The ethnic phenomenon.* New York: Elsevier

4

Teaching Multicultural Education

The emergence of multiculturalism, like any new social philosophy, has been accompanied by its share of fanfare and fantasy. When the federal policy was announced in 1971, some promoters thought "we had arrived" in terms of achieving a national identity based on an appreciation for cultural pluralism and diversity. Others saw multiculturalism as the most fruitful avenue by which to achieve national unity – a way to meet the challenges and overcome the shortcomings brought about by provincial variations, regionalism and intergroup misunderstandings. To date the formula has not worked in an "ultimate" sense even though there have been some admirable successes (McLeod, 1981; Stephan, 1981).

Substituting Reality for Fantasy

After two decades of growth and struggle an honest evaluation will pinpoint the limitations of multiculturalism as national policy. As an envisaged goal it cannot easily be surpassed, but as a "state of the union" it leaves much to be desired, if only because of the perpetually-operant forces of racism in the nation (Taylor, 1991). Hence, multiculturalism must be viewed as an ongoing process, not a state to be achieved. So long as there are regional differences, rapid social change and a constant discovery of new information, and so long as *any* credence is awarded the concept of pluralism, the process must and hopefully *will* continue in an unpredictable direction.

The reality of multiculturalism as an unattainable objective may jar goal-oriented politicians and educators towards possible disillusionment. This need not happen, however, because when it is viewed as a process, even a *slow-moving* process, multiculturalism delivers at least minimal results. Against this mandate it is easier to live with the reality of a society fraught with inequity. The resultant "tension" is still active, but more subdued. Besides, things worth pursuing are *supposed* to take time – so goes the slogan. The obvious continua of pluralism are less threatening even if not resolvable. For example, consider two of the controversial requirements of a pluralist society: (i) to permit subgroups to maintain a separate economic system as long as this does no damage to the general welfare of society; and, (ii) to make all subgroups responsible for contributions to the general welfare of society (Gordon, 1964; Friesen, 1983). Clearly the problematic phrases are: "does no damage," and "responsible for contributions." Who decides what "damage" is, or what comprises a "contribution?" By what criteria will a person be considered "responsible?" Does the dominant society dictate these criteria? Are they mutually discussed and worked out by the parties involved? Do the definitions have different meanings, depending on time and place? Do they change over time, and are they subject to the whims and/or serious social pressures of each new generation?

The above questions engender ongoing discussions commensurate with an continuing process. Hopefully, with each new debate, additional light will dawn in an effort to bring the nation one step closer towards the fulfillment of an admirable social ideology. This will require a tentativeness in solution-seeking, by developing the ability to feed on any and all ideas without becoming emotionally tied to their source. Educators will need to see social issues as many-sided, instead of two-sided; learn to appreciate the ideas of others instead of merely listening politely to them or trying to push our own; demonstrate a lack of mental set in attacking problems; and develop as many alternative explanations, hypotheses and viewpoints as possible in seeking solutions (Smith, 1965). This, of course, will require the maximum energies of an enlightened and dedicated society – dedicated, that is, to the goals of multiculturalism.

Contemporary Approaches

A look at some of the latest proposals in multicultural education may leave one with the impression that there is really no way to design a program that might not offend someone, somewhere. Perhaps that kind of sensitivity might be the proper place to start; listening might actually be more helpful, pedagogically speaking, than focusing on trying to do one's best for one's charges. In fact, the idea of eliminating the constant orientation of always wanting to do something for someone may be at the very foundation of the new multiculturalism.

The Search for Techniques

Educational practitioners are sometimes justly accused of being more concerned about method than philosophy. Classroom teachers often protest, "who has patience for assumption-gathering with thirty fact-hungry youngsters to teach?" So the objection goes, and with some justification, of course. The problem may be, however, that unless one is aware of the ground rules for a particular methodology, it's use may actually be a contradiction of what one believes to be philosophically acceptable. Techniques may be interesting or entertaining and even be enthusiastically adopted by one's pupils, but they may also violate some sound pedagogical principles. A physical education teacher who probably knew little about the basic philosophy of education used to divide his teams into the two cultural factions represented in the school on the grounds that "since they fought anyway, let them at least do it in a organized way!" Obviously, this approach grossly undermines anything that implies learning how to get along with others to say nothing of other multicultural concerns.

The increase in the number of books dealing with techniques for functioning in the multicultural classroom can be described as phenomenal. In fact, it is now possible to purchase books that merely list the sources purporting to give this kind of knowledge. Current emphases deal with building the pupil's self-esteem or teaching him/her to accept his/her colleagues on their own grounds. The general principles of such an approach have been outlined in an excellent book by Pamela Tiedt and Iris Tiedt (1979) entitled, *Multicultural Education: A Handbook of Activities, Information and Resources.* These authors suggest that we need to help pupils learn to:

1. see themselves as worthwhile human beings;
2. recognize their origin and cultural background as an asset;
3. attack meaningful tasks with the expectation of success;
4. interact positively with other children in the classroom;
5. recognize that the cultural backgrounds of others are valuable aspects of the pluralistic North American society.

Specific things the teacher can do to augment the above principles include:

1. using language that is free of sexist/racist connotations;
2. talking about people having varied characteristics other than race, sex or ethnic background; and,
3. avoiding the use of stereotypes or language that can hurt people's perceptions of themselves, thus limiting their potential.

Tiedt and Tiedt suggest that teachers initiate discussions that promote a fuller awareness of other people generally and deliberately plan their lessons so as to break down stereotyped thinking. The process requires careful planning of the day's activities particularly with reference to selecting materials and organizing classroom approaches.

Human Rights: The Larger Mandate

It will come as no surprise to proponents of multiculturalism to acknowledge a link with the larger mandate of struggling for a fuller recognition of human rights. (Nakamura, 1977; Ray, 1983; Ray, 1985). In a generic sense, multiculturalism is *part* of the human rights phenomenon, albeit a *significant* part. Multiculturalism makes a plea for equal rights regardless of cultural differences.

An equally convincing campaign could be launched for the importance of other human distinctives or differences, i.e. physical (including biological, racial and hereditary), and political or religious, to say nothing of differences in individual perception. This admission in no way diminishes the significance of noting cultural differences, although each categorical difference is also worthy of emphasis.

Towards a Definition

The notion of "teaching for the individual" has long been a valued slogan among educators, even though the multicultural component has only recently been emphasized. We have long been attuned to the idea of respecting *some kinds* of differences in schooling, for example, those differences derived from administrating intelligence tests. In addition, *physical* differences have received a disproportionate amount of attention, thanks to the field of sports. Reflective of a highly revered value of dominant society, schools tend to pay tribute to students who do well in sports. Consider, for example, the exorbitant salaries paid to grown men skilled at kicking around an inflated pig bladder in an open field (football), men deliberately physically bloodying each other (boxing), or hitting a small hard rubber ball across a field and then walking around looking for it (golf). Dare one add a reference to hockey or the play-acting of wrestling without running the risk of heresy? And what of monies paid to women who openly flaunt the "outstanding" physical features of their anatomy at high paid "fashion shows" or "beauty" contests. Perhaps this is not the time to mention that even forms of "beauty" are culturally-related. The bottom line, of course, is whether or not these forms of physical discrimination are justifiable. In a money-oriented society the question is merely academic; in a society at least half-interested in equity, the question is unsettling to say the least.

The sad realization emerging from the above considerations is that society's values disallow the suggestion that those who work with young children are worthy of at least the same pay as those who make goals in hockey or coach football. Apparently we are not yet ready to admit that the nurture and education of the next generation is as important as sadistic forms of "amusement" are. The fact that we justify one form of single-characteristic discrimination is insufficient grounds for advancing the practice to another sphere. Instead we must aim at the formation of a society which recognizes that those who promote the advancement of the "total person" are engaged in an undertaking which is at least as important as the sports "professions" indicated above. True, it may be a long and arduous campaign, but perhaps someday we *will* witness a greater appreciation than is now the case for the art-forms practiced by the early childhood educator, the nurse, the psychologist, the social worker and others who work in the domain of seeking to make improvements in the arena of human well-being and functioning.

One of the toughest situations a child (and later the adult), will need to deal with is the realization that some things "just aren't fair." Unfortunately, this *is* true; nature just isn't fair. Some people seem to have all the talent and beauty, others were lucky enough to be born tall (or short, or strong or whatever), and others have the advantage of being born and raised in a rich and plentiful society, or better still, landed in a family sporting that proverbial silver spoon in their mouths. In the meanwhile, due to no absolutely no fault of their own, many children will die in infancy because of the geographic, cultural and accidental location of their birth.

One of the most difficult challenges faced by those who auger for equality is to avoid launching a campaign for uniformity in human behavior. It is difficult to evaluate the success of this objective without some kind of measuring instrument. Too often that instrument reflects a distinct cultural bias, however, and its use inadvertently comprises a push for sameness with the inherent aim to "smooth out" human nature. Historical examples of deliberate attempts to smooth out human nature regardless of cultural characteristics are rampant. A well-known campaign of this kind was launched by European immigrants when they first came into contact with the Aboriginal peoples of North America. Under the slogan, "Christianize, educate and civilize," missionaries and government bureaucrats banded together to promote cultural assimilation among the young. Traditional Indian ways were condemned, and a foreign-contrived "age of enlightenment" was pursued. Now, several hundred years later, when those conditions have changed in so many ways, the question of how much success the invaders had in making over their claimed protege is most embarrassing.

To Illustrate

As history reveals, the campaign to assimilate Native peoples failed, even though a multiplicity of different kinds of activities and programs were initiated (Brookes, 1990). Failure has not necessarily deterred policy-makers, and the basic objective of annihilating Native cultures has been maintained as an underlying policy. The institution of schooling has been perpetually charged with the two-pronged responsibility of annihilating and transforming, and a variety of administrative arrangements have been devised by which to accomplish these aims (Piwowar, 1991). Before the turn of this century, schools were run by missionaries with government financial backing. After some ninety years of operation, administration of these schools was turned over to government control with a gradual move towards Indian participation (Friesen, 1991). More recently Native parents and leaders have successfully agitated for "local control of Indian education" and some strides have been made to accomplish this objective. Tired of what was termed "peripheral participation" in the education of their own children, Native leaders pressed for additional input. They wanted more say in schooling, not just with regard to such matters as bussing, school luncheon programs or discipline, but in regard to school policy, curriculum and hiring of school personnel. On July 14, 1970, a sit-in began at the Blue Quills School in Saint Paul, Alberta, by protesting parents who wanted control of their local school. Almost two months later, on September 1, 1970, Blue Quills became the first school in Canada to be administered by Indians, and set a precedent for what was to follow (Persson, 1986). By 1985, 450 of the 575 Indian Bands in Canada were administering all or part of the educational programs on the reserves.

Early reports on Native (local) control of education were exceedingly positive. A survey of 300 Native education programs in British Columbia in 1982 found that students in band-operated schools exhibited a higher success rate than students in provincial or federal schools. Teachers were viewed as being more sensitive to the traditional Native perspective, and Native involvement in education was increased. Students perceived the school in a more positive way, a moderate increase in attendance was noted. Native languages were more frequently spoken, student self-esteem increased and the parents and leaders felt that the school was more a part of the local community (C.E.A., 1984).

By now a certain reality overshadows the local control issue because educational monies handled by communities are still controlled by eastern Canadian government bureaucrats, i.e., the Federal Department of Indian Affairs. Most local administrators are non-Natives, since most Natives lack experience in governing what are essentially non-Native originated institutions. Translated into practice, this means that the "golden rule" still persists; whoever holds the gold, makes the rules! Still, many Indian leaders believe that their people will prevail, as they always have (Couture, 1985), and the "bugs" in Native control of education will eventually be resolved. With strong community support for this and other future innovations the vision for Native self-government will continue to be nourished and empowered (Morris and Price, 1991). If this prophecy is correct, the quest for Canadian unity via uniformity will have to focus on another target group.

A Tolerance for Process

Perhaps the hardest thing about growing up is the realization that things are not the way we once thought; nor are they necessarily the way we were told they were. This challenge includes having to adapt to the reality of a world without Santa Claus, the Easter bunny, the tooth fairy, and a whole host of other myths and fantasies. Black-and-white thinking has to be exchanged for a more relativistic perspective; the pursuit of permanent solutions must be replaced with an appreciation for tentativeness, with the end result that only sometimes workable and usually temporary approaches to immediate pressures can be attained.

These lessons have yet to be learned in the multicultural sector – wherever the belief is held that human acceptance and cooperation can easily be implemented on a widespread basis. For the most part, multicultural programs in Canada are *still* of the fun-food-festival-and-finery variety. Potluck dinners, ethnic dances and one-day conferences have definite limitations in this regard. Curiosity about other cultures, even a *healthy* curiosity does little to promote understanding of or even tolerance toward other peoples. To achieve anything in this regard is to recognize that multiculturalism even at its best is a *process* with an *end-in view,* not a prescription with an in-built guarantee (Friesen, 1985b).

Viewed as a process, multiculturalism generates a series of "problematic" continua within whose bounds there appear to be perpetual tensions. These continua include the pluralist versus assimilation make-up of society, social conformity versus independence and settling for even "small" successes in achieving tolerance. Ensuing discussions sometimes deteriorate into arguments about the extent to which individuals or groups should be "allowed" to persist in lifestyles which differ significantly from that of the dominant society. In the final analysis, how much tolerance should be tolerated?

The Classroom as Laboratory

Teachers have long struggled with the challenge of trying to incorporate a recognition for human differences without minimizing the preponderance of human similarities. This is not a particularly easy matter since respect for individualities is to be fostered in a nationally-recognized institution with a more or less standardized administrative model with a uniform curriculum and methodology.

The toughest challenge in multicultural education, regardless of the age level of the student, is to create an environment in which the "best" in each individual comes to the fore (Mitchell, 1991, 16). Subject matter per se is not necessarily a factor in the campaign to help students to accept themselves in terms of their total identity – physically, culturally, emotionally, etc. What *is* important is the role of sensitive educators who are willing to become familiar with the different cultural approaches to "common" learning situations in a given student body. Sometimes students who respond uniquely to classroom stimuli are reflecting cultural practices, and educators need to be cognizant of this. Students should be encouraged to search out other unique aspects of their cultural heritage as a means of trying to understand themselves. They should be able to conclude that their backgrounds are personal *assets* not handicaps. The urgency of this conviction is premised on the belief that every individual is worthy of making a contribution to society, and cultural background affords a special corollary potential to that contribution. The learning group within which students function should become part of the enabling process by fostering mutual acceptance among their colleagues. Individual students should be made to feel a part of the group while working out their unique personal and cultural agenda (Friesen, 1985a, 168-170).

While the above process continues, the educator/teacher is dutifully engaged in looking on, encouraging, enabling and facilitating. In any intermission, educators will need to address their own personal/cultural voyage – including struggles of identity and other crises. They will have to be careful that this process has a minimal effect on their students' agenda. Tough job, isn't it?

Practical Principles for Multicultural Teaching

Rather than list a series of exercises that might be used by teachers in multicultural classrooms the approach taken here is to suggest a set of principles which might be employed to determine the appropriateness of a given technique. This puts the onus on the teacher to justify philosophically why a particular approach should be used.

Knowledge of Culture

It practically goes without saying that teachers should be at least somewhat familiar with the cultural configuration within which they fulfill their professional duty. Two reasons may be cited. First, it may save the teacher some embarrassment in the long run and, second, it may save the student embarrassment. Both are vital components of effective educational functioning.

A few years ago two teachers, a husband and wife team, went to an African country for a two year teaching term. One day, shortly after their arrival, they found that their home had been broken into, and without giving the matter further thought, they notified the authorities. Within a few hours the culprit, a teenaged boy, was found and brought to trial. It was not difficult to locate or identify him, by the way, for he was found wearing a stolen t-shirt with the Canadian flag emblazoned on it. He was severely beaten later that day. Naturally, our friends were shattered by their part in the episode but their concern was shrugged off by the authorities whose task it was to fulfill local law-and-order. Their attitude to the outsiders was, "If you didn't want the boy punished, why did you report the crime?"

Another incident that shows the same kind of unfortunate cultural ignorance happened on an Indian reservation when the principal of a federal school was called in to answer to band council regarding the accusation that one of the teachers in the school had corporally punished a child. In giving his defense of the situation, the principal was anxious to convince the council of his command of things at school and to assure them that there must be another explanation for the episode. It is obvious that he was quite unaware of the strong allegiance of the tribe to the spiritual world when he uttered these words to the council: "I am sure that none of my teachers has actually struck a child, but if I am wrong and I find on investigation into the matter that it has happened, there will be the devil to pay!"

Instantly, every microphone of the eighteen band member council came alive as individuals shouted their response, "Take that statement back! Do you want to jinx us all?" Of course, the principal complied very quickly, but he also learned a valuable lesson on cultural awareness and sensitivity that day.

A lack of familiarity with lifestyles other than our own often produces negative attitudes, an abomination often perpetuated by the media. A columnist in daily newspaper in Alberta recently berated the actions of a Doukhobor woman in British Columbia who was determined to fast to the death unless what she considered atrocities against her people were remedied. The columnist suggested that she be sent home so she could "die where somebody cared about her cause" and thus save taxpayers a lot of money. That attitude finds ready support in Alberta school curricula where Doukhobors are still referred to as "those who march nude in public and burn schools in defiance of Canadian law." and this despite regular protests from the United Doukhobors of Alberta. Anyone even remotely connected with Doukhobor ways knows that the behavior in question refers to the activities of a very small but radical sect among Doukhobors. The vast majority of their people, Orthodox and Independents, are kind, hospitable and law-abiding citizens (Friesen and Verigin, 1989).

Cultural ignorance is still too common to allow the matter to rest on the basis that everything will turn out O.K. Revamping teacher education to include courses in multicultural education of itself is not sufficient. Even educators have their biases. In a recent group discussion in a course on multicultural education, a guest educator stated that all parents want the same thing for their children by way of educational objectives, namely, the ability to think critically. When questioned about that assertion by suggesting that Hutterites, for example, might not exactly desire that for their children, the retort was, "what do they want for their children? Do they want them to be stupid?"

Naturally, the matter is not that simple. There is a broad range of alternatives between children who can critically examine everything that is thrown their way and "being stupid." Hutterites are hard-working people. They pay taxes, live without contributing very much to social problems and "mind their own business." They do not quite want their children to be robots, but neither do they want to have their every order questioned by their young. To be ignorant of that value preference is to fail to understand Hutterite ways.

No one can be an expert on many cultures, but we can all be more sensitive to people by at least examining carefully one or two alternate styles of living. Travel in other countries can be a great help; in fact, even reading about international events with a sensitive heart will broaden one's outlook. Thus when the opportunity lends itself to visit or work in an unfamiliar setting, it behooves the teacher to "study the facts," to respect another's lifestyle by learning at least a little of its idiosyncrasies, its uniquenesses, its specialties. The next step then is cultural enrichment as new experiences are absorbed into one's repertoire of being.

Staying on Top

The principle of "life-long learning" certainly applies to multicultural education since new knowledge is rapidly becoming available on so many fronts. Practical and personal experience may still be one of the best routes by which to proceed. The field of special education which emphasizes the uniqueness of each child is paralleled by the concerns of the multiculturalists and those of the English as a second language movement. Keith McLeod (1981) offers these suggestions as a means of imbuing the total school program and atmosphere with multicultural concerns:

1. The total school program must be open to examination. We must ask the question, "are there institutional norms that promote ethnocentrism, racism and discrimination?"
2. Teachers must be frank with themselves. Are we as teachers free of ethnic prejudice, and if not, what prejudices do we have? Am I as a teacher secure in my own sense of identity?"
3. School programs should not focus on the "contributions" of a particular ethnic group but rather on the roles of various groups in the development of Canada. To regard ethnic groups as "contributors" suggests that the main dynamics are located in some superior group.
4. Every school subject may incorporate multicultural content.
5. Ethnic studies should not be limited to schools with particular cultural populations. In a sense we are all ethnics and we need to develop an awareness of multicultural dynamics in terms of human relations.
6. Students should not be taught that they are guilty of an offence if they exhibit an attitude of more prejudice against a particular group. Rather, they should be shown that their attitudes may have formed as a result of being conditioned to taste or preferences.

The responsibilities of teachers in multicultural classrooms can readily be labelled "an unfinished agenda" because of the tremendous challenge and dynamic nature of the discipline. Synthesizing the available resources will require a continual commitment and exploration. That, as any teacher knows, is what the profession is all about anyway.

Community Sensitivity

Few people are not bothered by the sight and sounds of an adult attempting to quieten a child in a busy shopping centre, and many feel very much like interfering when it begins to look like the larger of the two is taking unnecessary liberties with the younger. Native leaders tell us that they have had to put up with that kind of interference for centuries in their communities and yet it does not stop. Often, outsiders who feel sorry for Native people come to their communities with the intent of helping them. Then, instead of even trying to learn anything about how Native people have managed to survive through the centuries without the aid of their European brothers, it is simply assumed on the basis of the negative conditions perceived by the outsiders that Native people require assistance. "Well, assistance is what they need, and assistance is what they will get!"

Recent studies have shown that unwanted help often makes things worse for members of a culture that is temporarily off-balance. In the case of Native culture this imbalance has occurred because a synthesis between traditional Indian ways and the conditions brought about by the onslaught of the Industrial Revolution has not been achieved. Many Native spokespersons are saying that possibly the only conceivable way in which this can come about is when it is carried out by Native people themselves, on their own terms and in their own good time.

That solution may be somewhat unrealistic. What may be required is a continued facilitating effort by government and educators, albeit in a supportive, not manipulative role. In many communities this is exactly what is happening even though specified guidelines are not available.

Encouraging higher education in isolated Native communities often raises the expectations of participants to an unrealistic points. On completing their education they often find they have to leave their home community to find employment. The promises of higher education play a trick on them.

Observers of this situation may coldheartedly comment that this is "the way things are, that's progress" or "welcome to the world of 1993." Such perceptions are not without foundation. However, if the basic assumption that educating individuals should provide them with some opportunity for its application is taken seriously, then we need to take a second look at what is happening in Native communities. Upgrading schooling in these areas often introduces other kinds of problems, i.e. what to do with the skills and knowledge attained after graduating? The resultant dilemma is obvious to educators who work in the area of literacy promotion and skill development, and often they begin to experience a certain degree of confusion and perhaps guilt. If they continue to fulfill their obligation to provide the very best education possible, they consequently contribute toward the eventual disappointments experienced by unemployed Natives in their home communities. On the other hand, if such education is not provided in any form in Native communities, the children are robbed of what might be their only opportunity to attain the skills required for a technological age. Realistically, there are very few northern settlements today that can survive much longer via the traditional forms of livelihood – hunting, trapping or fishing. The futurists are probably right; no longer can any Canadians avoid coming into the "real world."

In the transition period between the old and the new it is likely that some of the costs will include a loss of revered ways and the neglect of those who have served the community well in the past, i.e. Native Elders. Personnel like educators, responsible for ushering in the new age, will often feel caught on the horns of a dilemma as they try to help forthcoming generations bridge the gap between the old and new.

It may be true that the community interference factor is most pronounced in the context of Native development, but its quandary is also evident with respect to immigrant groups. No one can be certain at what point newcomers to this country are made to feel at home or when their traditional values are disregarded. When a taxi cab company arbitrarily decides that none of its drivers may wear a turban head covering it may be responding to the pressures of the marketplace, but such regulations clearly violate certain rights of Canadian citizens regardless of their cultural or national origins. The same may be said of a teacher who deliberately attempts to encourage young Hutterite children to consider the freedom which living off the colony affords.

Those who find it necessary to function in a cultural context other than their own would be well advised to respect its workings. Such an attitude is evidenced by those who are not judgmental or evaluative of unfamiliar attitudes or behaviors and try not to be too secretive about their own orientation. Until complete trust between both sides has been established, the conditions to fulfill the agenda will not be met. On a corollary note there is always the possibility that an outsider may accommodate themselves so well to the new context that a subversive stance may be suspected. There have been times when Native leaders have felt that they have more to fear from those who understand and sympathize with their ways than from those who run roughshod over them. The former types may actually tempt Native people to consider adopting an alternative lifestyle and while doing so they may lose their own identity.

Towards "Meaningful" Multiculturalism

The charge that multiculturalism is agenda-oriented is valid. Multiculturalism did not originate in a vacuum, nor does it rest on a value-free philosophy. At its basis are a series of western humanist presuppositions which most adherents espouse. The essence of multiculturalism is a positive supportive commitment to our diversity (Wood, 1980, 7-14). Multiculturalists believe that all humans are members of a single species, and there are no biologically meaningful subspecies with in it. The concept of "race" is a social construct without a biological basis. Differences *between* human populations are smaller than those *within* them, and such differences as exist (e.g. differences in intelligence) are largely, if not entirely, the product of social environment (van den Berghe, 1981, 2-3). It is safe to say that Canadian multiculturalism is "home-grown" with some imported corollary notions. These have been incorporated through immigration, by diffusion and by personal choice. Multiculturalism must incorporate a constantly changing and hopefully flexible policy, and be reflective of underlying albeit emerging Canadian values. The following grid may serve as a workable approach.

Step One: Tolerance or "Minimal Multiculturalism"

The basic agenda of "good" multiculturalism is to advance past the minimal starting line of being tolerant of others. Tolerance means "putting up with, but not necessarily liking" those who "insist in traversing in our life-space." Tolerance is also a somewhat patronizing concept because it implies a superior position on the part of those doing the tolerating. Tolerance per se implies no need for further learning, since the basic objective is simply to muddle through a particular situation. Tolerance in this context is a dead-end street, void of even the slightest potential of gaining additional meaningfulness from human interaction.

Step Two: Understanding and Acceptance – An Improved Mandate

Not content with the notion of mere tolerance, multiculturalists have for some time been agitating for a deeper level of interaction, namely to promote cultural understanding and acceptance. Once we decipher the rationale for people's behavior, it is argued, we will be a step closer to creating a healthy society, capable of encouraging a bonding among the various societal factions. To "understand" implies taking time to "walk in someone else's shoes for a while, to study other lifestyles and value systems, to take relativity seriously. This does not mean that students of culture need to study a multiplicity of cultures other than their own, but to study at least *one* different configuration which features *somewhat* extraordinary values and structures. By expanding one's view past the immediate, and not regarding one's own cultural perspective as the standard by which other cultures are measured, one cannot help but be affected (hopefully positively) through contact with a differing rationale. To understand implies that new knowledge has been attained, but the *use* of knowledge can also be directional. In other words, varying applications can be made of knowledge. Knowledge, when it is attained, is usually categorized by the learner in terms of being useful or not useful, positive or negative. Knowledge is rarely left in an non-evaluated state. Here, multiculturalism reveals its subjectivity because it is commonly held among multiculturalists that knowledge about cultures should be *appreciated,* and not treated in a neutral sense nor disregarded. This belief impacts a specific value mandate upon classroom teachers who thus have the responsibility of helping their students to *accept* new data as valid and useful with the encouragement to students that they add it to their repertoire of *valued* knowledge.

This is easier than it sounds. It is one thing to learn about differences or to discover why people behave the way they do, but it is quite another to have to *appreciate* what they do. Ours is not a society without ethnocentric leanings, and most of us are not too willing to give a blessing to what we might perceive as unorthodox or "weird" beliefs and behaviors for no good reason other than to be generous. This, then, is the *rub* of multiculturalism. To what extent can we dare to promote specific values in a school system that is allegedly cognizant of pluralist value systems? Have educators a right to insist on their fulfillment on the grounds that they reflect national values? What is the penalty for cultural "deviance" and how is it enforced? Does the extension of tolerance apply also to the individual who *refuses* to appreciate cultural differences and is content merely to *tolerate* them? What happens to the individual who refuses even to go so far as to *tolerate* differences?

Step Three: Endorsing and Encouraging Diversity

The final step to completing a multiculturally-inspired education is to *encourage* diversity. This will be the most difficult challenge because, as in the case of Quebec, diversity-seeking citizens may opt for complete separation. Opposition to French diversity has long been a sore point in Canada, particularly in the west, spurned on the grounds that it may lead to a breaking up of Canada. On the surface, this objection has the ear-markings of genuine national concern; a quick analysis will show that it more likely belongs in the realm of regional jealousy which is one of the potential prices to be paid for a truly pluralist society.

The cost of blocking the enhancement of unique cultural preferences is to inherit a unified, uniform society. Undoubtedly efficient to the core, such a potentially mundane existence is attractive to very few individuals, unless, of course, that society would be constructed in accordance with *their* particular value system! Obviously such a recipe would have appeal to would-be reformers with a specific schedule in mind, but it clearly exhibits an anti-pluralist stance.

Meanwhile, back in the world of reality for the teacher, which is the classroom, the challenge of seeking to *enhance* differences becomes a very personal undertaking. Preparation for such a career emphasis must include an understanding of the theoretical conceptions and ideologies of ethnic pluralism and multiculturalism, the study of philosophical assumptions concerning multi-cultural education, a study of the different characteristics and sociopolitical experiences of ethnocultural communities, and learning skills and techniques for teaching ethnically different students (Gay, 1986, 173). In addition, the inertia of traditional pedagogical habits motivate teachers toward the employment of the technocratic or classroom management model of teaching by interpreting multicultural concerns in the language of the dominant social science disciplines. Unfortunately, this model provides prospective teachers with a limited context or framework for understanding the dynamics of a culturally-diverse classroom (Kasprisin, 1991). If one perceives of the school as a microcosm of society it becomes important to learn how to develop a pluralist atmosphere in the classroom. Guidelines by which to accomplish this will include helping students to accept themselves with all of their characteristics, and learn to see others as having equal worth and dignity. This can be done by introducing exercises that encourage students to become aware of their own personal strengths and to identity areas in which they need to grow. They should be encouraged to express positive feelings for other students and participate in cooperative activities in group situations to help each other. Practical ways to achieve this is to help students to learn the facts about their family origins and identity the many (or singular) group(s) to which they belong. By studying the ethnic communities resident in their local neighborhood they will become familiar with the contributions made by diverse cultures and, hopefully, become convinced of the importance of understanding and acceptance among the peoples of a nation as a step towards achieving world peace (Tiedt and Tiedt, 1979, 7-9).

In spite of the thorny nature of teaching in a multicultural context, the teacher is still responsible for creating a positive learning environment and so must select an appropriate method. If the statement that "a philosophic-minded and mature person is one who can act in an ambiguous situation and still be prepared to live with the consequences" is correct, then multicultural teaching can be so characterized.

Borrowing from some of the authors cited earlier we can establish a number of reliable pedagogical principles which will ensure the creation of a healthy learning atmosphere for children regardless of their cultural affiliation:

1. Encourage students to accept themselves in terms of their total identity – physically, culturally, emotionally, etc., particularly with regard to what their peers or superiors might perceive of as atypical traits. Of course, the tendency of some pupils to ridicule even such minor differences as physical shape and height will likely prevail, but the effects of even this kind of harassment can be rebuffed by one who "knows who he is." As John Kehoe (1979) of the University of British Columbia has suggested, "Emphasizing the things about us that are similar is more pedagogically sound than emphasizing differences." By doing this we can reduce the emphasis on differences between us and develop a meaningful communality.

2. Present alternative cultural explanations for normative behavior. Most children are curious about different ways to celebrate Christmas, but the lesson will be more appreciated if such unusual practices can be demonstrated. In other words, if unique customs can be actively described or demonstrated by a member of a subculture resident in the community it will be much more effective. A Sikh colleague recently indicated that his children experienced very little difficulty with acceptance by their classmates, and when asked to explain how this had come about, he had a twinkle in his eye. "As soon as the school year begins I invite my children's peers to our temple for a visit," he said, "and there we go through the ritual of our services with them, carefully explaining every facet of the experience. Then we answer all questions, provide the youngsters with a bit of refreshment and send them home. From that day on they become friends of my children because they have been able to come into their lives in a very special way."

Fear of the unknown may be very real but there may be a ready solution for such a situation, namely, provide an explanation for the unknown. This formula even works with adults, as evidenced by some who grow up to adulthood with preconceived (and false) notions about the Hutterian Brethren. Once inside such a home I have seen many a jaw drop in surprise when the warmth and hospitality of these folk is experienced first hand. More than once, on leaving a Hutterite home, I have heard these former skeptics say, "Well, I never knew they were such fine people."

3. Encourage children to learn about and appreciate the unique contributions of their own culture. This is a tall order, especially if one is not familiar with the historical development or cultural theme of a given culture. This may require a little research, but without exception, it will be fruitful. For the better part of this century, Native youngsters have been taught in school curricula that their people accomplished very little by way of technology before the Europeans came. Even a little historical digging quickly shows the fallacy of such a view, for before the European invasion, North American Indian tribes did very well in such areas as agriculture, architecture and engineering and in making other scientific advances. Their mounds, pueblo remains and other ruins attest to a significant period of development. The same may be said of other groups who have claimed North America and have been pressured to abandon all elements of their previous lifestyle after arrival on this continent. As our society gradually absorbs varying value systems into its very essence, hopefully, members of still other groups will feel increasingly at ease in sharing their way of life with the mainstream of Canadian society.

4. Assist every child in realizing that he/she is worthy of making a unique contribution to society. At first glance this statement appears to suggest that each individual ought to make a certain kind of contribution to our society, but that is not what is meant. The fact, nature and extent of that contribution

is not important. What is essential, however, is for the pupil to believe he can make a contribution if he so desires, along the lines he chooses, and that it will be appreciated.

5. Assist the pupil in becoming part of the group while at the same time maintaining his or her own identity. No group identity is so important that it can demand a complete obliteration of personal uniqueness and require a total melding into the body politic. This lesson was probably portrayed most vividly during the nineteen-sixties when the young people of America developed a counterculture to remind the nation that they were people too. Surely that kind of radical action should not be required in a free nation in order for individuals to be assured of their personal worth and identity.

6. Be yourself; a phoney can be detected by even the youngest student. It is one thing to be sensitive and understanding, but an obvious case of oversell occurs when an individual tries to appear to enamored of a lifestyle different from his own that he either pretends his own is somehow inferior or not worthy of adherence. Neither stance is honest, neither stance is justified. In the final analysis, depending on the cultural context, no one configuration can be superior to any other. Thus to "convert" from one to another or to deny one's own background may be to leave a component of oneself unacknowledged. Few ethnic groups really desire to attract many adherents anyway because they realize that their own system is best for their own members. Furthermore, it is entirely conceivable that those who find other ways of life immeasurably superior to their own have never examined thoroughly either of the two systems. As the old Greek philosopher put it, "The unexamined life is not worth living." If this is so, we might as well start with examining our own culture.

   Pretending to have no values of one's own shortchanges the people one meets or works with. A mutual relationship of the kind implied by the teaching-learning situation demands a giving of oneself, of who one is. This cannot be accomplished when a significant part of "personhood" is held back.

7. Accept each student as an individual. It is entirely possible to make too much of individual differences, be they a cultural derivative or a unique physical or personality trait; on the other hand, to eliminate references to differences entirely by suggesting that "people are people" is similarly too simplistic. The beginning point of teaching a lesson is to determine where the student is at in terms of a particular learning situation. This is done not by cataloging unique personal qualities but by an overall professional assessment of the student's readiness and orientation. The progressive educators of a few decades ago left us with the slogan that "the child is the sum total of his experiences" which, translated, means that all personal characteristics – attitude, behavior, physical components, etc. – contribute to learning read-

iness. Every student will be unique in at least one of these ways, but that fact should be recognized, not enlarged upon.

The ultimate criterion for measuring one's success in attempting to promote self-appreciation on the part of an individual student is to witness their seeing themselves as worthwhile. On that basis their interactions with others can be positive and they will be able to attack meaningful tasks with every expectation of success.

When that expectation becomes a reality, multicultural education at its best will have been realized.

It will be tempting for educators to formulate a workable philosophy of multiculturalism and implement it as an effective pedagogical package. Viewed as a process, however, multiculturalism must remain the object of ongoing analysis and emendation (Piper, 1988). Treated any differently, its attending operationalization may stagnate and bypass important arising needs and thereby defeat its own purpose.

References

Brookes, Sonia. (1990). An analysis of Indian education policy, 1960-1989. Unpublished M.A. Thesis, The University of Calgary.

Canadian Education Association. (1984). *Recent developments in Native education.* Toronto: Canadian Education Association.

Couture, Joseph E. (1985). Traditional Native thinking, feeling and learning, *Multicultural Education Journal,* 3(2), November, 4-16.

Friesen, John W. (1983). *Schools with a purpose.* Calgary: Detselig Enterprises.

Friesen, John W. (1985a). *When cultures clash: Case studies in multiculturalism.* Calgary: Detselig Enterprises.

Friesen, John W. (1985b). "Establishing objectives for a multicultural program," *History and Social Science Teacher,* 21(1), Fall, 32-38.

Friesen, John W. (1991). *The cultural maze: Complex questions on Native destiny in western Canada.* Calgary: Detselig Enterprises.

Friesen, John W. & Michael M. Verigin. (1989). *The community Doukhobors: A people in transition.* Ottawa: Borealis Press.

Gay, G. (1986). Multicultural teacher education. *Multicultural education in western societies. J.A. Banks & J. Lynch, eds.* London: Holt, Rinehart and Winston.

Gordon: Milton M. (1964). *Assimilation in American life: The role of race, religion, and national origins.* New York: Oxford University Press.

Kasprisin, Lorraine. (1991). The Education of teachers for a multicultural society. *Multicultural Education Journal, 9(2)* November, 29-34.

Kehoe, J. W. (1979). *Prejudice and the role of the school.* Vancouver: University of British Columbia.

McLeod, Keith A. (1981). Multicultural education: A decade of development, *Education and Canadian multiculturalism: Some problems and some solutions,"* Saskatoon: Canadian Society for the Study of Education, Eighth Yearbook, 12-26.

Mitchell, Samuel. (1991). There is more than one way to play the multicultural game. *Multicultural Education Journal,* 9(1), May, 12-20.

Morris, Joann Sebastian & Richard T. Price. (1991). Community educational control issues and the experience of Alexander's Kipohtakaw Education Centre. *The cultural maze: Complex questions on Native destiny in western Canada.* John W. Friesen, ed. Calgary: Detselig Enterprises, 181-200.

Nakamura, Mark. (1977). The human rights challenge. *Multiculturalism,* I(2), 6-7.

Persson, Diane. (1986). The changing experience of Indian residential schooling: Blue Quills, 1931-1970, ndian education in Canada, volume 1: The legacy. Jean Barman, et al., eds. *IVancouver: University of British Columbia Press, 150-168.*

Piper, David. (1988). Multicultural teaching: Critical-reflective approaches. *McGill Journal of Education,* 23(1), Winter, 5-16.

Piwowar, Elizabeth Ann. (1991). Towards a model for culturally compatible Native education. Unpublished Master of Arts Thesis, The University of Calgary.

Ray, Douglas. (1983). Human rights in education, *Multiculturalism,* VI(2), 3-7.

Ray, Douglas. (1985). Human rights and the multicultural perspective, *Multiculturalism,* IX(1), 10-12.

Smith, Philip. (1965). *Philosophic-mindedness in educational administration.* Columbus, Ohio: Ohio State University.

Stephan, Werner. (1981). Panem et Circenses? Ten years of multicultural policy in Canada, Canadian multiculturalism: Some problems and some solutions. Saskatoon: Canadian Society for the Study of Education, Eighth Yearbook, 3-11.

Taylor, K. W. (1991). Racism in Canadian immigration policy. *Canadian Ethnic Studies,* XXIII(1), 1-20.

Tiedt, Pamela L. & Iris M. Tiedt. (1979). *Multicultural education: A handbook of activities, information and resources.* Boston: Allyn and Bacon.

van den Berghe. Pierre L. (1981). *The ethnic phenomenon.* New York: Elsevier Science Publishers.

Wood, Dean. (1980). Multiculturalism: Appreciating our diversity. *Accord,* November/December, 7-14.

5

Multiculturalism as a North American Challenge

Although Canadian multiculturalism is flourishing in comparison to developments within the regions of her southern neighbor, the United States, it is interesting to note the comparisons and differences between the approaches of the two nations. The idea of conceptualizing cultural pluralism as a possible societal format is a fairly recent derivation in the United States even though the country may be described as a nation of immigrants. Between 1820 and 1970, more than 45 million immigrants, mostly from European nations, took up residence in the United States (Bennett, 1990, 86). Initially the plan was to assimilate all newcomers into the American way of life, but to help them, by force if necessary, to become part of the great melting-pot. The official view of both government bureaucrats and educators regarding immigrants nearly a century ago was to ". . .break up their groups and settlements, to assimilate or amalgamate these people as part of the American race, and to implant in their children, so far as can be done, the anglo-saxon conception of righteousness, law, order, and popular government. . ." (Cubberly, 1909).

In its most academic form, cultural pluralism relies on the process of compromise characterized by mutual appreciation and respect between two or more ethnic groups (Friesen, 1985). It implies a commitment to the development of all cultural groups, and even hints at governmental assistance in overcoming the cultural barriers which would impede their full participation in society. In effect, cultural pluralism, or its counterpart, multiculturalism (Fleras and Elliott, 1992, 314), has been delineated as a new social policy. As an expression of a social goal, it suggests respect for and support of the heritages and cultures of the various ethnocultural groups within a given society, with the end-in-view of providing equity for all citizens.

It was early in the 20th century that the concept of cultural pluralism first received any serious measure of national attention. Philosopher Horace Meyer Kallin (1882-1974) came to America from Poland around the turn of the century and argued strongly against the deliberate assimilation of immigrants, claiming instead that they be allowed to retain their cultural heritages even though becoming patriotic American citizens (Kallin, 1924; Bennett, 1990). It was not until the protest movements of the 1960s, i.e. civil rights, women's liberation, Black power, and Vietnam War protests, however, that his ideas were afforded much attention (Gay, 1983). Gradually the policy evolved, at least in theoretical form, that cultural minorities should be encouraged to be proud of their ethnic heritage instead of being ashamed of their differences (Tiedt and Tiedt, 1990). Along with this development was the suggested shift to a new expectation of public tolerance and acceptance of unique cultural lifestyles. Cultural pluralism is even currently touted as a healthy national composition, but not necessarily of enhancing ethnic group identity, as is sometimes charged, to the point of causing fragmentation or intergroup antagonism. According to some observers, multiculturalism is widely viewed as a developing national policy (Bennett, 1990).

There are numerous barriers to fulfilling the commitment to multiculturalism in the United States, including an fuzzy definition, lack of financial resources and the fact that supportive studies are conducted by academic ethnocentrics who end up promoting a form of academic ghettoization (Grant and Millar, 1992, 211). In light of the relatively recent origins of multiculturalism it is well to keep in mind that social movements come and go even if at any given time they are viewed as more or less permanent fixtures. House suggests that nationalism, for example, is a recent player (late 18th century) on the international scene, but at the height of its intensity it drives people to the point that they become willing to die for their nation and ethnic community. Apparently, nationalism was generated in part from shared print languages. When cheap newsprint became available, many speakers of the vernacular also became readers for the first time. People began imagining themselves as part of communities which stretched beyond themselves and their immediate villages, even across time. House contends that language is the major instrument of nationalism, and the school is used to teach the local nationalistic vernacular. He admits that nationalism may be economically inspired, but points out (citing Hobsbawm), that some scholars see it as a transitory phase of capitalism which is bound to dissolve as nations become economically obsolete units and are drawn into larger economic entities (House, 1992; Anderson, 1983; Hobsbawm, 1990).

A second wave of nationalism flourished in America during 1820-1920, when one could witness deliberate attempts to prevent popular nationalist movements overseas by utilizing the apparatus of state cultural and educational institutions to promote loyalty to the mother country. Ironically, today similar tactics are employed by pluralist exponents.

Complications and Complexities

The challenge of formulating a functional mix of multiculturalism with the democratic process often produces tensions with national implications. As Gordon has pointed out, when pluralism *is* encouraged, questions quickly arise pertaining to the extent to which separatism can be practiced without risk to the general national welfare. If culturally divergent groups are awarded the right to preserve the basic elements of their lifestyle, at what point does this arrangement run the risk of interfering with the rights of others? To what extent does the existence and practice of cultural separateness contribute towards the welfare of the nation as a whole? (Gordon, 1964, 16-17). In Gordon's words:

> The major problem, then, is to keep ethnic separation in communal life from being so pronounced in itself that it threatens ethnic harmony, good group relations, and the spirit of good will which a democratic pluralistic society requires, and to keep it from spilling over into the civic arena of secondary education to impinge on housing, jobs, politics, education, and other areas of functional activity where universalistic criteria of judgment and assignment are necessary and where the operation of ethnic considerations can only be disruptive and even disastrous. The attainment of this objective calls for good sense and reasonableness on the part of the average American citizen. . . . (Gordon, 1964, 264)

Gordon's phrase, "good sense and reasonableness" offers the clue to appreciating the complexity of cultural pluralism as an applied goal. It is difficult to conceive of a situation where pluralism is void of educational, civic and political ramifications because these represent the very arenas in which applications are undertaken. Moreover, ethnicity *does* affect schooling, class membership and earnings, although to understand this phenomenon fully, it is necessary to also take into account other sources of inequality (Li, 1988, 125). Opponents of cultural pluralism have aptly pointed out that a truly multicultural and multiracial society is hard to govern because of the difficulties in forming and maintaining functional political coalitions. Tensions among groups may erupt because of competition for housing, jobs or other resources. The debates over the outcome, content and processes of schooling will similarly be a major concern (Henry, 1990).

A democratic society is by definition committed to discussion and debate as the various issues propelled by freedom of speech are deliberated. At the core of such discussions is a potential analysis of the nature of democracy itself, which in the case of a pluralist society, is similarly open to debate. The dominant group will logistically set the limits of acceptable democratic behavior, and define what is normative behavior. Still, there are numerous examples to indicate that the parameters of defined "normative" behavior are easily violated. Here is a partial list:

1. refusal of Amish people to send their children to school;
2. the Mormon practice of polygamy;
3. Jehovah Witnesses refusing to salute the flag;
4. Vietnamese boys not taking orders from female teachers;
5. Blacks starting Afrocentric schools; and,

6. Hindu men burning brides because of insufficient dowries (House, 1992); and

7. State legislation forbidding the use of animals as religious sacrifices.

Here are some specifically *Canadian* examples, equally illustrative, even though Canada *officially* lays claim to being a truly multicultural nation.

1. government restrictions on Hutterite land purchases because of citizens' objections to their communal lifestyle;

2. removal of Japanese Canadians from their homes and confiscation of their goods and businesses during World War Two solely on the grounds of their allegedly undesirable visible (racial) appearances;

3. government refusal to honor land Aboriginal claims on grounds that they involve heavily-populated urban areas;

4. refusal of the Quebecois government to allow non-anglophone immigrants to be taught in English in provincial schools;

5. refusal of the Alberta government to allow French to be spoken in the legislature even though French is an official national language; and,

6. public objections to the new policy that members of the Sikh faith can wear non-traditional head-gear when joining the Royal Canadian Mounted Police on the grounds that the uniform, which essence is a gift from Britain and which has already changed its head-gear in four major ways since the inception of the RCMP in 1874, somehow violates a long-established and much revered *Canadian* tradition.

House points out that there are definite differences in the way Canada and the USA perceive multiculturalism. He suggests that Americans are brash nationalists, while Canadians tend to be closet nationalists. Differences between U.S. and Canadian approaches to multiculturalism are symbolized by the melting-pot and mosaic metaphors (House, 1992, 137). A Canadian sociologist, John Porter, defined Canadians (in contrast to the Americans), as conservative, authoritarian and more oriented to tradition, hierarchy, and elitism in the sense of showing deference to those in high status, and united in defense of these values against the egalitarianism and aggressiveness of American culture (Porter, 1987). As House notes:

> Both societies experienced immense migration from 1850 to 1914 and again since World War II. In the most recent decade, 1980 to 1990, for example, the Hispanic population of the United States increased by 7.7 millions, a 56 percent increase. Twenty-five percent of the U.S. population is now minority, up from 20 percent in 1980, the largest population change this century (Barringer, 1992). New immigrants then and now have been greeted with hostility manifested in nativist movements (House, 1992, 137).

Those who worship unquestioningly at the shrine of democracy are sometimes shocked to discover that its format can be subject to change without inflicting permanent damage. Undoubtedly the changing ethnic composition of the USA has political, philosophical and pedagogical ramifications as the various shifting segments of society impinge their opinions upon the democratic process, possibly even redefining its traditionally-revered essence. Gay suggests that world developments are causing some Americans, at least, to reconsider their country's traditional role of international dominance and unquestionable leadership in world affairs (Gay, 1992, 46). Recently, in an attempt to summarize the feelings of the American people on the topic, then USA presidential candidate, Bill Clinton, accused President Bush of being too concerned about international affairs and neglecting the needs of the American people. The fast-changing international scene is hard to keep up with, let alone adjust to, even from a democratic perspective. Japan's economic and technological might has severely threatened America's influence in the world marketplace, and the increasing rate and magnitude of foreign investments in North America generally has raised doubts about the validity of a North American continentalism. There are other happenings: the crumbling of the communistic bloc in Eastern Europe, the reunification of Germany, escalations of tensions in the Middle East and the relaxation of South African government policy on apartheid. The involvement of the United States in these situations is extensive and has expanded the contextual parameters of multiculturalism to global dimensions. The resultant situation is not one for which the traditional American "quick-fix" orientation will necessarily produce a ready solution (Gay, 1992, 47).

Re-Focussing Multiculturalism

The central focus of a liberal democracy, such as that of Canada or the USA is a respect for individual equality and the economic marketplace. A further interpretation promulgated by liberal multiculturalists is that the members of the body politic will have respect for differing cultural identities *and* for the common bond that makes them a society. The difficulty that emerges from the discussion is that *group rights* are not an entity in the United Nations context because in delineating its parameters of recognized rights that body foresaw that minority or group claims could be dangerously threatening to the national stability of some member nation-states. Against that context, ethnocultural communities or minority groups have no *international* grounds for claiming collective recognition. Individuals *do* have rights, however, and these are supposed to be protected by national and international law, and as such furnish the individual with the freedom to choose to retain or not to retain cultural connections or identity. That freedom is a fragile commodity, however, in a world where human rights are beset by ideology and orthodoxy, where diversity is rejected and dissent is stifled (Berger, 1982; Kallen, 1989).

All of this places the urgency of multicultural policy and practice on extremely precarious grounds and raises doubts about the efficacy of the pluralist principle. Glazer, for example, construes ethnic membership as an individual, private, voluntary matter, like belonging to a club or choosing one's associates or deciding which college to attend. He treats ethnicity as a matter of personal choice and argues against any measure of group rights, stressing instead that only *individuals have rights,* not groups (Glazer, 1988). To illustrate, House emphasizes that Aboriginal rights in America are treated as *gifts* which can be revoked; they are not rights. He suggests that only when a minority culture is actually threatened are special rights justified. Even then, no cultural custom or practice should be permitted if it violates the individual rights guaranteed by the nation even if it is argued by the minority in question that the practice is essential to the maintenance of their culture (House, 1992, 143-144).

A similar situation prevails in Canada where ethnicity has been entrenched in law and is allegedly protected by the Federal Charter of Rights and Freedoms (Friesen, 1992). In effect the charter has made little difference since its inception, and even its goal of encouraging national unity has been "fragile and often threatened by intolerance" (Trudeau, 1990, 366). In essence, the implementation of the spirit and intent of the charter is dependent upon the will and spirit of the people (Ray, 1985, 10). For example, the charter does not have the authority to override existing laws that violate human rights. This is because parts of the charter are interpretive; they do not *confer* rights, but rather allow for a behavior translation which is supposed to be consistent with "the preservation and enhancement of [the] multicultural heritage of Canada" (Leal, 1983, 25). Thus the charter is a passive instrument, at best indicative of a long-range social goal or envisaged ideology. It is not meant to be a spur; it is meant to be a brake. It prohibits racial discrimination in law, but it cannot require governments or citizens to promote racial (or cultural) equality (Matas, 1991).

Against this background it would seem logical to conclude that a genuine North American multicultural society is still a long way off. In the meantime the sloganizing about multiculturalism will no doubt continue, hopefully, with the eventual end that a closer correlation will emerge between official policy and practice. Undoubtedly world events and the changing national cultural composition will auger strongly as related factors in the transition.

Implications for Schooling

The above conclusion raises serious questions about the potential importance of multiculturalism as a reachable educational objective. A brief review of past educational approaches will illustrate the quandary that educators will find themselves in when trying to match school procedures to social reality.

Perhaps multiculturalism, like nationalism and other such themes, has had its day, even before it culminates in a full fruition. In the meantime as dedicated educators continue to attempt to transform an underlying assimilative stance towards a culturally pluralist format we would do well not to neglect the other factors that distinguish human diversity, i.e. other distinctions or uniquenesses which weigh heavily in the campaign to define the human species more sharply in an effort to better achieve equality for all. These include the physical aspect (including biological, racial or hereditary), and the political, social, psychological and religious, to say nothing of individual differences in perception. This in no way diminishes the significance of noting cultural differences, although each categorical difference is worthy of separate emphasis.

Introducing the Case Studies

Schooling is one of the most frequently employed avenues by which ethnocultural leaders have attempted to preserve their community's values and culture. This orientation is evident in each of the five case studies presented in the following chapters. Both charter nations, French and English, hoped to perpetuate their values systems through schooling, including language as well as institutional structures such as religion. One Anabaptist group, the Hutterites, pride themselves on their four and one-half centuries of effective cultural maintenance, thanks largely to their unique form of private schooling. Similarly, the multitude of subgroups within the ranks of another Anabaptist group, the Mennonites, all pay homage to the particular form of schooling which their sub-constituency has espoused, as a major factor in perpetuating their way of life.

The fourth case study offers an intense look at a specific ethnocultural school, namely that operated by the Chinese community in Calgary, Alberta. In this chapter, Dr. Kim Sheung-King Lan, a former principal of the Calgary Chinese School, explores specific ways in which schooling may be employed as a vehicle of cultural maintenance, i.e. its function in promoting cultural identification, ethnic self-identity, intercultural sensitivity, and appreciation of other cultures. Finally, a case study of the Sikh community in Canada reveals how various social institutions, including the school, play a role in maintaining ethnic cohesion. This study is particularly important as an example of an ethnocultural group who face constant opposition and oppression. Their diligence and perseverance is truly an example of cultural persistence in a not-too-friendly multicultural society.

References

Anderson, B. (1983). *Imagined communities: Reflections on the origin and spread of nationalism.* London: Verso.

Barringer, F. (1991). Census shows profound change in racial makeup of the nation. *New York Times,* A1, A12.

Bennett, Christine I. (1990). *Comprehensive multicultural education: Theory and practice.* Second edition. Boston: Allyn and Bacon.

Berger, Thomas R. (1982). *Fragile freedoms: Human rights and dissent in Canada.* Toronto: Irwin.

Cubberly, E. (1909). *Changing conceptions of education.* Boston: Houghton-Mifflin.

Fleras, Augie & Jean Leonard Elliott (1992). *Multiculturalism in Canada: The challenge of diversity.* Scarborough, Ontario: Nelson Canada

Friesen, John W. (1985). *When cultures clash: Case studies in multiculturalism.* Calgary: Detselig Enterprises.

Friesen, John W. (1992). *Multiculturalism in Canada: Hope or hoax?* Edmonton: Alberta Teachers' Association.

Gay, Geneva. (1983). Multiethnic education: Historical development and future prospects. *Phi Delta Kappan,* 64: April, 560-561.

Gay, Geneva. (1992). Multicultural education in the United States. *Beyond multicultural education: International perspectives.* Kogila A. Moodley, ed. Calgary: Detselig Enterprises, 41-66.

Glazer, N. (1988). The affirmative action stalemate. *The Public Interest,* 90: 99-114.

Gordon, Milton M. (1964). *Assimilation in American life: The role of race, religion and national origins.* New York: Oxford University Press.

Grant, Carl A. & Susan Millar. (1992). Research and multicultural education: Barriers, needs and boundaries. *Beyond multicultural education: International perspectives.* Kogila A. Moodley, ed. Calgary: Detselig Enterprises, 201-214.

Henry, III, W.A. (1990). Beyond the melting pot. *Time,* 135: 28-31.

Hobsbawm, E.J. (1990). *Nations and nationalism since 1780.* Cambridge, Mass.: Cambridge University Press.

House, Ernest R. (1992). Multicultural evaluation in Canada and the United States. *The Canadian Journal of Program Evaluation,* 7(1), 133-156.

Kallen, Evelyn. (1989). *Label me human: Minority rights of stigmatized Canadians.* Toronto: University of Toronto Press.

Kallin, Horace Meyer. (1924). *Culture and democracy in the United States.* New York: Boni and Liveright.

Leal, H.A. (1983). Multiculturalism and the Charter of Rights and Freedoms. *Multiculturalism,* 8(1), 24-28.

Li, Peter S. (1988). *Ethnic inequality in a class society.* Toronto: Thompson Educational Publishing Co.

Matas, D. (1991). The Charter and racism. *Currents: Readings in Race Relations,* 7(1), April, 14-15.

Porter, John. (1987). *The measure of Canadian society: Education, equality and opportunity.* Ottawa: Carleton University Press.

Ray, Douglas. (1985). Human rights and multicultural perspective in Canada. *Multiculturalism,* 9(1), 10-12.

Tiedt, Pamela L. & Iris M. (1990). *Multicultural education: A handbook of activities, information and resources.* Third edition. Boston: Allyn and Bacon.

Trudeau, Pierre Elliott. (1990). The values of a just society. *Towards a just society.* Thomas S. Axworthy & Pierre Elliott Trudeau, eds. Markham, Ont.: Penguin.

6

The Charter Nations: A Prevailing Clash

Most histories of North America civilization concentrate on European beginnings on this continent and disregard the Aboriginal record almost entirely. To some extent this was due to the orientation of the incoming explorers whose perspective was that of invaders and conquerors. They did not come to learn or share but to dominate and transform. In addition, the culture of the Aboriginal peoples was founded on the oral tradition and thus no written records were available for the invaders to peruse if that had been their orientation. It has often been observed that if Canadian history had been written by Aboriginal authors the emphasis of the last several centuries would have been much different. Most historical records depict Native peoples as defeated and powerless, while contemporary Native writers tend to stress the durability and persistence of Native cultures (Couture, 1985; Dickason, 1992; Sioui, 1992). They point out that even after five hundred years the Native Sacred Circle of Life, which symbolizes the interdependence and equality of all living things and the earth itself, has remained unbroken (Moore, 1992). Against this backdrop Canadian Native peoples are planning to participate more actively in the various sectors of the nation's future development, including literature and history, in the centuries that lie ahead.

The First Clash

When Christopher Columbus set sail for North America his homeland of Spain was at the height of her imperial power. Land-space, however, was at a premium, and a popular prospective for relocation and starting a new life was America. Thus the motivation for a North American exodus developed a two-pronged purpose – to provide a source of hope for a new start for the crowded multitudes of Europe and a target for economic exploitation. Subsequent history shows that to some extent both goals were realized by incoming peoples.

Even a cursory survey of Canadian history points to the influence and contributions of the French in Canada. School readers include accounts of Jacques Cartier, for example, who set sail for New France from St. Malo on April 20, 1534. Following the beaten track of the Breton fishermen, he passed through

103

the Strait of Belle Isle and entered the Gulf of St. Lawrence. He landed at the Bay of Chaleurs, as he named it, an area which separates New Brunswick from the southeastern tongue of the Province of Quebec. He landed, planted a cross, and solemnly took possession of the land in the name of the King (Tracy, 1908). Official settlement of the area did not take place until 1608, however, when Samuel de Champlain founded the city of Quebec. Within the next twenty-three years the cities of Trois Rivières and Montreal were also established.

In July, 1629, a year after the first visit, and English fleet again sailed up the St. Lawrence, anchored at Quebec City, and demanded the city's surrender. Champlain as founder of the city was understandably upset by this move and travelled to England to intercede with the king to return control of Quebec to the French. This happened three years later in July of 1632. In the meantime the fur trade continued as usual and the Jesuits campaigned for a spiritual harvest among the Indians of the territory, mostly in Huron country. The mission of the Jesuits was not necessarily endorsed by the Indians who often held conferences to decide the fate of the missionaries. From time to time chapels were attacked and priests beaten. In addition, some of the priests developed ideological differences with the elite clergy who were linked to France (Driedger, 1989, 166). It was the local inhabitants who continued the Quebec nation after the British conquest. In the meantime, the Jesuits (or Black Robes as they came to be called), prevailed and went on their way teaching, nursing, helping and baptizing, all for the "glory of God" (Tracy, 1908, 84).

The French Colony

Over the next 150 years, nearly 10 000 Frenchmen migrated to the new colony and New France became firmly established on the St. Lawrence River. The rate of immigration was low, averaging only sixty-three persons a year (Burnet and Palmer, 1988, 18). Although French Roman Catholics were pre-ferred immigrants in the colony represented many different countries – Austria, Poland, Portugal, Scotland, Spain, Switzerland, China and Africa. The develop-ment of agriculture and trade and the establishment of religious, judicial and political institutions provided an expanding base for communities that enjoyed a distinctively French and Catholic way of life. According to Scott, "The exclusion of all Protestants . . . kept the society tightly knit and sharpened the notion of a missionary group dedicated to the propagation of the Catholic faith in the New World" (Scott, 1958, 54). The French settlers brought with them abundant religious and civil traditions, authoritarian practices of rule and feudal social relationships which continued to influence the French Canadian ways of life well into the 19th century and which have survived in modified form to this day.

From the base of original colonization, the French continued exploration into the interior of the continent, opening areas for future settlement and control of vast areas in North America. In the 1630s, Jean Nicolet reached Lake Winnipeg and from 1731-1743 Pierre de la Verendreye and his sons explored as far west as the Rocky Mountains. For over one hundred years thereafter, French voyagers and missionaries travelled throughout the west.

The colony of New France soon became embroiled in a tremendous power struggle between France and England, a struggle which was translated into conflict with religious overtones in the new land. According to Lower, "The self-governing British colonies of the Atlantic coast, predominantly Protestant in character, were distrustful of the autocratic, imperialistic regime in New France, a Roman Catholic community" (Lower, 1973, 38). It proved that the slow westward movement of British settlement into territories claimed by France that precipitated the final war for control, the Seven Years War of 1756-1763. Following the British victory, the Treaty of Paris was signed giving most French possessions in North America to the British. This victory is often referred to as "the conquest" by French historians and represents a watershed which figures prominently in the minds of French Canadians when interpreting the Canadian past. It was also the event that marked the end of the French empire in America (Morton, 1965).

National Adjustments

Following the conquest, problems with rival commercial interests in the fur trade, legal matters and the authority of the Catholic Church led to the passing of the Quebec Act in 1774. The Act essentially recognized the individuality and separateness of Quebec and also permitted a return to the conditions of New France, except that London acted in the place of Versailles (Lower, 1973). Commercial rivalry continued to plague Quebec, and in an attempt to satisfy the interests of competing French and English interests, the Constitutional Act of 1791 was passed, dividing Quebec into the provinces of Upper and Lower Canada. The act essentially created a political division which distinguished itself in two cultural groups and provided for their governance, but it changed little else.

The years that followed were marked by the struggle for responsible government, culminating in the Act of Union of 1841 which united Upper Canada and Lower Canada into the Province of Canada. The other British North American provinces of Nova Scotia, Prince Edward Island and Newfoundland were engaged in similar struggles. An arrangement that would unify the provinces for economic or political purposes had been discussed at intervals since the end of the 18th century. The loss of the favored position that colonial markets had enjoyed until 1849, the threat of American annexation in the west, and the inter-provincial interests that followed the introduction of the railways led to a renewed interest in political union. The British North America Act of 1867 made the union a reality by creating the Dominion of Canada which included the four provinces of Ontario (formerly Upper Canada), Quebec, (formerly Lower Canada), New Brunswick and Nova Scotia. The Quebec Commissioners concluded their consideration of the events by noting that the Union of 1867 met the common needs of the provinces. They also suggested that the primary reason why the French bloc joined Confederation was because "it had been given every conceivable promise that it would be able to govern itself in autonomous fashion, along with all its institutions, according to its special way of life and its own culture (Lower, 1973, 109). Naturally, English observers who were not party to the agreement saw the arrangement as the selling out of English Canada.

The New Confederation

At the time of Confederation, Canadians of French descent, living mainly in Quebec and New Brunswick, accounted for approximately thirty percent of the Canadian population. The BNA Act gave English and French equal status in Parliament and the courts of Canada, and in the courts and legislation of Quebec, thus recognizing the cultural duality of Canada. However, the French language had no official status in any other provincial courts and, more importantly, was not protected in any of the nation's schools (Cook, 1966). Although the fathers of Confederation showed a fair amount of interest in education and its legislative control, it was very characteristic of these typical British Americans, with their strong denominational affiliations and frequent sectarian biases to have schools. Their primary concern, however, was not the role of language but the place of religion in the schools (Creighton, 1970).

During the period of French rule and for many years following the treaty of 1763 by which Canada became a British colony, the only schools in Lower Canada were operated by the Roman Catholic Church or by private individuals. Proposals to establish non-denominational schools were strongly opposed by Roman Catholic leaders. The first step towards state control of education came about in 1801 with the passage of the colonial government of "An Act for the Establishment of Free Schools and the Advancement of Learning in this Province." The act provided for the establishment of free common schools when a majority of citizens petitioned for one and were willing to bear the costs for its operation. Roman Catholics objected to the provisions of the act because of obvious attempts to give the Church of England a prominant role in education. Protestants equally disliked the act because of the authoritarian type of control which it provided. As a result, very few schools were established under the act of 1801 (Cheal, et al., 1962, 45).

The French Perspective

It was the two elements of language and religion that continued to dog the struggles of French Catholics in western Canada, especially since those distinctive cultural features of French Canada were confirmed only in those parts of the Dominion in which they had already been established by law or custom. Section 93 of the BNA Act gave the provinces the right to legislate in respect to education. Moreover, since the western provinces were not yet created, those cultural features confirmed in the older provinces were given protection in these outlying areas. Thus an inherent contradiction was created; while the federal government recognized the duality of cultures in Canada; it gave the *provinces* jurisdiction over the very means by which that duality could be protected or destroyed, namely the school.

Immediately after Confederation, the French schools issue dominated national and provincial elections. Many Anglo-Canadians were convinced that the terms of Confederation had been too generous to French Canadians, and they became determined to make Canada, except for Quebec, as homogenous as possible. One by one the provinces exercised their authority over school matters by legislating uniformity and establishing "national" schools.

When Manitoba came into Confederation in 1870, protection was given to separate school systems and French was to be the second official language in the legislation and in the courts. In 1890, however, Manitoba passed a public school act ending the dual system and making English the language of instruction in publicly-supported schools and declaring it to be the sole official language of the province. In Ontario, the French-speaking minority took their case to the Supreme Court only to have it decisively ruled that Section 93 provided absolutely no legal protection for education in the French language within separate schools.

French-Canadians have traditionally perceived that language and religion are central to the maintenance of their culture. They believe that the state of cultural health of a national community may be measured with a fair precision by the state of health of the language which is spoken, and firstly by its conservation, its survival. French Canada does not conceive of education divorced from religion. Religion must be at the very base of all conscious living and must form the soul of all thinking. All education accordingly, is a study of God and there is no such thing as secular education (Saint-Denis, 1940, 25).

Traditional French Canadian historians were primarily concerned with legal, political, religious and linguistic questions. Although they placed varying degrees of emphasis on the church, they all glorified a past in which French Canadians were free of British dominance. They looked to the past to discover values that would help French Canadians resist the threats of the present. They emphasized Catholicism, conservativism, order, stability and agrarianism. It was only these traditional values that could save French Canada from the anti-clericalism of France and the materialism of its neighbors in the rest of Canada and the United States.

The modern historians who emerged after World War Two rejected tradition and opted for change. They exposed what they called the "myths" of rural life, fear of the state, and the idea of a spiritual mission, and claimed that their cultural survival could only be achieved through an interventionist state and provincial autonomy. Some of them promoted Quebec separatism. The modern interpretation of cultural survival remained largely confined to Quebec and the traditional view continued to prevail in the west.

The ideology of cultural survival is a direct response to the British conquest of 1760. Because French Canadians are a "conquered" people and a minority, they place a great deal of emphasis on group rights. It is hard for people of English speech to understand the feelings of those who must pass under the yoke of conquest, for there is scarcely a memory of it in all their traditions (Lower, 1977, 65). By contrast, English Canadians, comfortably engulfed in the majority culture, can afford to be more concerned with individual rights. Anglo-Canadians view majority rule as fundamental to a just society, whereas French Canadians view representation by groups as the basis of a just society. For most French Canadians there are only two groups in Canada – French and non-French (or English). For them, the recognition or inclusion of more groups or support for multiculturalism would undermine this reality. The French leaders who came to the west fostered the traditional interpretation of cultural survival based on the implicit assumption that it can only be attained through community solidarity and strong leadership.

The British Perspective

Until the 19th century the history of Upper Canada (now Ontario), was a story of intercultural relations between Aboriginal peoples and British and French immigrants. The Maritimes featured a slightly enhanced multiculturalism with the addition of other national groups. In Ontario, however, British ethnic groups – English, Scottish Lowlanders and Highlanders, Northern Irish (Scotch Irish) and southern Irish, and Americans dominated the social scene. They also shaped the economic, political, educational and religious institutions of the province. Much of the development of the province showed American and British impact and French influence was barely noticeable. French Canadians tended to be isolated in rural areas and competed with Irish lumbermen and construction workers as members of an emerging proletariat (Burnet and Palmer, 1988).

The French peasantry of the St. Lawrence Valley practiced a lifestyle similar to that which they had left in Europe. They duplicated on North American soil the pre-Reformation peasant society of the Old World. They saw little need for striving; to them life was a series of ritual acts such as being born, coming of age, marrying, begetting, and dying. Each stage, when properly performed, brought its own degree of success and satisfaction (Lower, 1977, 68). By contrast:

> Into this unchanging world, there comes bursting the hurly-burly of the English man of business. He has long since cut his associations with the soil. He wants to get things done. He has ends to gain. He has an object in life. That object is one comprehended only remotely by the peasant (Lower, 1977, 69).

Building a British Canada

After the signing of the Treaty of Paris (1763) it fell to the British to originate a policy for nation-building. Implicit in the treaty was the assumption that large-scale immigration would occur and the fur trade would be perpetuated. In that sense the treaty gave the area a degree of stability it had not previously known (Hamilton, 1970a, 88). The residents of New France felt abandoned, however, for they had depended upon the mother country for government, educational structures, commerce and cultural leadership. Thus they turned to the Roman Catholic Church for leadership but that route proved to be only partially satisfactory since the Church of England (Anglican) religion of the invaders fostered different ideas about educational structures and objectives (Giles and Proudfoot, 1990, 10). The successful national conquest would have to include a cultural takeover if conflict was to be averted. Schooling was selected as the primary vehicle through which "appropriate" acculturation would be accomplished.

From the outbreak of the American Revolution, Nova Scotia became the nearest haven for those in the thirteen American colonies who believed they could not support the revolutionary cause. Between May and November of 1783 approximately 14 000 to 15 000 came to that area of Nova Scotia which the following year became the Province of New Brunswick. In general the Loyalists tended to reinforce the provincial elite whose Anglicanism and conservative outlook were rapidly becoming entrenched in government councils. In March, 1783, a group of Anglican clergymen met in New York to discuss the future of Nova Scotia and concluded that two steps were necessary to ensure the province's cultural flavor – the establishment of a colonial episcopate and a literacy institution. In a legislative session of 1789 an act was introduced to establish King's College and providing for its support. This act seemed to jolt many Nova Scotians out of their lethargy which ultimately culminated in the passing of "An Act for Encouraging the Establishment of Schools Throughout The Province" in January, 1808. This was followed in 1811 with the passage of the Grammar School Act which empowered the Lieutenant-Governor in-Council to appoint trustees in counties not already served by grammar schools (Hamilton, 1970a). By the end of the first quarter of the 19th century, education became the chosen vehicle by which acculturation would be undertaken through both public and private means.

A similar situation developed in New Brunswick. Its formal educational history commenced with the coming of the Loyalists. Their leaders brought with them a well-defined concept of the role that education could play in the new colony. They saw the school as an agent of both the church and the state and responsible for perpetuating the image of a "sane" British society that would embrace the ideals of an aristocratic society. In an effort to preserve their cherished ideals at the level of higher education, a college charter was approved by the New Brunswick legislation on March 9, 1793. Although early drafts of the charter suggested that it would be open to individuals of all faiths, the final version in 1800 restricted such privileges to members of the Anglican Church. In addition, the president and faculty were to be of the same religious persuasion (Hamilton, 1970b, 107).

In 1805, the foundation for secondary education was laid in New Brunswick through the passing of "An Act for Encouraging and Extending Literature in the Province." Part of the act provided for the provision of two grammar schools in "each and every county" of the province for the instruction of youth of both sexes in the English language and writing and arithmetic. The schools were to be under the direction, regulation, control and management of the Justices of Peace for said counties (Hamilton, 1970b, 109).

Prince Edward Island was envisaged to be an extension of British feudalism from the beginning. The census of 1798 indicated that half of the island population of 4 372 was Scottish, but by 1827 the population had increased to over 70 000 with a healthy influx from both Ireland and Scotland. Oddly, arrangements for schooling were meagre in the early stages of the province's growth. Private schools and itinerant schoolmasters met most of the population's needs supplemented by a series of home schools. In 1821 a national school was opened in Charlottetown but it was not until 1825 that the province passed its first Education Act entitled, "An Act for the Encouragement of Education in the Different Counties and Districts of the Island" (Hamilton, 1970b). The fact that teachers were required to obtain certification from a local clergyman implies the nature of educational content and objectives to be promoted.

In Upper Canada the development of the province and the evolution of education were parallel. The Loyalists arrived in 1784 and established their first school at Kingston two years later. Seven years later the first land grant was issued for the support of grammar schools and the establishment of a university was announced. From the beginning, however, there were two influences affecting educational development in the province – British *and* American. A juxtaposing of divided loyalties emerged in the Loyalist community, initially fuelled by the fact that, on the surface at least, they were faithful to their British origins. Deep down, however, they had been conditioned by the new-found freedom of their adopted homeland – they were now Americans (Wilson, 1970, 191). The result was an educational philosophy with a practical bent mixing an equality of concern with a concern for quality in educational services (Nash, 1975).

Illustrative of British educational conservativism was the work of John Graves Simcoe who argued for a two-tiered system of schooling. He chose his advisors largely from well-to-do families of Loyalist background who favored a "proper" education for those who would become the nation's leaders and a lesser form of education for people in the "lower degrees of life" (Johnson, 1968; Wilson, 1970, 193). The American influence was evident in the writings of Richard Cochrell who wrote the first book on educational theory in North America in 1795 (Cochrell, 1949). Although born in England, Cochrell was impressed with and advocated the American educational model on such items as discipline and pedagogy and the establishment of teacher examination practices. The debate between influences probably reached its height after 1844 when Egerton Ryerson became superintendent of the province's educational system. Ryerson advocated a system of education that was democratic, universal, compulsory, free and practical, and was bitterly opposed by John Strachan, first Anglican Bishop of Toronto. Although ordained a Presbyterian, Strachan converted to the Church of England and became a consistent advocate of the recognition of that Church as the rightful, indisputable authority for the proper conduct of schooling in the colony (Patterson, et al., 1974, 131). He also wanted the common schools under clerical control to counteract "dangerous American tendencies," through the use of American textbooks and the hiring of American-trained teachers, but he lost the battle. Nonsectarian schools became the order of the day (Francis, et al., 1988a, 221). Some observers note that this double philosophical influence persists in Ontario to this day.

The religious dualism of Upper Canada was similarly manifest in its economic makeup. Although the bulk of the province was involved in agriculture in the early part of the 19th century, the timber trade was also being developed. The farm population was considerably removed from the area in which the lumber trade was being promoted, and was thereby sheltered from its disturbing influence. Any cultural clash between the two groups occurred alter 1814. The continuing influx of newcomers, the increasing mobility of the population and the growing numbers of rural dwellers who migrated to urban settings cause increasing social strains upon social organization.

One of the institutions required to absorb the results of these adjustments was the school. The isolation of farm homes and the urgent requirements of farm children to provide labor made school attendance difficult to enforce. In addition, the lines forming to mark off the Loyalists from the American settlers were extended by suspicions caused by geographic isolation (Clark, 1971). There is some indication that the reluctance of the Anglican Church to adapt itself to frontier conditions yielded up the province to American influence which is later evidenced in the formation of a universal school system under the progressive leadership of chief school superintendent, Egerton Ryerson. Critics also point out that the disparity between urban and rural education currently evident in Ontario is a longstanding tradition in Ontario and continues to shortchange those who migrate to the city where they are forced to enter the lower levels of the occupational world (Humphreys, 1971).

Developments in the West: The Role of Schooling

Historians divide the history of western Canada from 1768-1962 into three periods. Since 1962, Canada has been described as in the formative phase of developing a multicultural nation (Friesen, 1985). During the first period, from 1768-1890, the west was characterized by a balance of anglophone and fracophone communities. During the second period, from 1890-1917, the demographic base was radically altered as the result of a large influx of eastern Canadians and European immigrants. The third period, from 1917-1962, has been characterized by attempts to assimilate all non-anglophones to ensure the cultural dominance of anglo-Canada (Jaenen, 1979). Naturally the school figured strongly in these campaigns and frequently became the primary vehicle by which the objectives were to be reached. A brief examination of this development will illustrate the tremendous struggle of French Canadians in the west to preserve their culture and identity through education.

Colonization Of The West

The French in western Canada were actively engaged in providing schooling for new settlers well before Confederation. Their pattern of schooling was introduced by Father (later Bishop) Provencher in 1818 near what is now St. Boniface. At the same time two other priests organized a school at Pembina on the Red River. The Hudson's Bay Company, which owned the land, strongly encouraged these missionary-educators as much as possible giving them free transportation to the area, providing land grants, building schools and churches, and allotting funds for the purchase of books for religious instruction. The company's interest in supporting educational efforts was not altogether altruistic since, according to the resolutions of the Council for Norther Development in 1828, education was the means by which to achieve "the more effectual civilization and moral improvement of the families attached to the different establishments. Among the resolutions for promoting moral and religious improvement, issued in 1885, were stipulations that fathers devote their leisure hours to teaching their children literacy, the Catechism and elementary education, and every father was to speak to his children in his own native language (Lupul, 1970).

Educational growth in the west was closely tied to parish growth, and by 1849 there were about a half dozen schools for a population of about 2 500 French Catholics. By 1879, this number had more than doubled, and similar schools were established further west around Edmonton.

The first western schools were usually crudely built log buildings with a single room and little by way of equipment. Religion was the primary subject matter. At St. Boniface, in 1869, some of the subjects studied by boys included sacred and secular history and algebra, while the girls studied Canadian history, music and ancient mythology. Secondary education presented a problem due to costs and the small number of students eligible for this level of schooling slowed its growth compared to elementary school developments. By the time of Confederation, two generations of missionary-educators had carefully supervised the growth of the school as a means of perpetuating French culture and religion.

The Act of Confederation was in large part theoretical and the actual building of the new nation through territorial completion still lay ahead (Creighton, 1970). The drive towards continentalism was made urgent by two external forces: Britain was anxious to relieve herself of the remaining territorial obligations in the northwest, including Rupert's Land, and the United States, in a desire for expansion, turned her eyes towards the vast and largely unpopulated west. These factors hastened the first post-Confederation government of Sir John A. Macdonald to annex these lands and effect the movement of thousands of immigrants, preferably those with agrarian inclinations, into the west.

At this time, the few thousand inhabitants of the northwest were Indians, a handful of non-Native fur traders and several hundred communities of Metis. Between 1896 and 1914, more than three million immigrants, mainly Europeans, settled in the west (Palmer, 1975). Before this movement got well underway, the northwest could be characterized by bilingualism and biculturalism featuring a demographic, institutional and constitutional balance between anglophones and francophones. By 1915, however, the French Canadian population had been reduced to no more than ten percent of the total population in each of the provinces of Manitoba, Saskatchewan and Alberta. It has been estimated that the French Canadian population in Canada today is descended almost entirely from the 65 000 people who had settled in New France by 1763 and this has not been enlarged by French-speaking immigrants (Palmer, 1975).

When Manitoba joined Confederation in 1870, francophones still represented a large portion of the population and the Manitoba Act included provisions for the province to be bilingual and bicultural with a dual system of denominational schools. Church schools were officially recognized in 1871. Of the 24 school districts in Assiniboia at that time, half were Catholic, reflecting the demographic balance between English and French. Catholic settlers in Manitoba were French-speaking and thus the two designations, French and Catholic, became coterminous. The act essentially blessed the denominational balance in education which the missionaries had established and assumed the balance would continue.

Perhaps sensing that this situation was precarious, the Catholic bishops sought to attract additional numbers of French-speaking people to the west. Their vision was the establishment of a Franco-Catholic bloc would enhance the position of their nationality in Confederation, while carrying forth the "civilizing" mission of the society from which most of them came (Painchaud, 1976). The Catholic Church became a strong proponent of francophone settlement in the west and set itself up as a colonizing agent and lobbied governments to achieve its objectives. The bloc settlements were designed to create a monolithic and homogeneous society in which the church, the parish, the school, the family and the rural way of life would complement one another. When bloc settlements became more difficult to establish, "chain" settlements were promoted.

Clerical leaders looked to Quebec as one source for new immigrants and from 1879 onwards, church leaders, politicians, missionary-colonizers and journalists sought to convince their counterparts in Quebec to promote the migration of Quebecois westward. The Quebec response was cool, however, since the province was preoccupied with the retention of French-Canadians. Concerned about depopulation as the result of an already massive exodus of Quebecois to the United States and not convinced that the future of French Canada lay in expansion to the west, the Quebec leaders really took no initiatives of any consequence.

When it became clear that French settlers would have to come from elsewhere, western leaders became involved in trying to repatriate former Quebecois from the United States and to attract settlers from Belgium and France. The results of these efforts were meagre.

In addition to the lack of enthusiasm of Quebec to send settlers to the west, there were other reasons for failure. The sense of defeat experienced by the French-speaking bishops stemmed in large part from their ideology. They were conservative-minded, staunch believers in the agrarian way of life, somewhat paternalistic, and above all, determined to build a society in which the church would be predominant.

There were three long-term effects of the colonization and immigration programs carried out by the church. First, the bloc settlements not only survived, but became bastions of the French fact in the west. By the same token, the chain settlements led to the isolation of a number of French-speaking communities and actually facilitated in their assimilation. Second, the French-speaking population in the west gradually became one of a number of minority groups. Third, the power of the predominantly French-speaking Catholic Church was drastically reduced (Painchaud, 1976).

The failure of the colonization program was poignantly symbolized by the Manitoba School Question which marked not only the end of biculturalism in the west, but also the end of the recognition of the rights of Catholics in the field of education.

The Struggle for Bilingualism

It was the influx of several million European immigrants in the early 20th century that threatened cultural dualism in the west and ultimately the type of schooling which the French Catholics deemed important. French-Canadian nationalists such as Henri Bourassa, M.P., viewed Prime Minister Laurier's energetic immigration policy as a direct threat to the French presence. Bourassa and his associates charged the government with deliberately attempting to swamp the French minority with immigrants of dubious European extraction and a lack of organization to attract immigrants from France, by granting cheaper railway ares to immigrants from Europe than for those who wished to go west from Quebec. They also accused the government of failing to provide adequate funding to repatriate French-Canadians in the New England states and allowing grossly inadequate medical examinations of immigrants who then "infected the French with their diseases" (Petersen, 1975). Despite these protests, European immigrants continued to flood the market.

This view had some merit in light of Prime Minister Laurier's pessimistic statement in 1896 when he admitted that he had never had great confidence that Canada could ever have many immigrants from France. He believed that French people preferred to remain in France so immigration options would do better in Britain (Petersen, 1975). The relationship between immigration and education became of utmost importance to politicians since the school was viewed as the means by which to assimilate immigrants and promote a feeling of Canadian nationalism and/or British imperialism (Stamp, 1970). Moreover, the dual confessional school no longer coincided with the sociological contours of the increasingly multicultural landscape of the west.

In Manitoba, an apparent solution to this problem was an act passed in 1890 by the legislation which created a centralized department of education to replace the existing dual confessional board of education, and abolished Catholic public schools in favor of national schools. This act was formulated without consultation with French school authorities, and their opposition to the changes was immediate. It was also motivated by Ontarians who had swarmed into Manitoba bent on transforming it in their own image and likeness. They represented more than anglophone cultural imperialism; they also represented the secular and materialist culture of the 19th century industrialized societies which sought salvation in scientific discovery, technological advance and material progress (Titley, 1990, 77). The result was that the French minority obtained an unfavorable ruling in the supreme court and was deeply shocked that their educational interests were not protected in the Manitoba Act which was modelled on Section

93 of the BNA Act. Desperately, they appealed the decision. The second verdict was favorable, but the issue was far from being resolved.

In 1896, a federal election was fought in which education was the central issue. Ironically, the winner was the Liberal Prime Minister, Wilfred Laurier, a French Catholic who refused to give a specific pledge to protect French Catholic rights in Manitoba. His triumph was largely the result of the vote in Catholic Quebec, which was enamored with the notion that Laurier was one of them, and bitter that the Conservative government had authorized the hanging of Metis leader, Louis Riel. Shortly thereafter, a compromise, known as the Laurier-Greenway agreement between Manitoba and the federal government was enacted. It was agreed that the non-denominational nature of the Manitoba schools would remain; *any* religion could be taught by any denomination but only at the end of the day and under certain conditions, and where ten pupils spoke French (or any other language), a bilingual teacher could be employed. The compromise denied state aid to separate schools and required that Catholics support public schools financially. It did stipulate, however, that if requested, trustees had to provide a certified Catholic teacher for every twenty-five Catholic pupils in a rural school or forty in an urban school. These results were basically unsatisfactory to the Roman Catholic bishops and they subsequently launched an unsuccessful appeal to church authorities in Rome (Lupul, 1970; Jaenen, 1978).

By 1915, one-sixth of Manitoba's schools, mostly French, were bilingual. Many students knew little English and in the absence of compulsory laws, about 75 percent of children did not attend. The lack of bilingual teachers also compounded the problem and this situation precipitated educational reform. In 1916, public school education was made compulsory for children between the ages of seven and fourteen and the bilingual clause was repealed. Apparently the feeling against bilingualism was so strong that even the study of a second language was omitted. Faced with an electorate which refused to accept cultural duality, the politicians readily succumbed to the temptation to sacrifice minority rights on the altar of political success.

Despite these developments, the western Canadian French continued to cling to their language and culture. The nature of block settlements favored cultural retention and teachers in these French-speaking municipalities defied the law and continued to use French as the language of instruction in the public schools. Another factor that helped preserve French culture was the all-French education of fracophone elites at the high school and university levels provided by the Jesuits at the College de Saint Boniface.

Further west the situation was a little different. Before the provinces of Saskatchewan and Alberta were created out of the old Northwest in 1905, the federal government controlled the territory, and as a result state aid to separate schools was ensured. In 1877, additional federal legislation gave status to the French language and these provisions recognized the bilingual and bicultural reality of the Northwest at the time. Opposition to this cultural duality developed and the public and separate school districts were merged into a central authority which ensured that preference would be given to public schools. By 1892, the Board of Education also made English the official language in all schools but allowed French as the language of instruction in the primary grades. F. W. G. Haultain, Premier of the Northwest Territories, set out to establish a system of "national schools" which would be universal and compulsory, and in which civic and commercial ideals would replace religious and sectarian ideals in the interests of a more tolerant and united national sentiment, less driven by differences of culture, race, creed and class.

Haultain appointed David James Goggin as superintendent to head up his new school system and Goggin energetically undertook the task. As an unabashed national imperialist, Goggin perceived of the British empire as "the most splendid possession ever entrusted to any people" (McDonald, 1974). A great deal of his time was taken up with the formation of corollary institutions and clubs dedicated to an adoration of British culture. He clearly believed that children of all different races, creeds and customs should be gathered into the common school and there "Canadianized." Goggin perceived that those these children may enter the school as "Galacians, Doukhobors or Icelanders," they would come out as Canadians. A common school and a common language (English) would produce an homogenous citizenship necessary to the development of a "greater Canada" (McDonald, 1974).

The French in Saskatchewan and Alberta fared slightly better than their counterparts in Manitoba. When Saskatchewan became a province it inherited school legislation from the old Northwest, but controversy erupted in 1911 over school taxes and eventually developed into a much larger emotional issue. Anglo clerical leaders charged that French clerical schools were perpetuating non-anglo saxon ideals and features, and using the schools to foster their own sectarian ends. Thus the teaching of French and foreign languages was lumped into one category in spite of pleas by the French community for recognition of their special place in Confederation. By 1981, the issue had become a political football and cultural and linguistic uniformity were seen as the panacea for all of the province's ills. Following pressure by French leaders and much political wrangling, legislation was enacted which restricted teaching in French to the first grade but allowed it to be a subject of study for one hour in each day.

School controversies were less marked in Alberta, but in 1916 the province passed legislation which restricted the study of any language to the last hour of the school day and only in the first two grades. Thus a system of bilingual education in the west had ended by the time the first World War broke out. The initial motivation to allow bilingual education may have been based on the notion that such a system would deliver ethnic social disintegration and assimilation. Proponents did not foresee possible ethnic cultural transmission as an end result of such a policy. In fact, however, the spectre of national disunity resulting from cultural diversity inaugurated a third phase marked by concerted efforts to assimilate non-Anglo Canadians into the mainstream of Anglo society, using schooling as the means by which to accomplish this objective.

The Push for Assimilation

The aftermath of the first world war included a campaign to assimilate non-anglo Canadians into a unified Canada. Lest politicians be held solely responsible for these efforts, it is helpful to point out that educators shared this perspective. They worked diligently to instruct their pupils in good English useage, proper civic attitudes and matters such as personal hygiene, proper dietary habits, good sportsmanship and patriotic lore. Naturally, these objectives were couched in anglo terms and featured anglo interpretations. Protestant church leaders, especially Methodists and Presbyterians, accepted responsibility for building a Canadian nation conforming to the religious, moral and social values of the dominant English-speaking majority. For members of these institutions, Protestant Christian values were coterminous with Canadian national values (Barber, 1975).

Even though these attempts were aimed at new unacculturated immigrants, French-Canadian Catholics did not escape being tarred with the same brush, and were often relegated to the status of foreigners. Catholicism was considered by Protestants to be inferior, misguided, and even dangerous since the Catholic Church apparently fostered superstition. Moreover, the hierarchical structure of the Catholic Church was considered contrary to true democracy since its restrictions on individual freedom was both destructive to individuals and to the state.

Because of the very real presence of the Catholic Church in the west, and its dominance by a French-speaking hierarchy, Catholic religion and French culture became synonymous with the English-speaking Protestants. Moreover, because ultramontane archbishops waged public battles to preserve a separate French-Catholic identity in western Canada, their public profile was high. Many saw the French language and the Roman Catholic religion as mutually reinforcing, and as representing a bulwark against the encroachment of Protestantism. English-speaking Canadians rejected the notion that the school should be utilized to preserve the French-Catholic identity. They did not see any danger of French cultural losses because French children in the west were always surrounded by their own people in an almost totally French atmosphere. Why would the French worry about that?

The press for uniformity prevailed and was intensified by the time of the second world war where politicians saw European societies as alien to the Canadian way of life. This translated into a school curriculum with an emphasis on teaching national (and British Empire) pride and an awareness of the evils of the military oligarchy of Europe. Young anglo-saxon rural teachers worked hard to assimilate the "hordes of foreign children" (including French-Canadians), into the anglo-dominated Canadian mainstream (Jaenen, 1979).

This situation prevailed until the 1960s when provincial governments replaced existing school legislation. In 1967, the Manitoba government amended its legislation to allow one of the two official languages to be used as a teaching language in the public schools. Earlier, in 1961, Saskatchewan passed legislation to allow for the teaching of oral French in all schools, but only at the discretion of the local school board. In 1968, the Saskatchewan government also made a commitment to begin teaching French in the schools. In Alberta, an amendment to school legislation permitted the more frequent use of French, and in 1968 instruction in French was permitted from grades one through twelve for half of the school day. The question still remains as to whether these changes went far enough to meet the educational objectives of French Canadians in the west.

The Perpetual Clash

Canada is a society rife with contradictions. One of the most striking features of our society is the great disparity which exists in its reward structure and the consequent vast inequalities in the distribution of "tangible goods" among its members (Young, 1990). The French, for example, have been under-represented in the professional and technical occupations, as well as in the upper echelons of business and industry for many years (Richer and Laporte, 1979). Their struggle for cultural maintenance has culminated in the rise of French nationalism represented by the formation of the Parti Quebecois which is dedicated to a separate Quebec. For the Parti Quebecois, the separation of the Province of Quebec is a necessity if French culture is to be preserved in Canada. Despite the defeat of a referendum in 1980, in which sixty percent of Quebecers voted to remain in Confederation, the Parti Quebecois has not greatly modified its objectives (Driedger, 1989, 194).

As observers have noted, it cannot be denied that the image of French Canadians as one culture has a degree of validity (Ossenberg, 1971, 103). There is a lack of consensus on the desirable nature of the future Quebec society, however, and for some, a separate Quebec society with institutions reflecting the French-Canadian view would be the logical alternative to the present Canadian society that favors assimilation (Richer and Laporte, 1979, 83). A second view represents a retreat to the past, and relishes the once significant part that the French played as an equal partner in Confederation. Still another perspective is that Quebec culture needs to be brought up-to-date in order to participate as an equal partner in a multicultural Canada (Rioux, 1987, 215). If this should be accomplished, there is a price to be paid – that of at least partial assimilation. Thus, French-Canadians find themselves in a perpetual conflict between their status as Canadian citizens and as members of a French-Canadian nation

(Anderson and Frideres, 1981, 87). As the threat of assimilation continues to weigh heavily on the French their community is forced to continue to search for ways to give their language and culture new vitality (Francis, et. al., 1988b, 363).

The French fear of being swallowed up in a national campaign to develop an anglophone nation has deep historic roots. As far back as the spring of 1868, a group of intellectuals met in Ottawa to launch the Canada "First Movement." The group sponsored candidates in the election of 1874, but soon thereafter dismantled (Francis, et al, 1988b, 40). Their concerns, however, have been evident over the last century in the actions of many different individuals and groups. For example, Charles W. Petersen (1868-1944), a western agrarian editor, wrote about the need for the development of a distinct (anglo) Canadian nationality. In his words, "We cannot be satisfied with the position of a 'polyglot boarding-house.' We must either keep strangers out, or we must assimilate them. There must be no half measures" (Jones, 1989, 18). In the 1960s, recognizing that British Canada had a clear lead in determining the nationalist flavor for the country, Canadian sociologist John Porter, insisted that ethnic and cultural differences should be ignored in the interests of equality (Porter, 1965). In the meantime the Canadian government has strongly endorsed a multicultural policy. While it has not brought about equality of opportunity for all Canadians, it is certainly a step in a very different direction. Perhaps the day will come when equity *is* achieved for all Canadians regardless of their time of arrival, cultural and linguistic differences, or color. Perhaps it is not too much to envisage the day when symbolic pride will even become a matter of personal and national pride (Burnet and Palmer, 1988).

French Canadians living outside Quebec face a tougher challenge because of their isolation from possible forms of institutional completeness. In rural Manitoba, for example, the traditional French ideology of "rural-clerical ideology of conservation has been challenged by a new generation which has sought to effect change by altering the internal structures, attitudes and values of the old system (Hebert and Vaillancourt, 1971). However, in another study, targeting fourth-generation French-Manitobans it was found that the belief systems of adolescents were quite similar to that of their parents in terms of actual religious practices, but varied more in terms of actual religious beliefs (Backeland and Frideres, 1977). Comeau and Driedger compared ethnic identity factors among students at The University of Manitoba and found that French students placed a high emphasis on religion and ranked second only to Jewish students (Comeau and Driedger, 1978). Finally, Li and Dennis surveyed French residents in Gravelbourg, Saskatchewan, which is sometimes seen as a cultural centre for francophones in southern Saskatchewan. Their survey indicated that one-third of the respondents (residents) had shifted from a French mother tongue to English at home. It also showed that those who had experienced a language shift at home were more likely to use English outside the home. The study concluded that "the cultural enclave had failed to provide a strong support to the French language in a situation where anglophones are the majority in the provincial context" (Li and Dennis, 1983).

As the force of assimilation continues to prey upon unsuspecting minorities new alignments also appear. In the case of the French community, a new kind of Canadian – the bilingual/bicultural Canadian – is an emerging reality. According to one study, French-Canadians make little distinction between bilingual English Canadians and bilingual French Canadians, who are being recognized as a separate entity. It appears that bilingual people comprise an entirely new reference group regardless of the ethnicity of its incumbents (Taylor, et al., 1978, 164). Perhaps this development will offer a new kind of hope to French-Canadians, but it will not likely put a stop to the continuing clash of varying cultural backgrounds in Canada.

References

Anderson, Alan B. & James S. Frideres. (1981). *Ethnicity in Canada: Theoretical perspectives.* Toronto: Butterworths.

Backeland, Lucille, & J. S. Frideres. (1977). Franco-Manitobans and cultural loss: A fourth generation. *Prairie Forum,* 2:1, 10-15.

Barber, Marilyn J. (1975). The assimilation of immigrants in the Canadian prairie provinces: Canadian perception and Canadian policies. Unpublished doctoral dissertation. The University of London.

Burnet, Jean R. with Howard Palmer. (1988). *Coming Canadians: A history of Canada's peoples.* Toronto: McClelland and Stewart.

Cheal, John E., Harold C. Melsness & Arthur W. Reeves. (1962). Educational administration: The role of the teacher. Toronto: Macmillan.

Clark, S. D. (1971). *The developing Canadian community. Ssecond edition. Toronto: University of Toronto Press.*

Cochrell, Richard. (1949). *Thoughts on the education of youth.* Toronto: The Bibliographical Society of Canada.

Comeau, Larry & Leo Driedger. (1978). Opening and Closing in an Open Society: A Canadian Example. *Social Forces,* 57:2, 600-620.

Cook, Ramsay. (1966). *Canada and the French-Canadian question.* Toronto: Macmillan.

Couture, Joseph E. (1985). Traditional Indian thinking, feeling, and learning. *Multicultural Education Journal,* 3:2, November, 4-17.

Creighton, Donald. (1970). *Canada's first century.* Toronto: Macmillan.

Dickason, Olive. (1992). *Canada's first nations: A history of founding peoples from the earliest times.* Toronto: McClelland and Stewart.

Driedger, Leo. (1989). *The ethnic factor: Identity in diversity.* Toronto: McGraw Hill Ryerson.

Francis, R. Douglas, Richard Jones & Donald B. Smith. (1988a). *Origins: Canadian history to Confederation.* Toronto: Holt, Rinehart and Winston.

Francis, R. Douglas, Richard Jones & Donald B. Smith. (1988b). *Destinies: Canadian history since Confederation.* Toronto: Holt, Rinehart and Winston.

Friesen, John W. (1985). *When cultures clash: Case studies in multiculturalism.* Calgary: Detselig Enterprises.

Giles, T. E. & A. J. Proudfoot. (1990). *Educational administration in Canada.* fourth edition. Calgary: Detselig Enterprises.

Hamilton, William B. (1970a). Schools and schools in Nova Scotia. Canadian education: a history. J. Donald Wilson, et al., eds. Scarborough: Prentice-Hall, 86-105.

Hamilton, William B. (1970b). Society and schools in New Brunswick and Prince Edward Island. *Canadian education: A history.* J. Donald Wilson, et al., eds. Scarborough: Prentice-Hall.

Hebert, Raymond & Jean-Guy Vaillancourt. (1971). French Canadians in Manitoba: Elites and ideologies. *Immigrant groups.* Jean Leonard Elliott, ed. Scarborough: Prentice-Hall, 183-187

Humphreys, Edward. (1971). Equality? The rural-urban disparity in Ontario elementary schools. *Education Canada,* 11:1 (March), 34-39.

Jaenen, Cornelius, J. (1978). The Manitoba School Question: An Ethnic Interpretation. *Ethnic Canadians: Culture and education.* Martin L. Kovacs, ed. Regina: Canadian Plains Studies, 317-332.

Jaenen, Cornelius J. (1979). French Roots in the prairies. *Two nations, two cultures: Ethnic groups in Canada.* Jean Elliott Leonard, ed. Scarborough: Prentice-Hall, 136-153.

Johnson, F. Henry. (1968). *A brief history of Canadian education.* Toronto: McGraw-Hill.

Jones, David C. (1989). *Wake up, Canada: Reflections on vital national issues.* Edmonton: University of Alberta Press.

Li, Peter S. & Wilfred B. Dennis. (1983). Minority enclave and majority language: The case of a French town in western Canada. *Canadian Ethnic Studies,* XV(1) 23-25.

Lower, J.A. (1973). *Canada: An outline history.* revised edition. Toronto: McGraw Hill Ryerson.

Lower, Arthur R.M. (1977). *A history of Canada: Colony to nation.* Toronto: McClelland and Stewart.

Lupul, Manoly R. (1970). Education in western Canada before 1873. *Canadian education: A history.* J. Donald Wilson, Robert M. Stamp and Louis Philippe Audet, eds. Scarborough: Prentice Hall., 241-264.

McDonald, N.G. (1974). David J. Goggin: Promoter of national schools. *Profiles of Canadian educators.* Robert S. Petterson, John W. Chalmers & John W. Friesen, eds. Toronto: D. C. Heath, 167-185.

Moore, Christopher. (1992). The First People of America. *The Beaver, 72:5, October/November, 53-56.*

Morton, W.L. (1965). *The Canadian identity.* Madison: The University of Wisconsin Press.

Nash, Paul. (1975). Quality and Equality in Canadian Education. *Canadian education and ideology: Readings.* John W. Friesen, ed. Lexington, Mass.: Xerox, 3-12.

Ossenberg, Richard J. (1971). *Canadian society: Pluralism, change, and conflict.* Scarborough: Prentice Hall.

Painchaud, Robert. (1976). The Catholic church and the movement of francophones to the Canadian prairies, 1870-1915. Unpublished doctoral dissertation. University of Ottawa.

Palmer, Howard, ed. (1975). *Immigration and the rise of multiculturalism.* Toronto: Copp Clark.

Patterson, Robert S., John W. Chalmers & John W. Friesen, eds. (1974). Profiles of Canadian educators. Toronto: D. C. Heath.

Petersen, William. (1975). Canada's immigration: The ideological background. *Immigration and the rise of multiculturalism.* Howard Palmer, ed. Toronto: Copp Clark, 22-33.

Porter, John. (1965). *The vertical mosaic: An analysis of social class and power in Canada.* Toronto: University of Toronto Press.

Richer, Stephen Pierre E. Laporte. (1979). Culture, cognition, and English-French competition. *Two nations, many cultures: Ethnic groups in Canada.* Jean Leonard Elliott, ed. Scarborough: Prentice- Hall, 75-85.

Rioux, Marcel. (1987). The development of ideologies in Quebec. *Ethnic Canada: Identities and inequalities.* Leo Driedger, ed. Toronto: Copp Clark Pitman, 98-222.

Saint-Denis, Father Henri. (1940). *French-Canadian ideals in education: French-Canadian backgrounds.* Toronto: Ryerson.

Scott, F. R. (1958). French-Canada and Canadian federalism, *evolving Canadian federalism.* A. R. M. Lower, et al. eds. Durham, S.C.: Duke University Press.

Sioui, George E. (1992). *For an Amerindian autobiography.* Montreal: McGill-Queen's University Press.

Stamp, Robert M. (1970). Education and the economic and social milieu: The English-Canadian scene from the 1870's to 1914. *Canadian education: A history.* J. Donald Wilson, Robert M. Stamp & Louis-Philippe Audet, eds. Scarborough: Prentice-Hall, 290-313.

Taylor, Donald M., Nancy Frasure-Smith & Wallace E. Lambert. (1978). Psychological development of French and English Canadian children: Child-rearing attitudes and ethnic identity. *The Canadian ethnic mosaic: A quest for identity.* Leo Driedger, ed. Toronto: McClelland and Stewart, 153-168.

Titley, E. Brian, ed. (1990). *Canadian education: Historical themes and contemporary issues.* Calgary: Detselig Enterprises.

Tracy, Frank Basil. (1908). *The tercentenary history of Canada from Champlain to Laurier, MDCVIII-MCMVIII.* Three volumes. New York: P. F. Collier & Son.

Wilson, J. Donald. (1970). Education in Upper Canada: Sixty years of change. *Canadian education: A history.* J. Donald Wilson, et al., eds. Scarborough: Prentice- Hall, 190-213.

Young, John R. (1990). Equality of opportunity: Reality or myth? *Canadian education: Historical themes and contemporary issues.* E. Brian Titley, ed. Calgary: Detselig Enterprises, 161-172.

7

The Hutterites: Avoiding a Cultural Clash

Almost everyone in Western Canada has an opinion about Hutterites. Ironically, despite the number of popular source-books available which explain the lifestyle and value system of Hutterites, many people still hold unsupported beliefs about Hutterites, including their alleged failure to pay taxes, their lack of contribution to the economy and their buying up huge portions of farmland and forcing the destruction of small towns. Each of these complaints can be refuted by available evidence, but this has not abated the continual harassment with which the communal people have to contend (Gross, 1965; Hostetler, 1977).

On the other side of the ledger is the reality that the toughest challenge that the Hutterites face to continuing their way of life is internal. Their Anabaptist orientation makes them subject to a strong individualism which leads to disagreements and possible splintering. Like the other Anabaptist groups, Mennonites and Amish, they have also had their share of subdivisions. In addition, the lure of the outside world continues to appeal to Hutterite youth, and as interaction with members of the outside world increases, so does the temptation to leave the colony. Only the future will reveal the extent to which the challenge of cultural maintenance will be met.

This chapter will briefly outline the history of the Hutterites, present their basic beliefs and describe the challenges they face in Canada. Finally, it will present their views on schooling as the best guarantee for their cultural perpetuity. The genesis of the Hutterites can be traced to the period of history known as the Reformation and, more specifically, to the rise of the Anabaptist movement. During the sixteenth century in Europe it became popular to question the Catholic interpretation of the Christian faith and church procedures and the resultant controversies spawned a vast number of church denominations and splinter groups. The term "Anabaptist" refers to the practice of re-baptizing individuals who had been baptized as children and confirmed in their youth. The "rebaptizers" argued that the Sacrament (or ritual, as they referred to it), was invalid for children because they were unaware of what was happening to them when they were being baptized (Klaassen, 1973).

Basically the principles of Anabaptism include:

1. The Bible is an open book for all and constitutes the sole guide of faith and practice, particularly the New Testament.
2. The church is an independent, voluntary group of believers banded together for the purpose of worship. This implies a rigid separation of church and state and disavows the concept of compulsory state church membership.
3. Infant baptism has no place in a voluntary institution because it is the sign of initiation into a universal state church.
4. The office of magistrate cannot be filled by the Christian. Government, however, is a Divine institution ordained to protect the righteous and punish the wicked. The Christian must be obedient to his rulers, pray for them, and pay taxes to support the government.
5. The Christian cannot take up the sword. Love must be the ruling force in all social relations. It is wrong to kill, either as an individual or by judicial process or military force.
6. Christians should live secluded from the evil outside world.
7. Church discipline is to be secured through the "ban" which is used to exclude the disobedient from the rights of membership. Its practice may appear to be severe but its ultimate objective is to bring the individual to repentance.
8. The Lord's Supper is to be regarded merely as a memorial of the death and suffering of Christ, and not as containing the Real Presence.
9. It is wrong to take an oath. Christ taught his disciples to give and keep their word without swearing (Harder, 1949, 21-22).

Hutterian Beginnings

The above principles were adopted by a variety of followers. One such adherent, Jacob Hutter, a hatter by trade, established himself with a group of people who added the principle of communal property to the list of beliefs. Although his background is not well known, Hutter was elected leader of this group in 1533, a position he held for three years, during which time he managed to establish strict discipline and order in his church and implement the principle of common property. He was martyred in 1535 (Horsch, 1931; Peters, 1965). After his death the pattern of life for Hutterites quickly became marked by fear and flight. Persecution of Hutterites had been under way since the early 1530s. Originally the Hutterites fled to Moravia in order to escape their enemies but as the years went by their protectors, the Moravian nobility, lost power and the Imperial Government of Vienna took control. It soon became popular to comb the countryside for Anabaptists and force them to flee to the mountains and caves. As if this were not enough the Turkish wars were calamitous for the entire population, and by 1620 the entire protestant nobility of Bohemia and Moravia had left the country. Two years later, without their guardians, the Hutterites faced an army led by Cardinal Dietrichstein who had been ordered to "drive the Anabaptists out of the land" (Peters, 1965, 17-19). Dietrichstein himself tried to make it easier on the Hutterites by asking them to renounce their faith but he had little success.

As the first century of their history ended, Hutterites became homeless wanderers. They left Moravia and sojourned to Slovakia where the King of Hungary had less power to protect them than their previous benefactors. Later they relocated in other parts of Europe and managed to live in peaceful isolation in Russia for a century between 1770 and 1842. In 1842, the Russian Government decided to relocate the Hutterites. Then in 1864, a law was passed which made Russian the compulsory language in all schools and placed Hutterites under the supervision of the state. A few years later compulsory military service was introduced.

As these infringements on their freedom increased, the Hutterites could "feel the walls closing in on them" and they made plans to escape to America, a new land of freedom. In 1874 about 800 left the Ukraine and settled in South Dakota in three colonies named after the leader of each colony: Lehrerleut, Dariusleut, and Schmiedeleut. Although similar in almost every way, the groups do not intermarry even to this day (Hofer, 1991).

By 1915, the total number of Hutterites had increased to 1 700, the colonies to seventeen and two of these had been established in Montana (Pitt, 1949; Palmer, 1972). Expansion into Canada also occurred and by the end of 1918 the Dariusleut had developed six colonies (Bruderhof) in Alberta and the Lehrerleut, four. The Dakota Schmiedeleut colony expanded to Manitoba. By 1971 there were eight-two colonies in Alberta with a combined population of about 6 732. The total Hutterite population in North America today is 30 000 souls, living in over 300 colonies, two-thirds of them in Canada, and the rest in the United States (Preston, 1992).

A search of historical documents authored by Hutterites themselves reveals the following beliefs, according to John Horsch:

1. The Holy Scriptures are the final authority for revealed truth.
2. All descendants of Adam inherit a sinful nature, but through redemption man can be saved in spite of his original sin.
3. The need for a consistent Christian life on the part of the believer is essential, but this does not mean that the   propensity to sin is destroyed.
4. The Church is made up of all baptized believers; the community of goods is an essential characteristic of the true Christian church.
5. The community of goods is the "highest command of love."

6. Christ, by precept and example, enjoined upon His followers the principle of non-resistance.

7. Since war is forbidden, Christians are not allowed to become partakers in   the sin of making swords, spears, guns nor any such weapons.

8. Civil government is ordained of God and its commands, such as that of paying taxes, are to be obeyed. In the case of war, however, the Christian is to remember that "we ought to obey God rather than man."

9. Christians are not to go to court against one another.

10. A true brotherhood cares for the sick and the afflicted, the feeble-minded and invalid folk.

11. On the matter of believing versus unbelieving marriage partners, a believer   ought not to marry an unbeliever. However, if after marriage one of the   partners denies the faith the couple may still live together. Divorce, even   under such circumstances, is forbidden.

12. Religious convictions are to be practiced in an uncompromising way. This   means that the Christian should avoid non-Christian events and all forms   of dubious behavior.

13. The Christian faith is to be deemed of the utmost importance, even to the   extend of dying for it.

14. Church discipline is to be practiced as a means of encouragement and strengthening. There cannot be a New Testament church without the use of discipline.

15. Ritualism shall have no place in the church – pictures, instrumental music,   statues, towers or bells – all are a deterrence to worship (Horsch, 1931).

A Hutterite Statement of Faith

A deceased leader of the Fairview Hutterian Brethren of Crossfield, Alberta, the late Paul Tschetter, Sr., authored the following statement explaining Hutterite beliefs and practices. Before his death he gave permission to have it included here.

Declarations on Hutterian Brethren
and Their Assembly During Their Trying Times

We, the undersigned residents in the Province of Alberta, have associated together for religious purposes, by the name of the Hutterishe Bruder Gemeinde of the Province of Alberta. We have assembled ourselves together as a body corporate, pursuant to the constitution and laws of the Province of Alberta for the purposes of promoting and engaging in communal activities, these being:

carrying on the Christian religion, Christian worship, and religious education and teachings according to our religious beliefs. We act together as one being and have, hold, and enjoy all things in common. We are all of one mind, heart, and soul, according to the word of God, as revealed to us. We pray to God for our government to recognize and protect us as conscientious objectors. May God shield us from any discrimination from all godless rulers, be they kings, queens, presidents, or any who are involved in leadership and power. We ask the government to punish the unjust and assist the just. Again I want to say that we are a humble defenseless sect of people. Our scriptural convictions oppose any assistance to war, but we do not oppose assistance to those that are in need of food, clothing and shelter.

The Organization and Assembly of the Hutterian Brethren

I want to state in abbreviated form, the origin, time of establishment, and organization of the Hutterites' communal society, as envisaged by our Lord Jesus Christ with his 12 disciples. Since then it has operated like a colony of bees or a herd of sheep with their shepherd, and some of the people involved in this have been

Jacob Hutter in the year 1528

Hans Amon in the year 1536

Leonhard Lanzenstil in the year 1542

Peter Rideman in the year 1556

To mention additional names is not essential. I must state that, after they were established and communalized, the Hutterite colonies had to undergo great opposition and discrimination. Hutterites were subject to torture by the most painful methods. Some were skinned alive or hanged to scaffolds and stoned to death, or sawed apart by saws, or strangled; many were confined to a press, and stretched so that you could see the sunshine through them, and were then beheaded. Some were crucified or buried alive as was Peter's Riedeman's wife, Nela. Some sacrificed their lives in boiling lard contained in big vessels. Many of them were drowned in rivers or indiscriminately deprived of their belongings which they had earned by working day and night by the sweat of their brow. They were confronted with barbarism and insulted and speared with swords, hanged alive by their hands and feet in smoke houses, and smoked to death, or all their fingers and toes were cut off and they were then released in this state. This torture and discrimination seemed never to cease. All these actions continued to take place because Christianity and the Holy Spirit controlled them. They were not irresponsible but reaching heaven was their only goal. Many thousands of them were tempted and compelled by force to cease from Christianity, but everything was in vain. Thousands and thousands converted themselves from the darkness of this world, to the light. They were men and women and teenagers who vowed their lives to God even if it meant dying for Christ's sake, be it by fire, water, or sword, according to God's will. The covenant they made was not broken. They chose and accepted death, and that with cheerful, and bold hearts. Their goal was to reach and enter the Kingdom of Heaven. (Life on earth was unimportant). Many strange sights and signs were witnessed by onlookers during their trying times as they perished from this forsaken world to enter the Kingdom of Heaven. Surely they will shine like the sun in their Father's Kingdom. For our Lord says, "I am the Road, the Truth and the Everlasting Life. No one can reach Heaven except through me, and this is the narrow Path."

Obedience to the Government

We do believe that government was approved of by our Lord Jesus Christ. Paul calls the government the servant of the vengeance of God, to guard and protect the just, punish the unjust, and build and construct righteousness. We never intended to disobey our government. Our Lord says, "Obey the government and be prepared to all good works, orders, rules, and regulations and all activities which are not against God and his commandments and Scriptural Religion." But, we are fully prepared to oppose orders that are contrary to our beliefs; to obey God more than man.

Service in Government

No Hutterite is allowed to serve in government, possess a seat in any cabinet, serve as a prime minister, premier or any other representative officer. Therefore, no citizenship papers have ever been required or taken. Any government carries out revenge. How can we take revenge, when God's word tells us, "The Vengeance is Mine! I will repay," says the Lord. We are opposed to taking matters to court, or any other world justice, as the Lord suggested.

One does not overcome evil with evil, but one overcomes evil with good. We find in His scriptures, that at the time of His capture, He could have protected Himself from any enemy. He could have asked His Heavenly Father for more than a million escorts or war servants, or body guards equipped with defence weapons. But, this He rejected because He had to fulfill His Father's will and carry out His duty. That is why He left His Heavenly Kingdom and His Father and came to live among godless people. Peter, His disciple on earth, drew his sword when they came to arrest Jesus, but the Lord commanded Peter to put away his sword for he who uses the sword shall perish through the sword. (If any man sue thee at the Law and take away thy coat, let him have thy cloak also.) Matthew. 5:40. But we do not oppose assistance to those who are in need of food, clothing, and shelter. (Again, whosoever smite thee on thy right cheek, turn to him the other also.)

Hutterite Schooling and Education

Attending public schools has never been opposed or even rejected by Hutterite Colonies. All children from the ages 3-6 have to complete kindergarten. Two appointed women are in charge of this school. The morning bell rings at 7:20 a.m. Three meals are served. After lunch at 11:00 a.m., it is compulsory for them to sleep and rest. At school, they are disciplined, taught and drilled to obey, honor and respect their parents and others. Also table manners and a few other subjects are taught. The first commandment with promise – honor thy father and thy mother that thy days may be long upon the earth – is especially stressed. Parents are also instructed: provoke not your children to wrath but bring them in the nurture and admonition of the Lord: Ephesians, 6th Chapter.

The knowledge of God, His will, and His commandments are taught. The children are instructed in the rules and regulations of the colony, and taught to be tidy and clean. When reaching the age of six years, they are discharged from the school and proceed to attend German Bible school and also the Public School.

German Bible School and Public School

The Bible teacher opens the school at 7:30 a.m. with singing and long prayers. Testament readings, writing, studying biblical lectures, memorizing, singing Christian prayers from our history books follow. The history of the Bible is read and studied. They are trained to be conscientious. They are instructed to obey God's commandments and the reason why He was delivered and transferred from heaven to this earth. They receive an education which familiarizes them with basic apostolic doctrine. Upon reaching the age of fifteen years, they are discharged from this school and also from the dining room where they were served by the teacher and his wife, and are now admitted into the working classroom. They are still required to attend the Sunday Bible school. They begin assignments with the working class after having received all full knowledge of God and His will along with regulations and religious rules of the colony. At age eighteen and over, they can receive Baptism on their familiar conviction, or true confession of faith.

To Become Baptized and a Member of the Colony

1. The Church of Christ is the community of the believing and the pious, the people of God who do and have abstained from sinful life. Into this community we are brought through submission, that is into the Spiritual Ark of Noah in which we can be preserved.

2. It is not a human deed but an act of God. Just as Mary through faith and the Holy Spirit conceived Christ when she placed her will into God's will, and said; "here I am, a servant of the Lord, be done unto me according to thy words," thus, we must also receive Christ in faith. Then He will begin and complete His work in us.

3. Let each be mindful that the church has the key and power to loose and to bind, as Christ has commanded, which means to put away the sinner and to receive the contrite. What the church binds is also binding in heaven according to the words of Christ. Matt. 16:19.

4. Each should first count the cost that will come. But, one is not to counsel with flesh and blood, for they that would enter the service of God must be prepared for tribulation, for the sake of the Truth, and the faith, and to die for Christ's sake, if it be the will of God, be it by fire, water, or the sword. Now we have house and shelter, but we know not what will be on the morrow.

5. Therefore, no one should join for the sake of prosperous days. He who will not be steadfast with all the godly, to suffer the evil as the good and accept however, the Lord may direct as good let him stay away. For whoever does not act voluntarily, will not be forced.

6. We desire to persuade no man with smooth words, as it is not a matter of human compulsion or necessity, for God wants voluntary service; whosoever can not render that cheerfully and with hearty pleasure, let him remain in his former station.

7. Let no one undertake to join the church for the sake of another. The wife for the sake of the husband nor the husband for the sake of the wife, not the children for the sake of the parents, for that would be in vain. It would be building upon the sand, having no permanence. But instead, one should build upon the rock, trying to please God alone. For each must bear his own burden, upon that day.

8. One must submit to follow brotherly admonition, address and punishment. He must also practice and apply the same with respect to others in the house of God, so that no one may fall into strange sins.

9. One should submit himself in obedience to God and his church. He should not be obstinate or do only according to his own desires, but instead permit himself to be guided for the good and necessity of the church, in whatsoever is known to be right.

10. No one shall have private possessions any more, for one gives and surrenders himself to the Lord and His Church, with all that he has and is

able to do. This is as it was in the original apostolic church, when no one said that his possessions were his, but all things were common to them. This we regard as the safest way and the most perfect foundations. Of this we are all well assured in our hearts.

11. This we now plainly state to everyone beforehand, so that we may be under no obligation to return anything to any one afterwards. Therefore, if any one should undertake to join us and later feel it impossible to remain and wish to have his possessions returned, let him now stay away. Keep his own and leave us in peace. We are not anxious for money and possessions, but desire godly hearts.

12. Whosoever has wrong dealings that are punishable in the world, be it that it is owning men or that he has defrauded them, or if anyone has involved himself into matters of marriage, or is engaged to be married, he shall first straighten these matters out. For if anyone should conceal any of these things from us, and should in the meantime have himself baptized and we should learn of these matters afterwards, we shall be compelled to excommunicate him as one who came into the church improperly and by falsehood. Therefore, let each one be truly warned. Amen.

Social Organization

Hutterian religious beliefs provide the foundation for daily practice. Every age level on a colony has specific patterns and expectations attached to it beginning with early training, education, baptism, marriage and, finally, full responsibility in colony life. Older men who retire from leadership positions remain in their capacity as advisors and interpreters of the old ways; older women help with child raising, admonishment, and the distribution of colony allotments to individual families (Hostetler & Huntington, 1967). The bureaucratic organization of the colony usually involves six levels:

1. *The colony.* This presupposes informal participation in an organization which permits members full access to authorized privileges and guarantees care, food, shelter and other basic benefits.

2. *The church.* The church consists of all baptized men and women although only the men have voting privileges. They are also allowed to decide major colony matters and determine who will hold leadership positions.

3. *The council.* Five to seven men are selected by the church to fulfill an executive function. The first or senior minister, the assistant minister, the householder or steward (colony boss), and the field manager (field boss) are always on the council which is charged with care of daily matters such as granting privilege to travel, settling minor matters, and other activities pertaining to the smooth functioning of the colony.

4. *The informal subcouncil.* Hostetler notes that this body is frequently so informal that it need not be mentioned. It consists of four individuals – minister, assistant minister (sometimes), householder and field manager. They may meet after breakfast, for example, to assign daily chores (Hostetler, 1977).

5. *The householder.* This person serves as liaison with the outside world. He makes arrangements about economic matters and is largely responsible for the economic prosperity of the colony.

6. *The head preacher.* This individual is responsible for the overall life of the colony, moral, spiritual *and* economic. He is elected by the people and ordained to carry out the "will of the Lord" in the church. Although his powers are sometime seen as extraordinary by outsiders, his own flock sees him as exercising spiritual discretion.

7. *The assistant minister.* Generally speaking, every colony has an assistant minister, and his role is particularly important in the event the colony "splits up" or "branches out." This usually happens when the number of persons, "souls," the Hutterites say, reaches about a hundred; at that point one of the ministers (usually the assistant) goes with the group which leaves to establish a new colony while the senior man stays behind to continue the spiritual work in the mother colony. Like the senior minister, the assistant is elected, and no particular formal training is necessary since the only requirement is spiritual wisdom and discretion. It is only the recognition of the minister's gifts *by the people* who constitute the church, that matters.

Without elaborating unduly on colony life, yet rendering the essence of its format and functions, the following elements should be noted.

Sex Roles

Each colony has two operant subcultures, that of the men and that of the women. Women are believed to be inferior to men, intellectually and physically, and they seem quite prepared to accept this arrangement. After marriage, the bride leaves her people and takes up residence on the groom's colony. Here she takes up her place with the other women whose primary duties include caring for children, teaching, and household activities. To a certain extent women rotate their jobs with the exception of a few fundamental positions of responsibility such as head cook, gardener or kindergarten teacher. These are usually abdicated when the women reach retirement age. Because of significant social changes in philosophy over the years, undoubtedly influenced by outside sources, however, a "women's movement" is evident in the colonies today, and their voice is being heard with increasing authority (Peter, 1987).

Men's jobs are much more formalized. Almost all baptized men above the age of twenty-five hold regular occupational positions with well-defined expectations. In addition to those positions mentioned previously is that of German teacher, since Hutterites operate their own school system in addition to the schooling required by the provinces. Teaching German school is a seasonal task and thus the teacher is often charged with other chores in the summer or off-season (Mann, 1974).

Disciplinary Action

The most serious method of punishment for wrongdoing is the practice of *shunning* by which the offender is deliberately neglected and ignored by other members of the colony. He/she eats alone and does not participate in colony life until the assigned period is over or until he/she fully repents. Another control mechanism consists of reporting another's wrongs to the preacher. It is considered both ethical and compulsory to do this since the underlying principle of reporting is the other's spiritual benefit. "All men slip," it is said, and apparently to be reported is part of the restoration process. All members are responsible for their brother's/sister's spiritual welfare and when they observe their fellow believers engaging in misdemeanors they are expected to make full disclosure to the colony superior (Knill, 1968).

On very few occasions is an offence serious enough to demand that a Hutterite leave the colony even though shunning, when enforced may also have familial implications. In one of the more dramatic cases on record in Manitoba, a Hutterite was asked to leave his colony because he had converted to the Jehovah's Witness religion. It was felt that his conduct and beliefs would hinder and interfere with the work of the colony. When he left, his wife and family also went with him (Peters, 1965). In another case, in 1980, the Schmiedeleut people of Manitoba excommunicated an entire colony, the Pine Creek Colony, because they would not bow to the bishop's orders (Preston, 1992).

External Relations

Everyone is welcome to visit a Hutterite colony because opening the door to strangers is interpreted as a form of evangelism. Generally speaking, Hutterites do not advertise their existence, nor do they seek actively to participate in the world around them. Conversely, they "let the world come to them if they want anything of the Hutterites." The Fairview Colony near Calgary is perhaps an exception for they virtually encourage visits. During peak months they average two group visits per week, most of them children from local city schools. Hutterites hold no public conferences, though they meet amongst themselves or with other colony representatives, conduct no mass evangelism campaigns, and distribute no literature. Still, their informal network enables to keep in touch with one another about such matters as church functioning, schooling and even economic matters.

Outsiders rarely join the Hutterite Church, but this *does* happen on occasion. In Manitoba there are only about a dozen recorded instances of people converting to colony beliefs, while in Alberta there have been isolated instances. It may be surprising to note that there is a Hutterite colony in Japan which was started as a mission project by the Alberta Dariusleut. Apparently, a group of Japanese tourists visited a local colony and were so impressed with the way of life that they returned home to establish a colony of their own. They subsequently requested and were given advice and assistance from local leaders who visited Japan on several occasions. The colony currently numbers 50-60 people who for the most part earn their living by working off the colony because their land holdings are too limited to sustain an agricultural base.

When someone indicates his desire to join a colony they are accepted willingly but they must go through a year of probation. If, after the year is over, the would-be-converts decide to remain on the colony, they are allowed to do so only on the condition that they fulfill all requirements demanded of them (Peters, 1965).

In light of their openness to strangers, it is difficult to understand why Hutterites have been discriminated against to such an extent. Most ill feelings toward them centre on the following myths.

Myths and Objections

Following is a summary of some of the most publicized beliefs and practices for which Hutterites have been publicly held in contempt.

Land Expansion

When the Hutterites immigrated to Canada in 1918 there was only a mild stir compared to the opposition they were later to encounter. The most vigorous campaigns conducted against the Brethren were in connection with land purchases and possibly the most serious offence against them was committed by the Social Credit Government of Alberta who actually legislated against land expansion by Hutterites. This law, the Communal Properties Act, was later repealed because it contradicted the Bill of Rights established by the later Conservative Government. In 1972, a government-approved committee discovered that, in fact, the Hutterites controlled a total of only 292 129 hectares of land and if they were allowed to expand at their own rate, they would possibly control 370 684 hectares by 1976. The Hutterites *did* purchase more land when the Communal Properties Act was repealed but ten years later the additional amount which they owned amounted only to 1.2 percent more farmland (Zwarun, 1983). In light of this evidence, observers can find little evidence to substantiate the fear of an alleged Hutterite takeover of prairie farmlands.

Population Growth

Many Western Canadians are apprehensive that if the Hutterite population increases at a fast rate, they may actually outnumber the total population of non-Hutterites in their particular province. While this notion may be supported by statistics which show that the Hutterite population did double every 17-20 years about two decades ago, this is hardly enough evidence to suggest an immediate Hutterite takeover. In Alberta in 1971, the Hutterite population was about 1/2 of 1 percent, a total of 6 732 people (*Report on Communal Property*, 1972). Since then, the population growth rate has been slowly declining. A soils professor at the University of Alberta, the late Professor C.F. Bentley, once estimated that by the year 2302 there could be as many as 20 594 432 000 Hutterites. A more conservative figure, based on doubling of their numbers every 17-20 years shows that in Manitoba, for example, there would be fewer than 20 000 Hutterites by the year 2000. In actuality the 1992 statistics indicate a total of 6 000 Hutterites in Manitoba (Preston, 1992). Since Hutterites have a low death rate, and they do not generally practice birth control it means that a woman may go on having children well past the age of forty; thus, it is not surprising that their population continues to climb. In seeking to determine population estimates, however, it might be just as well to take the Hutterites' attitude of letting nature take its course.

Payment of Taxes

Considerable public consternation has found expression as a result of the allegation that Hutterites do not pay taxes. Between 1949 and 1960 Hutterites indeed were exempt from doing so because of their recognized status as organized charities (Palmer, 1972). Presently, Hutterites *do* pay taxes, according to a special formula, although for a time their tax status was not clear. The Lehrerleut and Schmiedeleut, for example, had an agreement in the 1960s whereby they arranged with the Minister of National Revenue to pay income taxes for every person aged nineteen and over, calculated on the basis of total income divided by the number of people in a colony. When the Communal Property Committee reported in 1972 they were still paying these taxes.

The situation with the Dariusleut was not as straight-forward. After a significant campaign on the part of the federal government to wrest their share of taxes from the Dariusleut, whom they saw as a profit-oriented enterprise, an agreement was reached in 1981 similar to that practiced with regard to the Schmiedeleut and Lehrerleut (Janzen, 1991, 284).

It is not difficult to realize why people have the impression that Hutterites do not pay taxes when one considers the way corporations function. There is also the fact that the lifestyle of Hutterites enables them to use more of their income for expansion than other citizens. They have no use for radios, television sets or many of the appliances and luxuries "needed" by the average citizen. Little money is used for personal comfort and travel, and almost all is spent on the improvement of the soil and property (Hostetler, 1961). If everyone wanted to live by those standards there would probably be more than enough money to support the average Canadian home independent of any form of government assistance.

Military Exemption

The original agreement which the Hutterites negotiated with the government when they came to Canada gave them the privilege of exemption from military duty. Later, during World War I the public grew quite resentful when Hutterites did not contribute to the "Victory Bond" drives, so it was charged that they were using their government granted exemption as an excuse to keep their "cowardly boys" on the farm (Palmer, 1972). Actually, there is evidence that Hutterites bought some war bonds, although they refused to accept interest for them, and they also contributed liberally to the Red Cross (Janzen, 1990). Perhaps the culmination of prejudice against the Hutterites was provoked with the help of angry farmers and members of the Canadian Legion when in 1942 they successfully lobbied for the Land Sales Prohibition Act which was to prevent the sales of lands to "aliens" as the Hutterites were classified. The act was later changed because of the term "aliens" and another act was passed in 1944, specifically referring to Hutterites and Doukhobors; it remained in effect until 1947.

Community Destruction

It is frequently argued that community life is destroyed when Hutterites move into any given prairie town because they refuse to participate in local affairs or shop in local stores. An Alberta Government investigation published in 1972 shows some interesting findings. When the cancelled cheques of some colonies were examined, for example, it was found that money had been spent in this order: (1) local community, (2) nearest small city, (3) Calgary, Lethbridge or Edmonton. Actual statistics for one colony included this breakdown:

> It was found for a Southern Alberta colony that $120 000 (nearly half of the total expenditure) was spent in the immediate trading centre, $128 000 in Lethbridge, $8 000 in Calgary, $8 000 in Edmonton and $17 000 in other

centres. A second colony showed similar results with about 1/3 spent in the immediate trading centres (*Report on Communal property,* 1972, 22).

It is difficult to substantiate allegations that where money is concerned Hutterites are breaking down local communities or municipalities. In 1971 colonies paid $892 575 in taxes to local communities and or municipal districts and $192 752 in income taxes. Thus the average tax paid per person by Hutterites in 1971 was $300 and that paid by the average Albertan farm person was $251. In light of these findings little additional research has since been done in this area.

Freedom and Individualism

A re-occurring concern about Hutterites relates to the lack of freedom experienced by their children. It is true that the baptism vows enacted by adults on a colony include the vow that, should they leave the colony they will forfeit all goods to the colony and this has been tested in the courts and upheld. The public is concerned because Hutterite children grow up with very limited alternatives insofar as life choices are concerned. When and if they should ever leave the colony they face the virtual impossibility of adjusting to the outside world (Hoer, 1991). There are also those who observe that the education of Hutterite children is second-class and that these children deserve better. Frequently public outcries for the closure of Hutterite schools is based on the principle of "rights of children." In 1962, a Conservative Party leadership convention went so far as to call for the breaking up of existing Hutterite colonies and forcing them to live on individual farms "so that they can enjoy the freedom of our country" (Palmer, 1972, 48).

Thinly-veiled forms of prejudice though they be, these claims show only too clearly that the opposition against Hutterites takes many forms and is generally based on fear informed by emotion (Friesen, 1977).

Education

There are over a hundred public schools operating on Hutterite colonies in Alberta today with all of their costs borne by the colonies on which they operate. Public taxes pay for the teachers' salary, based on the education tax portion of property taxes, but when this amount is insufficient to pay the teacher's salary, the colony is billed for the balance. In addition, the provision and maintenance of the buildings and utility costs are provided by the Hutterites themselves. Three colonies, Brocket, Monarch and Felger have been sending their children to regular public schools while another colony utilizes correspondence lessons for grades one to eleven. At Vulcan, Alberta, a few years ago, a local school board decided to ask the courts to determine the legality of the operation of public schools on Hutterite colonies. Opponents to these schools claimed their opposition originated not from prejudice but from concern for "the preservation of the public school system." A related plank in their anti-Hutterite platform was the notion that school boards could be guilty of giving special considerations to religious or ethnic groups. When the dust had settled, the complaints were ignored.

The public school on a colony essentially functions like any other such institution except that its pupils are probably all from a few Hutterite families (Fitch, 1978). The provincial curriculum is followed, homework assigned, and discipline administered. These schools do not exist because of transportation costs or community attitudes but because colony leaders have requested them. They fear that the integration of their children into the outside world will assimilate undesirable dominant values and reduce their familiarity with the German language. They do not oppose public schooling per se since minimal literacy, a valued Anabaptist principle, is necessary for reading the Scriptures. If the state insists that literacy be taught in a particular manner, the Hutterites gladly acquiesce to the requirement. If, however, there is enough latitude in the law to allow for the location of public schools on the colonies, Hutterite leaders are willing to bear the extra cost in order to get what they want. In many cases local leaders have been able to develop good rapport with teachers of English schools and even to exert a little pressure to ensure that certain emphases will be included and others avoided. For Hutterites, the arrangement has been satisfactory (Mann, 1974).

Hutterite Cultural Retention

For observers, one of the most intriguing aspects about Hutterites has been their uncanny ability to have maintained their way of life virtually intact, for well over four and a half centuries. Recently, however, scholars have detected factors that affect the Hutterite system which suggest its slow but steady disintegration and perhaps demise.

Cultural Threats

Two decades ago, Frideres predicted the end of Hutterite colonies as a result of the Canadian provincial governments', especially Alberta's, systematic program of discrimination pertaining to land purchases (Frideres, 1972). Subsequent events have proven the thesis to be somewhat misguided, but alternative explanations for the same phenomenon have been proffered Another view recognizes that Hutterite society is a tightly-structured society, and that fact alone may account for their tenacity. Despite this observation the fate of Hutterite culture may still be in peril because of the increasing rate of defection of their members, a gradual erosion of ancient values and the weakening of rigorous discipline (Boldt, 1980). Citing the case of the Schmiedeleut Boldt points to examples of more liberal dress codes, violations of traditional taboos such as television and radio, and more lavish household furnishings. In addition, Hutterite operational policies have changed in the case of he Schmiedeleut, at least, who also grant greater autonomy to their individual colonies (Boldt, 1980). The same situation applies to the matter of forms of "government assistance" as the Hutterites interpret them – family allowances, Canada pension, etc. These benefits were once regarded as forms of government handouts (Fretz, 1989, 236), but now some colonies allow their members to receive them.

There are other signs as well. Contemporary Hutterite women now more concerned about their health, have begun to object to having large families and a majority of them at a certain age surgically terminate their reproductive capacity. As Peter notes, this process is concomitant with the acceptance of a doctor/patient relationship in which the advice of the doctor carries greater authority than the traditional religious proscription of the community (Peter, 1982, 271). This new liberty has also affected a restrictiveness of Hutterite women in terms of sexual availability for their husbands and triggered a change in their self-perception and general assertiveness. As a result Hutterite women have become more selective in mate-selection and many are postponing marriage to a later age. Over the years as geographic stability has become more of a reality, the women have also been granted greater independence in organizing their work and have thus become a vital substructure in the functioning of the colony. Such comments as, "Our women wouldn't like that," or "the women won't do that," are frequently encountered among Hutterite men (Peter, 1987, 202).

There is some indication that the Hutterites have thrived in the past when their immediate environment has been hostile to their way of life. Hostetler implies that the absence of persecution by the outside world tends to maximize internal problems among the Hutterites and lessen cultural tenacity. Thus, even the forms of discrimination practiced against Hutterites in Canada may not be sufficient to provide their culture with the kind of victim complex it requires to maintain its cloistered order of life (Hostetler, 1977).

Birth-rate and Growth

Hutterite population statistics have been the target of interest for anthropologists at least since J.W. Eaton and A.J. Mayer published such a study forty years ago (Eaton and Mayer, 1953). The earliest estimates of population growth showed an annual rate of 4.12 percent per year, but in 1970 Hutterite sources estimated that the annual rate could be as low as 2.4 percent for the years 1969 to 1970 and to 2.2 percent thereafter (Peter, 1980a; Peter, 1987). Speculation about the various factors contributing to the lower birth rate among Hutterites includes the explanation that too many people on a colony simply augers against an orderly and effective assignment of chores. A reduced birth rate may be a solution to that problem and this has been achieved by delayed marriage and birth control. Boldt and Roberts discount these explanations on the basis that the raised marriage age among Hutterites is simply not significant enough to warrant a correlation with population figures. They also dismiss the idea that because young Hutterites encounter difficulties in finding suitable marriage partners they wait longer to marry, and they argue instead that the size of population pool has not diminished and since Hutterites enjoy more travel to other colonies, availability of marriage partners has certainly increased (Boldt and Roberts, 1980). In Peter's rejoinder to Boldt and Roberts, the notion that population decreases among Hutterites may induce their disintegration is discounted on historical grounds; they have demonstrated several times previously a capacity to make notable, adaptive value shifts. Twice, for example, colonies in one region of Russia abandoned communal living, first for a period of seventy-two years (1690-1762) and then for forty years (1819-1859). How did they manage to re-establish that structure after such lengthy periods of time? Undoubtedly the answer reveals their ability to make significant changes (Peter, 1980b; Hofer, 1982). Projecting Peter's argument allows for the conclusion that perhaps even the acceptability of "increasing worldliness" noted by Boldt, may not greatly affect the basic aims and structures of Hutterite society.

Hutterite Fragmentation

An inherent weakness in Hutterite philosophy which leads to fragmentation among them is their strong sense of individuality which stems from their Anabaptist origins. Although the communal authority appears to be paramount in deciding day-to-day operations, there are many instances where break-a-way groups have left the mainline Hutterian community and started fringe groups. To begin with, the three main branches of Hutterites in Russia, Dariusleut, Lehrerleut and Schmiedeleut eventually developed distinctions within their respective villages which developed full-blown differences when they migrated to North America (Friesen, 1985). In addition, when the Hutterites settled in the United States in 1874 there were 800 people who opted for individual land ownership instead of forming communes. Eventually, they became known as "prairie Hutterites," partly because they settled on prairie lands instead of along riverbanks as their more orthodox brethren did. They adopted the name, "Hutterite-Mennonites" for themselves and adopted a more assimilative lifestyle illustrated by a paid clergy, the establishment of a high school and college, and the use of musical instruments, gospel singing, choirs, and special music groups (Hofer and Walter, 1975, 141).

In 1920, a closely-related group to the Hutterites was founded in Germany by Eberhard Arnold. Started as a Christian renewal group, the members soon took up communal living as their form of economic organization. Although they had no knowledge of the Hutterites, the Society of Brothers, as Arnold's followers called themselves, learned about them in 1930. After visiting the colonies in North America, the Society members decided to affiliate themselves with the Hutterites but when they were expelled from Germany by the Nazis they relocated in England and Paraguay. Although an informal affiliation with the Hutterites was achieved, in 1974, the Society of Brothers adopted a new name for themselves, "Hutterite Society of Brothers," and continued to operate their own administrative structure. While the orthodox Hutterites maintained an agrarian way of life, the Hutterite Society of Brothers became engaged in the manufacture of wood-working products, especially children's play equipment under the trade name, "Community Playthings." Their American settlements are in Woodcrest (their headquarters) and Rifton, New York; Farmington, Pennsylvania; and Norfolk, Connecticut (Hostetler, 1983, 43).

Peaceful living has not always been a reality for the Hutterite Society of Brothers, and their turmoil has also affected the orthodox Hutterite community. Between 1959 and 1962 a schism developed in a power struggle between Arnold's son and son-in-law. The schism reflected a philosophical struggle between the intellectual and spiritual aspects of their lifestyle; there were those who saw their work as that of a more secular-oriented peace organization with world-wide connections, while others opted for a more cloistered way of life. Eberhard Arnold's son, Heini, who opted for the more sedate and spiritual lifestyle, won out and forced half of the 2 000 membership to leave the organization. Today the remaining membership is led by Christoph Arnold, grandson of Eberhard Arnold, the original founder.

In 1974, Jacob Kleinsasser, a Manitoba Schmiedeleut Hutterite minister, met with 71 ministers of the Hutterite Society of Brothers to study the feasibility of their joining forces. Kleinsasser became a bishop in 1978 and admitted the Society ministers and their churches to his constituency. This move was opposed by many of the more conservative elements of Kleinsasser's charge who feared that the merger could lead to a liberalizing of their way of life. Dariusleut and Lehrerleut colonies in Saskatchewan quickly disassociated themselves from Kleinsasser's actions. It was no secret that Kleinsasser shared some of the Society's attitude's towards education, for example; their youth usually completed high school and some of them even went on to college in order to become colony teachers.

On December 9, 1992, ministers from the Schmiedeleut colonies met at the Starlight Colony near Winnipeg to consider the complaints against Jacob Kleinsasser. The vote taken after two days of meetings resulted in 78 ministers siding with Kleinsasser and 90 voting against his leadership. A representative from the United States colonies registered an additional 29 votes in favor of Kleinsasser (*Mennonite reporter,* Dec. 28, 1992, 7). A major split has occurred, and Kleinsasser, as heir to the more radical legacy of the Hutterites, has been challenged to prove that his merger action will have more benefit than damage for Hutterite society (Preston, 1992).

Role of the School

Hutterite leaders believe that much of the credit for their successful cultural survival is attributable to their system of religious education instructed in the German language. All Hutterite children are taught German before they are taught the English language. Formal instruction begins in the home and is supplemented in the kindergarten where the curriculum consists of learning prayers, songs and related recitations. Children officially enter kindergarten at the age of three or four and remain there until the age of six when they are admitted to both the public school and the German school. The former operates at standard hours while the German school meets before and after English school and on Saturdays. The teacher is a married man, selected by the colony, and his role is defined by tradition. He is often a member of the colony council and his wife usually has parallel duties. She helps supervise the children's meals, since they eat in a separate room and not with their parents, and helps her husband instruct the girls in their work patterns and responsibilities. In special circumstances the colony may assign an older woman to assist the German teacher in fulfilling these obligations.

The colony school curriculum consists of learning the German language, reciting Biblical passages and hymns from memory, and practicing the writing of the German script. Much of the school content consists of admonishing the students about Hutterian beliefs and expectations. Punishment for disobedience may consist of three straps on the palm of the hand for a first offence or minor infraction, and additional blows depending on the seriousness of the offence. A serious transgression brings the child to the bench for strapping and more minor offenses are punished by measures such as standing in a corner or being scolded.

Progression through the curriculum in the German school is accomplished on an individual basis although the expected level of efficiency and type of discipline administered is fairly standard. The basic function of the school is to teach the Hutterite way of life. Its effectiveness is measured when children move beyond school age to full participation in adult life. Unlike the English school it is spiritually and emotionally tied to Hutterite living and constitutes not only a vital part of the composite picture but plays the key role in preparing the young for adult function (Hostetler and Huntington, 1967). When this does not occur, as in the case of an occasional delinquent, the German school teacher is at least partially blamed for having failed in his duty. The role of German teacher carries with it a moral and pedagogical responsibility and like most positions of leadership is held until retirement or unless obligations are seriously violated.

Under the supervision of the German teacher, the following socialization techniques are imposed on Hutterite children from age six to fourteen:

1. Most of the child's day is closely supervised by an adult;
2. Children learn patterns of interaction while working together and these will remain well into adulthood;
3. School activities are designed to provide interaction between siblings and peers and teach children how to function in both roles. Naturally the two memberships overlap, interact and supplement one another but persist with traditional modification until the peer group embraces the whole colony;
4. School-age children are taught unquestioning obedience to Hutterite authority – parents, teacher, the colony, and any Hutterite adult. Disobedience is punishable by a variety of means including corporal punishment and must be borne meekly;
5. Children are not generally taught to think for themselves but taught that they will be told what to do. In turn they will be cared for, punished and protected by their authorities;
6. Praise and punishment basically guide the behavior of children and they do not need to feel particularly guilty about misbehaving because it is natural to sin. Theologically, children are not held personally responsible for sin and it is not their "fault" when they misbehave;
7. Internalization of Hutterian beliefs is gradual. Children memorize the rules and learn the verbal expressions of the system but it is not expected that they will really understand them until they are older; and,
8. Children learn to accept their proper place in Hutterian society by learning to accept its basic processes and conditions. They accept frustrations passively, hard labor as a routine, life uncluttered by material objects and even the cleansing process of pain and punishment as a kind of pleasure (Hostetler & Huntington, 1967, 67-68).

Ensuring the fulfillment of the above conditions is the primary responsibility of the German teacher. One teacher wrote:

I feel that the greatest challenge in my work is to put a good religious foundation under the children so that they may become respectable and honorable members of the Gemein. I always like to think of them as young tender plants in the Garden of the Lord where the school teacher's duty is to trim, weed and water as he finds necessary. Of course I realize that neither the planter nor the waterer can achieve anything without the Lord's blessing (Hostetler and Huntington, 1967, 72).

There are several reasons why German education is effective among Hutterites even though it is difficult to prove that it is singularly creditable for the successful retention of their youth and the perpetuation of their culture. Nor is it any guarantee for the future of colony life, particularly in light of the many obstacles which this century has imposed upon them.

First of all, Hutterian German education is comprehensive and synthesized. It incorporates all aspects of Hutterian living in its content and process.

Second, its ultimate purpose is preparation for adult living on the colony. Its objectives are slowly and gradually intensified throughout the learning process.

Third, the nature of German education is constraining in the sense that a questioning of procedures and content is simply not encouraged or expected (Hostetler and Huntington, 1967).

The German school and the role of the German teacher are seen as integral to the colony's existence. The school has the support of the leadership and members and its performance is of vital concern to all. It is not adjunct to the colony's existence and function. Rather, it *is* the essence of the colony.

Our society frequently credits or blames schooling for various social phenomena, something that is difficult to prove directly. In Hutterian society the extraneous factors in identifying causes are fewer in number, making it easier to determine the influence of German schooling. In the final analysis, however, successful maintenance of the Hutterian culture may be the ultimate criterion for judging the effectiveness of the German school.

References

Boldt, Edward D. & Lance W. Roberts. (1980). The decline of Hutterite population growth: Causes and consequences – a comment, Canadian Ethnic Studies, XII:3, 111-117.

Eaton, J.W. & A.J. Mayer. (1953). *Man's capacity to reproduce: The demography of a unique population.* Glencoe, Ill.: Free Press.

Fitch, Angeline C. (1978). Comparison of Hutterire and non-Hutterite children's cognitive abilities. Unpublished master's thesis, The University of Calgary.

Fretz, J. Winfield. (1989). *The Waterloo Mennonites: A community in paradox.* Waterloo, Ont.: Published Wilfred Laurier University Press for Conrad Grebel College.

Frideres, James S. (1972). The death of Hutterite culture. *Phylon, 33: September, 260-265.*

Friesen, John W. (1977). *People, culture & learning.* Calgary: Detselig Enterprises.

Friesen, John W. (1985). *When cultures clash: Case studies in multiculturalism.* Calgary: Detselig Enterprises.

Gross, Paul S. (1965). *The Hutterite Way.* Saskatoon: Freeman Publishing Company.

Harder, M.S. (1949). The Origin, Philosophy, and Development of Education Among the Mennonites. Unpublished doctoral dissertation. University of Southern California.

Hofer, Arnold M. & Kenneth J. Walter, eds. (1975). *The Hutterite Mennonites.* Freeman, S.D.: The Hutterite Centennial Steering Committee.

Hofer, John. (1982). *The history of the Hutterites.* Winnipeg: W.K. Printers.

Hofer, Samuel. (1991). *Born Hutterite: stories by Samuel Hofer.* Saskatoon: Hofer Publishing.

Horsch, John. (1931). *The Hutterian brethren: 1528-31.* Goshen Indiana: Mennonite Historical Society.

Hostetler, John A. (1961). Hutterite separatism and public tolerance. *The Canadian Forum,* 41: April,

Hostetler, John A. (1977). *Hutterite society.* Second printing. Baltimore, Maryland: Johns Hopkins Press.

Hostetler, John A. (1983). *Hutterite life.* Kitchener, Ont.: Herald Press.

Hostetler, John A. & Gertrude Enders Huntington. (1967). *The Hutterites on North America.* New York: Holt, Rinehart and Winston.

Janzen, William. (1990). *Limits on liberty: The experience of Mennonite, Hutterite and Doukhobor communities in Canada.* Toronto: University of Toronto Press.

Klaassen, Walter. (1973). *Anabaptist: neither Catholic nor Protestant.* Waterloo, Ont: Conrad Press.

Knill, William D. (1968). The Hutterites: Cultural transmission in a closed society. *Alberta Historical Review,* 16:3, summer, 1-10.

Mann, George Adolf. (1974). Functional autonomy among English school teachers in Hutterite colonies of southern Alberta: A study of social control. Unpublished doctoral dissertation. University of Colorado.

Mennonite Reporter. (1992). Hutterite majority in Manitoba rejects Kleinsasser leadership, 22(25), December 28, 4.

Palmer, Howard. (1972). *Land of the second chace: A history of ethnic groups in southern Alberta.* Lethbridge: *The Lethbridge Herald.*

Peter, Karl A. (1980). The decline of Hutterite population growth, *Canadian Ethnic Studies,* XII:3, 97-110.

Peter, Karl A. (1980). Rejoinder to the Decline of Hutterite Population Growth: Causes and Consequences – a comment, *Canadian Ethnic Studies,* XII:3, 118-123.-105.

Peter, Karl A. (1987). *Dynamics of Hutterite society: An analytical approach.* Edmonton: University of Alberta Press.

Peter, Karl A. & Ian Whitaker. (1982). The changing roles of Hutterite women. *Prairie Forum,* 7:2, 267-277.

Peters, Victor. (1965). *All things common: The Hutterian way of life.* New York: Harper Torchbooks.

Pitt, E.L. (1949). The Hutterian Brethren in Alberta. Unpublished master's thesis. University of Alberta.

Preston, Brian. (1992). Religion: Jacob's Ladder. *Saturday Night,* 107:3, April, 30-38, 76-80.

Report on communal property. (1972). Select Committee on the Assembly (Communal Property). Edmonton: Government of Alberta.

Zwarun, Susan. (1983). The Hutterites, *Western Living,* 18:10, October, 97-105.

8

Mennonites in Canada

Intra-community Pluralism

In North America the best known Anabaptist groups are the Mennonites, Hutterites and Amish. These groups are further subdivided into smaller segments and the Mennonites have by far the largest number of subgroups. Anabaptist groups generally subscribe to the fundamental beliefs outlined in the previous chapter but there is some divergence on what outsiders might call peripheral issues. Hutterites, for example, are the only group that believes in communal property while Amish and Old Order Mennonites believe in simplicity of living to the extent of farming with horses and using horse-drawn buggies for transportation. Mennonite groups generally may be differentiated from each other by a variety of beliefs and practices ranging from modes of baptism to the type of lifestyle or even clothing or hairstyle that is permitted.

The founder of the Mennonite faith was a Roman Catholic priest named Menno Simons (1496-1561). Like many other disillusioned priests of the Reformation period he participated in the counter religious movement in Europe and although his followers claim he never intended to start a separate order, this is essentially what happened. In 1536 he renounced the Roman Catholic church and aspired to help develop a new form of fellowship in keeping with New Testament principles, and by emphasizing the Anabaptist beliefs of Bibliolatry, individualism in faith, pacifism, isolation, practice of the "ban," and refusal to take an oath. In spite of the persecution that followed the Reformation, the movement spread to the German-speaking territory around Switzerland, to south Germany and ultimately to many other parts of the world (Smith, 1957).

As early as 1707, some of the Swiss Mennonites decided to immigrate to Pennsylvania, thus starting the flow of immigration that was to bring thousands of people to the new world. Mennonite and Hutterite immigrations to North America occurred in different time periods since these groups were essentially separate as a result of conflict over communal living. Although the Anabaptist movement provided these groups with a shared heritage, not all adherents were aware of the circumstances of their counterparts in other European countries. Mennonites and Hutterites shared many common beliefs, but the latter group was virtually unaffected by Menno Simons' personal beliefs because of the firm leadership they enjoyed in Jacob Hutter. Thus while both groups were part of a significant religious movement, their development took on some unique characteristics from the very beginning, which made their future identities and activities quite distinct from one another.

As the Reformation got underway the state church developed various means of controlling the rapid rise of heretic groups such as Mennonites, thus forcing them to flee to more tolerant countries. Furthermore, the nonresistant Mennonites were also perceived as a threat to the growing military power of Prussia, the leading European militaristic state. Many restrictive measures were imposed upon Mennonites; for example, they were forbidden to increase their land-holdings except by special permission, and they were charged extra taxes to make up for their lack of participation in military service (Bender and Smith, 1973).

In 1786 a delegation of Mennonites travelled to Russia to inspect lands offered them for occupation and to verify some other very attractive terms:

> Free transportation to Russia; one hundred and seventy-give acres of free land per family; a loan of $250.00 and support for each family at a cheap rate until the first harvest; complete religious freedom; complete freedom of language and schools; complete military exception; self-government within their settlements; no taxes for ten years and only a nominal federal tax thereafter. (Bender & Smith, 1973, 67)

The Russian offer was too good to turn down and carried only one restrictive clause: Mennonites were not to engage in evangelistic endeavors among native Russians.

Mennonite life in Russia was fulfilling and despite a major split in 1860, caused by a pietistic religious revival, (which birthed the Mennonite Brethren Church), the newcomers "lived happily ever after." However, less than a century after their immigration, the honeymoon was over and the Russian government began placing more emphasis on military power. In 1879, military exemption for pacifist groups was cancelled and despite many efforts to negotiate with the government, the thrust to Russify foreign cultures knew no exceptions. In 1873 a delegation of Mennonites visited Canada and the United States to determine the advisability of settlement there. Again the conditions of immigration were generous and the first Mennonites, 18 000 in all, relocated to North America between 1874 and 1880. About 6 000 arrived the first year; a third of them settled in Manitoba and the rest went to the States of Kansas (principally), Nebraska, South Dakota and Minnesota. In 1992, the Mennonites in Canada were nearly 200 000 strong.

One of the conditions of Mennonite immigration to Canada was the right to operate their own schools where Bible lessons and the German language would be taught. As though emulating a pattern, it was only a matter of a few years before the Manitoba government reneged on that privilege as well as the one granting military exemption. In 1890 the Manitoba Public School Act was passed declaring all public schools state-controlled, tax supported and non-sectarian.

English was the only language of instruction and the Union Jack was to be flown over every school. Again a compromise was sought with the appropriate officials and again a negative response was given. A series of petitions by the more conservative element of the Mennonite community was strengthened by public and press support but these efforts came to naught. In 1921, with guarantees similar to those they had received in Russia and Canada, over 5 000 Old Colony and Sommerfelder Mennonites began preparations for their move to Mexico; another 1 700 settled in Paraguay. The move, which finally got underway in 1922, was completed in 1929 (Heidebrecht, 1973).

Earlier, a community of Mennonites had left Manitoba to settle in Saskatchewan, but the long arm of the law soon caught up to them and the same story unfolded – public schooling or else. By 1932, this group embarked yet on another trek, this time to the Peace River country of Northern Alberta. Here tranquility was enjoyed until 1953 when the same issue drove thirty-five families to the British Honduras and thirty families to Worsley, Alberta. This example of migration is just one of many and merely serves to underscore the Mennonite strength of conviction.

A Compendium of Mennonite Groups in Canada

Canadians not familiar with the inner workings of the Mennonite network are often confused by the many varieties of Mennonites in Canada and are not aware of the vast sociological differences among them. As we shall later discover, an entire continuum pertaining to attitudes to education ranging form the approval of minimal literacy to the promotion of many different institutions of post-secondary learning, can be sketched. It would probably not be helpful to delineate all of the thirty-odd groups in Canada, but a brief description of some of the more commonly recognized divisions will now be provided. The two major divisions are the Swiss Mennonites, who migrated from their home country to the United States in the late 17th century and those groups which originated in Europe and transplanted to Russia between 1774 and 1786. These communities have been subdivided for a variety of reasons and some of these will be specified as a means of illustrating the Mennonite disposition to theological accuracy, individualism and congregational autonomy.

Swiss Mennonites

In 1683, about 2 000 families arrived in Pennsylvania constituting the first group of Mennonites in North America. In 1786 some of them migrated to Waterloo County in Ontario where their descendants still reside (Fretz, 1989). Often referred to as members of the "Old Mennonite" Church, their activities include providing leadership in publishing and education and operating many schools and colleges in the United States. In Canada they comprise three conferences with a combined membership of about 10 000, most of whom live in Ontario. The small northwest conference which functions primarily in Alberta has about seven congregations (Reimer, 1983).

1. Old Order Mennonites. In 1889, Abraham Martin and a few followers in Waterloo County, Ontario, decided to form a group that would eschew modernization and such "modern" church forms as Sunday School, English preaching and revival services. Essentially their way of life resembles that of the Old Order Amish who also farm with horses and travel around by buggy, but the two communities do not interact much and certainly do not encourage intermarriage. Old Order Mennonites reside in Waterloo County and have experienced at least two divisions since they began. They have nearly 1 500 members.

2. Church of God in Christ, Mennonite (Holdeman People). In 1859, John Holdeman of Wayne County, Ohio began preaching without the traditional call to ministry as a means of re-establishing true Apostolic succession. Popular doctrines of the new group were strict church discipline, non-conformity with the world, and the belief that revelation can come through dreams (Friesen, 1983a). In 1881 the church sent a preacher to Manitoba to conduct revival services which were successful in attracting many members of the Russian-originated Keingemeinde church to the numbers. Some of these members later settled in Linden, Alberta, and in the Peace River Country. Others moved to Abbotsford, B.C. and later to parts of Saskatchewan and Ontario. Their Canadian membership stands at about 2 500 in 30 congregations and their combined North American population is just over 12 000 (Yearbook, 1989).

3. Other fellowships of Swiss Mennonite origin include the Conservative Mennonite Fellowship, Conservative Church of Ontario, Fellowship Churches, Midwest Mennonite Fellowship, two independent congregations in Alberta at Stirling and Bay Tree, Reformed Mennonites, and a variety of scattered and autonomous congregations. Generally speaking, the bulk of these groups live in Ontario.

Mennonite Groups Originating in Russia

1. The Bergthaler Church actually derived its name in 1893 from the geographic area which its members occupied in Russia. They relocated to Saskatchewan as a conference of churches but officially disbanded in 1972 to merge with the General Conference Mennonite Church. Five independent congregations with a combined membership of 1 000 still function in Saskatchewan (Gerbrandt, 1970; Reimer, 1983).

2. The Chortitzer Mennonites also derived their name from a geographic location in Russia and maintained a strong agrarian lifestyle on settling in Manitoba. Some 2 000 strong, they are essentially religiously conservative but

demonstrate a somewhat unusual other-directed bent by supporting a number of missionaries in foreign countries.

3. Old Colony Mennonites. Essentially this group parallels the "Old Order" Swiss Mennonites in lifestyle, although they frequently drive automobiles and use mechanical, albeit somewhat outdated, means of farming. Church services feature singing from German hymnbooks without notes and sermons or repetitious monologues in the Low German language by lay, unpaid ministers. Members of this group, left Manitoba in the great school controversy in the 1920s for Mexico and Paraguay. A half century later most of them had returned and number about 4 500 souls in Canada.

4. The Sommerfelder Group. More conservative even than Old Colony Mennonites, the Sommerfelder have unpaid ministers, allow no choirs nor Sunday School and no musical instruments. Men are allowed to wear only dark colored clothing with no neckties and women must wear kerchiefs. Their settlements are found in Manitoba, Saskatchewan, Peace River Country in Alberta and Vanderhoof, B.C. with a combined membership of 4 000. They are originally a breakaway group from the Bergthaler Church.

5. Reinlaender Mennonites. This group, consisting of only six churches, broke away from the Sommerfelder Church in 1958 over the issue of electric lights and decoration in meeting houses. They *do* have Sunday School and youth groups but allow no musical instruments and approve only very conservative (black only) clothing. Their ministers are unpaid laymen and worship services are conducted in both the Low German and High German languages (Reimer, 1983).

6. Rudnerweider Church: later called, the Evangelical Mennonite Mission Conference (1959). Although quite lively and evangelical in today's terms, this group originated from a split in the Sommerfelder church in Manitoba in 1937. Their peculiarities include baptism by pouring, use of non-fermented grape juice for Holy Communion and the use of catechism for membership preparation (Epp, 1982). They do not have particular dress regulations and their preachers use an extemporaneous method of preaching. Their membership stands at 2 658.

7. Mennonite Brethren Church. This group was formed in Russia in 1860 as a result of a religious revival that swept through the established Mennonite churches at that time. Some of the original members came to North America in the 1874 exodus, settling in both the U.S.A. and Canada; their present Canadian membership is nearly 25 000. Their conference operates a variety of elementary schools, Bible Colleges and senior citizens homes. They are probably the most evangelical and liberal of Mennonite groups and support a very large domestic and foreign mission program. They are possibly the only Mennonites to insist on baptism by immersion.

8. Three other Russian-originated groups include: (i) the Evangelical Mennonite Conference which originated in Russia in 1812, and currently has 5 000

members in Ontario and the westerly provinces; (ii) the Evangelical Mennonite Brethren Conference, which originated in Mountain Lake, Minnesota, reorganized in 1889, and has 2 000 members in the four western provinces; and, (iii) the Evangelical Mennonite Mission Conference which began in 1937 as a result of a revival movement among the Sommerfelder Mennonite Church in Manitoba. This group has over 2 600 members in 23 congregations located in Manitoba, Saskatchewan and Ontario.

The General Conference Church

Also referred to as the Conference of Mennonites in Canada, this conference numbers about 28 000 members and is a truly Canadian endeavor. The group originated in 1903 when representatives from fifteen congregations in Manitoba and Saskatchewan met to share concerns and unify their structures. A second major influx of Mennonites from Russia in the nineteen twenties provided a generous increase in membership. The conference has twice changed its name because of reorganization but functions at present with five provincial conferences and maintains strong ties to the American conference. Culturally-speaking, there are no visible means of distinguishing this group from other Canadians, but idiosyncrasies of history, foods, common values and a strong unique religious orientation tend to deter them from entering into full integration (Friesen, 1977). In rural areas, a tendency to cloister themselves in communities contributes to the maintenance of their identity. In larger urban centres there are no Mennonite ghettos as such, but their practice of interacting basically with their own kind discourages non-Mennonites from joining their numbers to any significant degree.

Mennonite Cultural Distinctives

A debate that frequently arises in Mennonite circles is whether or not their various groupings should be conceived of as cultural or ethnic entities or merely as religious denominations (Toews, 1988). For the most part the debate over their identity does not extend beyond their community. Mennonite scholars, for the most part, concentrate their studies on the normative maintenance of their community, trying to isolate the basic features of the Mennonite community in an attempt to discover the forces which tend to disrupt or undermine the persistence of the community (Driedger and Redekop, 1983, 53).

Mennonite scholars such as Driedger describe their group as a social structural community in equilibrium – a stable predictable, little changing community where Gemeinschaft (fellowship) is the ideal (Driedger, 1975). Although the bulk of Mennonites tend to migrate to rural areas, recent decades have witnessed their urban migrations. Winnipeg, for example, is the Mennonite

Canadian capital with a community of 19 105 (Driedger, 1990). While sojourn-ing in the cities Mennonites have attempted to develop a functional lifestyle, carefully juxtaposing community welfare with required outside interactions. The traditional model for a rural to urban move consists of establishing territorial control in selected urban areas, and then transferring measured patterns of institutional completeness, cultural identity and social distance. This has not augured well for Mennonites in Winnipeg, for example, who have therefore tended to deal with the "outside world" through institutional operations such as the inter-church Foodgrains Bank, relief and material aid centres, thrift shops, self-help crafts, offender ministries, services to Aboriginal peoples, mediation services, Mennonite Economic Development Associates, and the Mennonite Central Committee (Driedger, 1990).

It is perhaps easiest to differentiate the Mennonite lifestyle from the domi-nant culture through the identification of minor eccentricities such as manners or customs. These have to do with everyday life, food habits, working and leisure, and religion as a basis for living. Socialization practices maintain these peculiar-ities, mainly through the home and to a lesser extent, the church. These practices can be referred to as "folkways" rather than entrenched cultural patterns (Smuc-ker, 1977, xiii)

Some of the more intrinsic elements of Mennonite culture include the Mennonite preference for the use of civil courts as a means of settling disputes, a preference for the maintenance of the German language, and the justification of basic literacy as a necessity for reading the Scriptures. It is quite likely that Mennonite culture will survive for at least a few more generations even though the most serious challenge facing the community is the threat of acculturation (Friesen, 1971). This concept needs to be differentiated from the process of assimilation in that the former term implies the cultural shifting of an entire people whereas assimilation may have an individual application.

In light of the foregoing it appears feasible to conceive of the Mennonite way of life as a culture rather than strictly a religious system. Of course its major structures and processes do not differ radically from the mainstream of Canadian life, except in the case of more eccentric groups like the Old Colony, Holdeman or Old Order Mennonites, but few subcultures in Canada do more than that. A basic definition of culture includes such components as language and stock, arts and music, cognitive data, sentimental elements, social structure and material aspects. Thus to "qualify" as a *subculture* it is only necessary that a social grouping differ *somewhat* from the mainstream in terms of several of these components. In this way, Mennonites certainly fall into the category of compris-ing a separate and distinctive culture. As Professor Winfield Fretz of the University of Waterloo has stated, "They (Mennonites) have a set of unique traditions, beliefs, customs and social practices that go beyond the conventional views of what constitutes a religious denomination . . . . What began as a strictly religious group has in the course of history also become a distinctive cultural group (Fretz, 1974).

The distinctive characteristics of Mennonites include a definitive heritage of European stock and German language. Until recently, most Mennonites were familiar with a variety of dialects originating from common European sources, i.e. Low German, High German or Swiss German. On the international scale the picture has changed somewhat because of missionary efforts of Mennonites who have established outposts and gained converts in nations whose inhabitants have maintained their own languages, e.g. India and Africa. In North America, however, Mennonites basically share a common European heritage. The younger generation is rapidly losing familiarity with their language of origin and this has caused some consternation among those elders who believe that maintaining language is essential to cultural survival. In sociological terms, language is obviously a significant element in differentiating subcultures and that fact alone may lend support to the argument that its loss by the younger generation will almost certainly result in a loss of cultural content and appreciation.

Although it may be contended that many of the eccentric beliefs of Mennonites are religious in nature, some of them are sufficiently unique so that when they are compared with the ideas of mainstream religious denominations they clearly belong to a separate category. The principle of the priesthood of the individual has been a primary contributing factor to the many splits among Mennonites, and even though the issues that arise often appear to be religious (or even Biblical) in nature, the related behaviors have more sociological than religious implications. Examples of these beliefs are pacifism, refusal to take an oath, endogamy, and, to a lesser extent, adult baptism, the abolition of the sacraments and the selection of ministers.

Students of Mennonite history are frequently overwhelmed by the many varieties of Mennonites and speculate as to the causes. The underlying rationale emanates from a fundamental religious orientation which has been translated into sociological terms, namely the intense historic Bibliolatry among Anabaptist groups. Transposed into behavioral terms, this belief has produced a rugged independence or self-reliance. Since individuals can interpret the Scriptures for themselves, the principle goes, they are also expected to act on their convictions. Examples of the intensity with which Mennonites adhere to this idea are the following: (i) in 1958, acting on conviction, a group of Reinlaender split from the Sommerfelder Church because of charges of worldliness. One of the issues in the split was the use of electricity in houses of worship; (ii) the Bergthaler churches of Saskatchewan are very similar in belief to the Sommerfelders, e.g. they have no formal conference organization, they worship in both Low German and English, they have no choirs or musical instruments, and their ministers are elected and unpaid. Still, they would not consider a merger with their sister group under any circumstances; and, (iii) in 1937 a religious revival began in a Manitoba district where the Sommerfelder church functioned. As a result, several individuals who had become religiously energized asked the church elders to make certain changes; they requested a more youth-oriented program of activities including Sunday school, choir practices and evening services. When the leaders refused to change, a split resulted, and the Rudnerweider (Evangelical Mennonite Mission) Church was born (Epp, 1982).

The origins of the Mennonite Brethren Church illustrate the lengths to which the group has gone in rectifying what they perceived to be past errors. When this group pulled out from the mainline church in 1860 there was some concern about the proper mode of baptism. They decided on adult immersion as a form, but concluded that an individual could only be baptized by a minister who had himself been properly baptized. As a result they proceeded in this fashion:

> Soon thereafter . . . in the month of September 1860, a wagon loaded with members drove to the water where we first knelt for prayer. Then we stepped into the water. Jacob Becker first baptized Bartel, then Bartel baptized Becker. The latter then baptized three others. (Toews, 1975, 56)

Many Mennonite factions have formed on the basis of individually-derived (Biblical?) convictions which have differed from those held by the parent group. In terms of the resultant behavior patterns, many beliefs have had immediate sociological implications and others have developed such as time went on. No doubt the Anabaptist predisposition to achieve Biblical exactness precipitates splintering, and it is probably safe to say that the resulting folkways have varied sufficiently from the norm to create a social uniqueness and/or pattern of deviance. When that occurs we are speaking about a cultural or ethnic minority, not a religious community.

Mennonites of all varieties have always decried a strong dependency on materialism even though the tenacity of that claim is hard to believe when one views the homes of some of the more progressive Mennonites of today. A continual theme of simplicity echoes throughout Mennonite history, however, and when congregations have divided there has still been a concern for an unadorned lifestyle. This concern is illustrated by the Mennonite Central Committee, a inter-Mennonite agency which is dedicated to welfare and relief work in overseas countries. Its philosophy is one of sharing through self-denial, and it is supported by a variety of Mennonite groups ranging from the vary conservative to the more progressive.

Groups like Quakers have also been concerned with a denial of materialism, contending that the essence of life is more than its substance. When this value is translated into lifestyle in any significant way, the words of Jesus are often cited in support, "For what shall it profit a man if he shall gain the whole world and lost his own soul?" (Mark 8:36-37). Patterns of simple living like that of the Old Order or Old Colony Mennonite often attract the attention of outsiders who fail to see the theological significance of their deliberate refusal to use modern conveniences. These groups have an answer for such criticisms, arguing that they do not expect their way of life to be understood. English-speaking apologists of those orders will often quote from the book of First Peter which states, "But ye are a chosen generation, a royal priesthood, an holy nation, a peculiar people . . ." (I Peter 2:9). It is not their intention to pursue peculiarity (or eccentricity) for its own sake but when a sociological trait is pronounced to the extent that it differentiates its adherents form mainline society, it may be concluded that sociology rather than religion can best provide an explanation.

Mennonite Philosophy of Education: A Continuum

European beginnings reveal that the Anabaptists have always had a genuine interest in education. The Mennonites of Prussia specifically were convinced that parents should provide at least elementary instruction for their children in order to perpetuate the German language and acquaint their children with the Bible and with Mennonite peculiarities. Instruction consisted of reading, writing, arithmetic and religion with much emphasis on memorization, drill and penmanship. Frederick the Great of Prussia had a liberal outlook and granted his subjects great freedom in religious and private educational pursuits. Similarly, Hutterites in Europe developed a well-organized system of compulsory education even thought they were living in an age when illiteracy was the common lot of the average man. While it is difficult to ascertain the extent of educational developments among the Amish in Europe, the fact that the Amish and the Old Order Mennonites in Ontario foster an independent system of education may be an indication that they recognize the need for consistency, and synthesis in the enculturation process. To this end they sponsor a system of private schools to ensure that the values fostered in their home and church environments will be reinforced at school (Hostetler and Huntington, 1971). A lack of this emphasis may have contributed to the demise of the Amish in Europe for it is only in North America that they can still be identified.

The role of education in the establishment of Anabaptist communities in Russia and North America is easily apparent. The earliest American settlements invariably featured parochial primary schools, but after the Pennsylvania school law of 1834 was passed, private schools began to dwindle and were practically eliminated by the middle of that century. The first Mennonite educational institution established in America was built in Germantown, Pennsylvania in 1702 and was supported by the improbable combination of Quakers and Mennonites. Five years prior to that the two communities had worshipped together in a common building, but the Mennonites soon recognized that if they were to maintain their separate identity they must have their own school and house of worship. Thus their first church house, a log structure, was built in 1708 and doubled as a schoolhouse for many years (Pannabecker, 1975). Further west in America, where frontier conditions prevailed, more recent immigrants established traditional church schools. Of these, the Gemeindeschule of the Zion

Mennonite Church established in 1853 in Donnellson, Iowa proved to have the greatest longevity (Hartzler, 1925). Today, the American Swiss Mennonite Church alone (Old Mennonite) sponsors 19 high schools and 93 primary schools (Horsch, 1983).

Mennonites in Russia

After colonization in the backward conditions of Russia had been achieved, Mennonites developed an extensive educational system of their own design (Heidebrecht, 1973). The first teachers were farmers, craftsmen or herdsmen who were ill-prepared for teaching, and poorly paid. The schools operated for the most part out of teachers' homes. By law the responsibility of school supervision lay with the elders and spiritual leaders of the community, but often the teacher was left completely in charge (Friesen, 1934). The first educational reforms were introduced by Johann Cornies through an organization called "The Society for Christian Education" which directed the building of the first secondary school in 1820. New teachers with Prussian background were hired, bringing with them educational innovations from Europe which featured the ideas of Johann Heinrich Pestalozzi, Johann Amos Comenius (Komensky) and others. By 1843 Cornies had laid the foundation for future Mennonite schools through a newly established Agricultural Commission which was granted considerable control over the school system by the Russian authorities. Some of the significant developments that came about included the erection of model schools, the creation of school districts, compulsory attendance, licensing of teachers, a planned curriculum and teacher conferences.

The educational theories of Pestalozzi and Comenius foreshadowed the progressive education movement in North America under the leadership of such educational philosophers as John Dewey. Central to the movement were these presuppositions: truth is relative, education is the sum total of the child's experience, and insight, which is individualized, is the sole objective of learning. While it is conceivable that the German interpretation of these ideas penetrated education in the Russian Mennonite context, there is no evidence that they influenced Mennonite education in North America in any way. In fact, research on the educational philosophy of Mennonite schooling is virtually non-existent, possibly because the implicit notion of cultural maintenance was so entrenched (Friesen, 1983b).

Most educational progress in Russian colonies came about in the area known as Molotchna. The more conservative leaders in Chortitza, particularly in the two daughter colonies of Bergthal and Fuerstenland, resisted many innovations, especially the introduction of the Russian language which they felt threatened their way of life. Generally the Russian Government was pleased with the content and direction of Mennonite schools and allowed religion and German to be taught for ten of a total thirty instruction hours per week. In the last fifteen years before World War l, Mennonite schools proliferated in Russia and by 1920, with a population of approximately 110 000, the Mennonites in Russia operated:

1. 450 elementary schools with about 16 000 pupils and 570 teachers (this included a school for the deaf);
2. Twenty-five secondary schools, two of which were considered business schools, with about 2 000 pupils enrolled and 100 teachers;
3. two teacher-training schools each with an approximate enrolment of sixty students;
4. one eight-year business school for boys with an enrollment of about 300;
5. a girls' gymnasium with 150 enrolled;
6. four Bible schools (Coward, et al, 1988).

The Mennonite exodus from Russia transpired for a variety of reasons, some of which were related to educational matters. Although Russian was taught in Mennonite schools as early as the 1830s and many more used it by the 1860s, the Russian State Department actually kept Mennonite schools under scrutiny from 1881 on, demanding that all instruction be in Russian except for religion and German language instruction. Russian teachers were provided for Mennonite schools with unqualified Mennonite teachers. The "straw that broke the camel's back," however, was not directly related to schooling; it was the passage of the universal military service law of 1874 (Dyck, 1967). Because military considerations were taken so seriously by the Mennonites, it is improbable that educational issues greatly influenced the exodus. Russian Mennonite schools may have been forward-looking in nature, but the marriage of primary progressivist educational concepts to the underlying desire for ethnic preservation had evidently not come about.

Mennonite Schools in North America

When the Russian Mennonites immigrated to North America, their educational concerns along with other peculiarities were simply transplanted on new soil. In Marion County, Kansas, three schools were built in 1877 with the rationale ". . . because we always had schools in the old country. . ." (Wiebe, 1959). The chief purpose of instruction was consistent – to teach children the German language and to acquaint them with the Bible. For this reason the Bible was also used as a textbook. Similar reasoning was evident in other American settlements, as evidenced by the Swiss German Mennonites who organized a school just two years after their arrival in Dakota Territory (Swiss German Centennial Committee, 1974). In Manitoba, Mennonites enjoyed complete school autonomy as guaranteed by Federal Government promises, a situation that lasted until 1878 when a census revealed that one-third of all Mennonite children were not registered with the public school board and were officially in private schools. Mennonites had little interest in government support for their schools because they felt that financial support implied governmental intervention (Epp, 1962; Epp, 1974). By 1907, governmental interference in Mennonite schooling was evidenced when the Roblin government requested that private schools fly the country's flag while in session. Objections and concerns were quickly raised, and private schooling in Manitoba was no longer as "private" as before.

Essentially the contemporary Mennonite rationale for a strong educational thrust is well summarized in a century-old statement drafted by seventy spiritual leaders at a Kansas Conference of preachers in 1877:

1. Where Mennonites are in the majority in a school district, and are in a position to exert a deciding influence, it is suggested that they organize school districts; but no recommendations are made in the matter of taking out citizenship papers.

2. Where it is impossible to wield a controlling influence in the public schools, Mennonites are urged to organize their own church schools.

3. The conference recommends the learning of the English language as well as the German for a double reason: (i) in order to facilitate communication with the American neighbors; and (ii) so that they may help to extend the Kingdom of God among the English-speaking people.

4. It is the opinion of the conference that in the matter of financial support the entire congregation in which the school is located is under obligation to assume this task as a common burden (Smith, 1927, 215)

Diversity of Educational Opinion

Some conservative groups among the Anabaptists, and Mennonites more particularly, have consistently endorsed basic literacy for their children. Hutterites and Amish, for example, are usually satisfied with minimal literacy, and do not necessarily connect schooling with the attainment of Biblical awareness. One of the reasons why some of the Amish migrated to Ontario from the U.S.A. in 1952, for example, was the absence of rigid school attendance requirements beyond elementary education (Gingerich, 1972). Moreover, they were allowed to have their own schools if they so desired. The Holdeman people have shown an equally lukewarm attitude toward schooling, and did not build their own schools in the United States until 1947. By 1969 they operated three in that country and soon thereafter built several in Alberta (Hiebert, 1973).

Developments in Secondary and Higher Education

Reports referring to higher education among Anabaptist groups in Europe are scant, but these increase with reference to Mennonite settlements in Russia in the 18th century and in the United States. The Russian situation before the Mennonite exodus, as previously mentioned, suggests a dual concern for the establishment of Bible schools as well as forms of secondary education. On arrival in North America all three of the larger Mennonite bodies were soon involved in setting up institutions of higher learning – The General Conference Mennonite Church (which originated here), the (Old) Swiss Mennonite Church as well as the Mennonite Brethren. Some scholars point out that the Bible school movement is largely a Mennonite Brethren phenomenon (Toews, 1975).

Prior to 1900 a comparatively small number of Mennonites secured a higher education, and those who did attend college or university frequently abandoned the church, tending to settle in non-Mennonite communities as teachers, physicians or lawyers, and affiliate with other denominations. One leader, Henry A. Mumaw sought to reverse this trend by establishing a number of schools such as the Elkhart and English Training School (later the Elkhart Normal School) in 1882, the Elkhart Institute of Science, Industry and Art in 1894, and the Elkhart Normal and Business College in 1898 (Wenger, 1966). Other efforts soon followed, Bluffton College in Ohio, Goshen College in Indiana and Heston College, Bethel College and Tabor College in Kansas plus others. Although historians have not addressed the matter, it is entirely conceivable that young people left their Mennonite roots because of difficulty coping with the philosophical or value disparity between their backgrounds and state institutions. Mennonite institutions were established to curb the trend of student attrition and it was assumed that Mennonite youth would choose to attend these institutions. Many did, but when some of them found that Mennonite schools failed to encourage critical thinking, they too left the Mennonite fold.

Conflict and Consensus

Developments in Mennonite education were not always void of controversy, spurned perhaps by the intense desire to "do what was right by our children" kind of thinking that dominated many of the early initiatives. In Gretna, Manitoba, a schism developed over the location of the Gretna-Altona high school, a conflict which was only partially ameliorated by the building of two schools, one in each community (Gerbrandt, 1970). Later, in Saskatchewan, in 1950, the board of Rosthern Junior College battled with the problem of releasing a very popular teacher (Epp, 1975), and, more recently, the release of the principal of the Mennonite Brethren Collegiate Institute in Winnipeg caused considerable consternation (Longhurst, 1982). Still, most Mennonite leaders assume that their own schools are absolutely essential for preservation of Mennonitism, and equate the loss of Mennonite identity with a failure to provide private schooling. Besides, there is evidence that public schools do not teach very much about Anabaptist history or Mennonite distinctives (Friesen, 1988). Also, whenever there has been a school controversy, outside authorities have argued that Mennonite children should be "liberated through public education," even if the government would have to force them to attend public schools (Janzen, 1990).

The question of whether or not to provide schooling for their children has rarely been an issue for Mennonites generally. On that point there is consensus. However, the amount and nature of that schooling, however, has varied in relation to the extent of their integration into the dominant society. Thus the diversity evident among Mennonites with regard to most issues is also evident with regard to schooling.

References

Bender, Harold S. & C. Henry Smith. (1973). *Mennonites and their heritage.* Scottdale, Pa.: *Herald Press.*

Coward, Harold, Christopher Bagley & John W. Friesen. (1988). *The evolution of multiculturalism.* Calgary: The Calgary Institute for the Humanities.

Driedger, Leo. (1975). Canadian Mennonite urbanism: Ethnic villages or metropolitan remnant? *Mennonite Quarterly Review,* 3: July, 226- 241.

Driedger, Leo. (1990). *Mennonites in Winnipeg.* Winnipeg: Kindred Press.

Driedger, Leo & John H. Redekop. (1983). Sociology of Mennonites: State of the art and science. *Journal of Mennonite Studies,* I, 33-63.

Dyck, Cornelius J. ed. (1967). *An introduction to Mennonite life: A popular history of the Anabaptists and the Mennonites.* Scottdale, Pa.: Herald Press.

Epp, Frank H. (1962). *Mennonite exodus: The rescue and resettlement of the Russian Mennonites since the Communist revolution.* Altona, Man.: D. W. Friesen and Sons.

Epp, Frank H. (1974). *Mennonites in Canada, 1786-1920: The history of a separate people.* Toronto: Macmillan.

Epp, Frank H. (1975). *Education with a plus: The story of Rosthern Junior College.* Waterloo: Conrad Grebel Press.

Epp, Frank H. (1982). *Mennonites in Canada, 1920-1940.* Toronto: Macmillan.

Fretz, J. Winfield. (1974). *The Mennonites in Ontario.* Waterloo: Mennonite Historical Society of Ontario.

Fretz, J. Winfield. (1989). *The Waterloo Mennonites: A community in paradox.* Waterloo: Published by Wilfred Laurier University Press for Conrad Grebel College.

Friesen, I. (1934). The Mennonites of western Canada with special reference to Education. Unpublished Master's Thesis. The University of Saskatchewan.

Friesen, John W. (1971). Characteristics of Mennonite identity: A survey of Mennonite and non-Mennonite views. *Canadian Ethnic Studies,* III: June, 25-41.

Friesen, John W. (1977). *People, culture & learning.* Calgary: Detselig Enterprises.

Friesen, John W. (1983a). *Schools with a purpose.* Calgary: Detselig Enterprises.

Friesen, John W. (1983b). Studies in Mennonite education: The state of the Art. *Journal of Mennonite Studies,* I: 133-148.

Friesen, John W. (1988). Concepts of Mennonites in school curriculum. Mennonite Quarterly Review, LXII:1, January, 56-77.

Gerbrandt, Henry J. (1970). *Adventure in faith: The background in Europe and the development in Canada of the Bergthaler Mennonite Church of Manitoba.* Altona, Man.: D.W. Friesen and Sons.

Gingerich, Orland. (1972). *The Amish of Canada.* Waterloo: Conrad Press.

Hartzler, John Ellsworth. (1925). *Education among the Mennonites.* Danvers, Ill.: The Central Mennonite Publishing Board.

Heidebrecht, Herbert V. (1973). Values of Mennonite youth in Alberta. Unpublished Master's Thesis. The University of Calgary.

Hiebert, Clarence. (1973). *The Holdeman people: The Church of God in Christ, Mennonite, 1859-1969.* South Pasadena, CA.: William Carey Library.

Horsch, James E. ed. (1983). *Mennonite yearbook & directory.* Scottdale, Pa.: Mennonite Publishing House.

Hostetler, John A. and Gertrude Enders Huntington. (1971). *Children in Amish society: socialization and community education.* New York: Holt, Rinehart and Winston.

Janzen, William. (1990). *Limits on liberty: The experience of Mennonite, Hutterite, and Doukhobor communities in Canada.* Toronto: University of Toronto Press.

Longhurst, John. (1982). M.B.C.I. Principal dismissed. *The Mennonite Brethren Herald,* 21:6, March 12, 12-13.

Pannabecker, Samuel Floyd. (1975). *Open doors: The history of the general conference church.* Newton, Ks.: Faith and Life Press.

Reimer, Margaret Loewen. (1983). *One quilt, many pieces.* Waterloo: Mennonite Publishing Service.

Smith, C. Henry. (1927). *The coming of the Russian Mennonites: An episode in the settling of the last frontier, 1874-1884.* Berne, Ind.: Mennonite Book Concern.

Smith, C. Henry. (1957). *The story of the Mennonites.* 4th edition. Newton, Ks: Mennonite Publication House.

Smucker, Donovan, ed. (1977). *The sociology of Canadian Mennonites, Hutterites and Amish.* Waterloo: Wilfred Laurier University Press.

Swiss-German Centennial Committee. (1974). *The Swiss-Germans in South Dakota (from Volhynia to Dakota Territory), 1874-1974.* Freeman, S.D: Pine Hill Press.

Toews, John A. (1975). *A history of the Mennonite brethren church: Pilgrims and pioneers.* Fresno, CA.: Board of Christian Literature.

Toews, Paul. (1988). Faith in culture and culture in faith: The Mennonite Brethren in North America. *Journal of Mennonite Studies,* 6: 36-50.

Wenger, J.C. (1966). *The Mennonite Church in America: Sometimes called old Mennonites.* Vol. II. Scottdale, Pa.: Herald Press.

Wiebe, David V. (1959). *They seek a country: A survey of Mennonite migrations with special reference to Kansas and Gnadenau.* Hillsboro, Ks.: The Mennonite Brethren Publishing House.

Yearbook: Church of God in Christ, Mennonite. (1989). Moundridge, Ks.: Gospel Publishers.

9

The Chinese in Calgary:
Schooling for Cultural Identity

Kim Sheung-King Lan

Introduction

Theorists contend that an effective way to maintain the survival of an ethnocultural community is to ensure that the needs of its members are fully met (Lewin, 1948; Newman, 1973). This implies having a positive identity with one's group and experiencing satisfying cultural experiences which are often fostered through institutional and informal socialization (Isajiw and Makabe, 1982). The problem of achieving and maintaining this quality of ethno-cultural life, however, is most challenging in an urban setting where the forces of interaction and assimilation are maximized. The purpose of this chapter is to illustrate how one urban ethnocultural community, the Chinese of Calgary, have managed to survive and flourish against such odds. The research data analysis suggested that the Chinese schools play an important role in the maintenance of the Chinese culture and cultural identity.

Canadian Immigration Policy Towards The Chinese

Being a vast country in terms of space, Canada has an abundance of natural resources with ample room for immigrants. Towards the end of the 1800s the large unanticipated arrival of immigrants, specially those from southern Europe (the less preferred European group), coincided with the opening of the Canadian west. This necessitated a shift in immigration policy from the relatively unrestricted free entry to some form of controlled entry. The Immigration Act of 1900, under the liberal government of Sir Wilfrid Laurier, classified immigrants into preferred and non-preferred categories in an ethnic pecking order based on conditions or requirements in Canada and the ability of immigrants to become assimilated (Palmer, 1982). Northern and western Europeans were the most preferred immigrants, central and eastern Europeans ranked second, and southern Europeans ranked third. Asians were restricted by a low quota. The Japanese were permitted under a "gentlemen's agreement," special treaties between 1894 to 1911 which systematically limited Japanese from entering Canada.

The Canadian government passed its first anti-Chinese legislation in 1885. A head tax for entry into Canada and a special resident tax were imposed on the Chinese immigrants. The head tax was increased from $50 in 1885, $100 in 1901, and $500 in 1903 to discourage Chinese immigration. A dramatic effect was felt in the first few years following 1903. No Chinese immigrated during the first half of 1904, only eight Chinese entered in 1905 and twenty-two in 1906. The deteriorating socio-economic and political situation in China revived the momentum for emigration. Although 55 739 Chinese, mostly males, entered Canada between 1901 and 1920, the net loss was 8 613. Population decline due to the unbalanced sex ratio, the federal government's guarantee for the re-entry of unemployed Chinese laborers after the war without the head tax, and the older Chinese returning to their homeland accounted for this phenomenon.

In 1921, the Chinese were not allowed to vote in the federal election and in 1923, the Chinese Exclusion Act was passed in spite of Chinese protest. The effect of the Act was immense. During the period of exclusion, 1925 to 1946, only seven Chinese came to this country. In the 1930s, the depression years, an Order-in-Council (PC 3173, 1931) was passed to further encourage Chinese to leave Canada. The Chinese Exclusion Act was repealed in 1947 and subsequent changes in the immigration legislation passed during the 1950s permitted Chinese to enter Canada through a family sponsorship program. In 1962, Canadian immigration policy changed from one of selection by nationality to one of selection by education and ability. After 1962, Chinese immigration increased steadily, particularly after the 1976 communist riot in Hong Kong and the 1989 Tien An Men incident in China. The imminent Chinese take-over of Hong Kong in 1997 has further encouraged Chinese emigration. By 1990 the total Chinese population in Canada was over 400 000. In spite of the fact that 42 percent of 1 785 000 immigrants admitted into Canada between 1977-1990 were Asians, the combined Chinese and east/southeast Asian Canadian population account for only 2.2 percent of the total population in Canada.

The Calgary Chinese and Chinese Heritage Language Schools

The first Chinese arrived in Calgary in 1886 after the completion of the Canadian-Pacific Railway. Rejected by the host society and for socio-economic security, the new arrivals segregated themselves forming the early Chinatown which was located along 9th Avenue east and Centre Street, next to the CPR station. Small businesses were opened up including stores, restaurants and laundries. The presence of Chinatown did not draw attention until the outbreak of smallpox in 1892. Violence broke out when the Chinese were blamed for the occurrence of smallpox. Three hundred Calgarians went on a rampage trying to drive the Chinese out of town until the Mounted Police intervened ("Hunting Chinamen," *Calgary Herald*, August 3, 1892).

In 1909, another Chinatown emerged on the other side of the track around the Chinese Mission on 1st Street S.W. and 10th Avenue S.W. In 1910, Chinatown was relocated to the present site (Centre Street and 2nd Avenue), when the previous site was sold by the non-Chinese owners (*Calgary Herald*, Sept. 28, 1910). The late 1910s and 1920s witnessed the formation of the Chinese National League, the Chinese Public School, a few family associations and the Chinese YMCA (later known as Calgary Chinese Mission). The depression years in the 1930s were especially hard for the Chinese. Provincial relief for the Chinese was $1.12 per week as compared to $2.50 for the non-Chinese.

The threat to Calgary's Chinatown occurred in 1966 when the Downtown Master Plan included a proposal to construct a parkway between 2nd and 3rd Avenue South which would result in the destruction of Chinatown. The proposal was defeated due to strong opposition from the Chinese community. In 1974, City Council delineated an area of forty-nine acres as "Chinatown." The approval of the Calgary Design Brief prepared by the Chinatown Development Task Force by the city in 1976 marked the revival of Chinatown to be a residential community and a focal cultural centre.

Chinatown in Calgary was not a place of residence for all Chinese since the early days. The trend to move out of Chinatown has continued since 1900. Mr. Luey Dofoo, who came to Calgary in 1900, reported that about 30 of the 100 Chinese in Calgary lived in Chinatown (*Calgary Herald*, Jan. 11, 1969). Baureiss' study in 1971 found that although Chinatown residents were mostly Chinese (534 out of 637 residents, and only 10% of the total Chinese population in Calgary), the large majority was found in other parts of the city. The "Project Chinatown" survey in 1971 and 1973 revealed a drop of 41% from 492 to 289 Chinese residing in Chinatown. In Lan and Friesen's study of 1988 (published in 1991), among the 12 030 Chinese living in Calgary, only 4-6% lived in Chinatown, most of them senior citizens and recent immigrants. Fourteen percent lived in the inner city area while 80-82% lived in the outer city. The zone distribution in Calgary was as follows: northwest 29%, southwest 19%, northeast 32%, and southeast 20%. The higher percentages occurred in northwest, the high socio-economic zone, and northeast, the low socio-economic zone. In the northeast, land and houses are more reasonable and it tends to attract new immigrants. Chinese professionals and the wealthier recent immigrants from Hong Kong prefer to live in the northwest, so that their offspring can commute easily to the university. Today, Calgary's Chinatown is a cultural, commercial and religious centre with close to 100 businesses and 60 operating social, cultural and religious organizations, including two Chinese schools and a newly-completed cultural centre.

Chinese Schools have been established at different time periods across Canada as the Chinese communities developed. Their purpose has been to transmit Chinese language, traditions and customs to the young Canadian Chinese. In Calgary, due to the unequal sex ratio of the Chinese population created by the discriminatory immigration laws, the first child of Chinese parents was born only in 1906. By 1920, there were about thirty Chinese children. To preserve the Chinese culture, the Calgary Chinese Public School was established. Initially, there were only six students and classes were conducted in the evenings (Baureiss, 1971: 45). In 1990, the student enrollment was 1 167 and classes were operated during weekends. Seven more Chinese language schools opened between 1975 and 1988 and two in 1991.

An increase in the number of Chinese language schools and student population since 1970s may be attributed to a number of reasons. The most important factor is the changing attitude of the host society as evident in the federal multicultural policy (1971), the Human Rights Act (1977), the Employment Equity Act (1986), and the Multiculturalism Act (1988). Other contributing factors are the cultural revival of first and second generation Canadian-Chinese, the recent arrival of large numbers of Chinese immigrants from South East Asia, especially from Hong Kong, and the failure of school boards to provide adequate public supported non-official language instructions.

The Study: Chinese Heritage Language Schools as an Agent in Promoting Cultural Identity

Although heritage language schools have been in Canada for a long time, their growth and development is a recent phenomenon. Studies by the Royal Commission on Bilingualism and Biculturalism (1969), O'Bryan, Reitz and Kuplowska (1976), Pannu and Young (1976) and Leung (1984), have barely scratched the surface in this field of research. The only in-depth study and systematic evaluation of the impact of heritage language schools was attempted by Bombas (1987) on the Greek day school in Montreal. The lack of interest can be attributed to the following reasons.

First, heritage language schools were and still are to a certain extent viewed by the public as cultural-linguistic preserving agencies contributing little to Canadian society. Second, most heritage schools are still functioning individually as separate units, in spite of the co-ordinating effort of heritage language school associations to provide assistance and to improve communication. Since they are community-operated and administered, the majority of them are only known to the supporting community. Most of them have "little to do with each other" as evident in Leung's study of ethnic schools (1984) in Alberta. Identifying these schools is a problem, not to mention the lack of response to question-naire surveys. This problem was encountered by the Royal Commission on Bilingualism and Biculturalism. Lastly, most of the heritage language schools rely on volunteers and teachers trained in their home country who may not be familiar with the Canadian educational setting, hence they are reluctant to be evaluated on their newly recognized status. They are also worried about having to justify their existence in order to obtain federal and/or provincial funding. The government and the public would perhaps like to see the impact of their moderate grants, but are afraid to tread on sensitive issues. However, evaluation is an integral part of the education process and is vital to quality instruction and the growth of the heritage language schools.

In Calgary, there are more than fifty heritage language schools offering a variety of language programs. The schools' objectives are mainly cognitive, although the affective and psychomotor objectives are indirectly involved. Among the heritage language schools in Calgary, the Chinese schools are the fastest-growing institutions. There were eight of them during the time of the present research in 1990. Two others were established in 1991.

Reitz' study (1980) suggested that the Chinese might be the most cohesive ethnic group in Canada. Friesen's research (1988) concluded that the Chinese in Calgary had effectively utilized purposive and non-purposive techniques in preserving their culture. The Chinese heritage language schools were cited as a purposive technique used to promote cultural identity. Among the Chinese heritage language schools in Calgary, the Calgary Chinese Public School, located in Chinatown, has the largest enrollment in Canada. The school had a student population of 1 167 in 1990 and has increased to over 1 600 in 1993 and offers fifteen high school credits in Chinese language instruction.

Delineating a Theoretical Base

The literature examining effective ways to ensure cultural identity and hence cultural maintenance is exhaustive, and a number of conditions and contributing factors have been identified. Positive identification with the group, often fostered through institutional and informal organizations (Isajiw and Markabe, 1982) and positive self-identity, are two conditions/identifiers for cultural survival.

Comeau and Driedger (1978) classified ethnic group identification into two components: institutional completeness (Breton, 1964), and ethnic cultural identity. Institutional completeness describes an ethnic community which pro-vides for all its own major cultural interactions within a specified ethnic milieu i.e. religion, schooling, sociability, etc. Ethnic cultural identity, the other com-ponent, incorporates six dimensions: identification with an ecological territory, charismatic leadership, historical symbols, ideology, an ethnic-specific culture and ethnic-specific institutions (Driedger, 1978, 14-10). In this section, institutional completeness will be discussed under ethnic-specific institutions.

Ethnic self-identity may be classified into three forms: ethnic affirmation, ethnic denial and maginality (Comeau and Driedger, 1978). The first form was regarded as a vitality-facilitating mechanism while the other two were considered vitality-inhibiting mechanisms.

Ethnic Group Identification

1. Identification with an Ecological Territory

Although there are many examples of ethnocultural groups who have elected to maintain a geographically-separated lifestyle from the dominant society, there are also groups who have been driven to separateness as a means of avoiding the discomfort of prejudice and discrimination (Allport, 1954). In Canada, Native reserves, Hutterite colonies, and the block settlements of the Québécois, Germans and Ukrainians serve as examples of geographic separateness, both rural and urban. Indirectly, negative regard for ethnic affiliation has inadvertently helped to ensure a stronger form of identity for some minority groups and consequently produced a stronger group cohesion. While it is commonly believed that rural segregation provides greater exclusivity, and hence assures a greater rate of cultural retention, similar correlation is indicated in urban settings. Reitz' survey of five Canadian cities positively correlated urban residential segregation with group cohesion (Reitz, 1980).

Among the Chinese in Calgary, residential segregation does not seem to be a major factor for ethnic cohesion as the majority of the Chinese live outside Chinatown. (For settlement pattern, refer to the section on "The Calgary Chinese" mentioned earlier with regard to studies by Baureiss 1971, Lan and Friesen, 1991)

2. Identification with Charismatic Leadership

Throughout history charismatic religious, political and minority group leaders have demonstrated their ability to attract and sway mass audiences. Examples of religious leaders would include Abraham, Buddha, Confucius, Jesus Christ, Gandhi, Guru Nanak, Mohammed and Martin Luther King. Political figures include Churchill, Hitler, Ho Chi Minh, Lenin, Lincoln, Jack Kennedy, René Lévesque and Malcolm X. Charismatic leaders often begin populist movements and rise to power in times of economic depression. They also use psychological means to influence their followers to mould a cohesive loyalty for a cause (Driedger, 1978). Individuals with a sense of mission often adapt a cause or an ideology to a current situation, linking it symbolically to the past, and using the media to effectively transform the present into a vision of the future (Driedger, 1977).

3. Identification with an Ideology

Religious and political ideologies play an important part in mobilizing followers. Strong ideological beliefs can motivate followers to a goal beyond cultural and institutional values and provide a kind of emotional rallying point for adherents (Glazer and Moynihan, 1970). There is evidence that a positive correlation exists between religion and ethnicity, and often doctrinal beliefs dictate personal attitudes and behavior (Driedger, 1974). Significant to this study are the traditional ideologies of cultural pluralism and assimilation. The former is often envisaged as an ideal objective in our society, and culture ethnic institutions, historical symbols and charismatic leadership are seen as the means by which to achieve that goal.

4. Identification with Historical Symbols

It has been conjectured that unlike rural minorities, who might perpetuate their social structure and community as ends in themselves, ethnic urbanites often require a sense of purpose and direction which they sometimes discover in searching out their ethnic roots (Driedger, 1978). The examination of one's cultural heritage may draw attention to historic symbols, for example, the holocaust for Jews. In a comparison of identity among seven groups of students from different ethnic origins at the University of Manitoba, Driedger concluded that ethnic heritage could have a positive influence on ethnic self-identity for French and Jewish students but a negative influence on Ukrainian, Polish and German students (1975). The study would seem to indicate that an appreciation of heritage can best be developed when positive historic symbols can be identified.

5. Identification with an Ethnically-Specific Culture

Four major components of ethnic identification connected to a specific culture include ethnic origins, mother tongue, ethnic-oriented religion and folkways (Anderson and Frideres, 1981). Driedger's research identified six cultural factors: language use, endogamy, choice of ingroup friends, participation in religion, parochial schools, and ethnic voluntary organizations. (Driedger, 1975). An investigative study involving students of seven ethnic allegiances at the University of Manitoba revealed that Jews and French rated the highest in terms of the tenacity of their cultural allegiance (identity), the Germans and Ukrainians ranked next, and the Polish, British and Scandinavian rated the lowest. The more residentially-segregated and ethnic-oriented French and Jews also ranked high on attendance in parochial schools, endogamy and choice of ingroup friends. The French also ranked high on language usage and church attendance (Driedger, 1975).

A number of reasons may be projected to explain the strong identity and high degree of institutional completeness of French students. Foremost would be the historical conflict over Charter group status, the French-British conflict in Manitoba over language and schools and the recent federal emphasis on bilingualism and biculturalism. In the case of Jewish students, historical conflicts over differential ethnic and religious values, high institutional completeness and mobility from immigrant status to high economic status have contributed to their high scores on endogamy, choice of ingroup friends and parochial education (Driedger, 1975).

Reitz' studies pertaining to ethnic cohesion/assimilation have centred around six components: basic ingroup interaction, ethnic self-identification, endogamy, language retention, residential segregation and ethnic church affiliation (Reitz, 1980). Reitz' findings confirmed three of Driedger's factors – language retention, endogamy and ethnic church affiliation as cultural components. He also found that ingroup interaction and ethnic self-identification were definitely related to each other and they were strongly related to language retention, less to endogamy and ethnic church affiliation and least to residential segregation. Furthermore, all six components of group ties/cohesion weakened somewhat less between the second and third generation than between the first and second generation. This supports the findings of Hansen (1962) that cultural revival was evident in the third generation. Hansen (1962), Nihirny and Fishman (1965) suggested that the third generation might be more interested in the abstract ideals of the ethnic culture than in establishing close bonds with the ethnic group. Breton's model of the life-cycle of immigrant communities (1964) predicted that ethnic communities would form, grow and disappear although he left open the time period for the life-cycle. Both Reitz and Breton agreed that in order for ethnic communities to survive indefinitely, they had to be constantly replenished by new immigrants.

Reitz' research involved four categories of ten ethnic groups: Chinese, North European, East European and South European. The Chinese ranked highest in ingroup interaction and in ethnic identification. They ranked second with regard to ethnic language retention, endogamy and ethnic neighborhood residence and lowest in ethnic church affiliation (Reitz, 1980). Reitz attributed the stronger subjective identification of the Chinese to their racial visibility, the weaker language retention to the more widespread knowledge of English and tendency to live away from Chinatown among the recent immigrants.

6. Identification with Ethnically Specific Institutions

The social organization of ethnic communities is crucial to their ability to hold and consolidate their membership. The concept of institutional completeness was coined by Breton to depict a community's efforts to provide for all social and personal services to their members (Breton, 1964). He elaborated the concept in terms of two indexes: the number of formal organizations – religious, welfare, and media – that a cultural neonate or newcomer might be involved in; and, the ethnic character of the persons with whom the immigrant was in contact. His findings showed that religious institutions had the greatest effect in keeping an immigrant's personal associations within the boundaries of the ethnic community, while welfare institutions had the least effect. In summary, Breton concluded that the more extensive the institutional completeness, the more the ethnic community would be able to attract and hold both neonates and newcomers.

A follow-up study by Breton indicated that the longer an immigrant spent in the host community, the more likely he/she would break the old ties within his/her ethnic community and form new outside attachments. Breton postulated that if the rate of immigration were to be slowed down considerably or reduced to nil, ethnic organizations would disappear or lose their ethnic identity, thus completing the life cycle of the community (Breton, 1964).

A number of studies have linked a weakened institutional completeness to increased assimilation (Vallee, 1969; Joy, 1972; Radecki, 1976). The contention is that as ethnocultural members begin to lose interest in ethnic affiliation, they move out past established boundaries and develop interests and relationships with dominant society.

Baureiss (1982) expressed concern about the conceptual base and the operationalization of the theory of institutional completeness in terms of two questions: 1) what emphasis should be placed on the relationship between a specific ethnic minority and the host society; and, 2) to what extent could the operationalization of the concept of institutional completeness do justice to the definition? Clearly the relationship of the ethnocultural communities to the dominant society could vary from one another, thus affecting both the rate and degree of assimilation into the dominant society. Baureiss also contended that inevitable assimilation was an implicit assumption underlying Breton's work. It ignored discriminatory practices against certain immigrants in society which pushed them into closure. It also disregarded the greater control of the ethnic community over its members more than any other institutional complex in the host society such as in the case of the Chinese (Lyman, 1974). Moreover, a lack of differentiation between formal organizations (part of the institutional structure) and institutions was evident in Breton's study. Baureiss concluded that unless the nature of formal organizations and ethnic institutional structure was assessed, the degree of integration or assimilation, and hence institutional completeness, would become problematic.

Related to the concept of institutional completeness are the opening (assimilation) and closing (differentiation) strategies employed by ethnic communities (Klapp, 1975; Comeau and Driedger, 1978). One of the realities for minority groups who are obviously outnumbered by dominant society members is to avoid being caught between the two worlds of the home community and the larger monoculture (Newman, 1973). Lewin discovered that a lack of sufficient ingroup security would result in ingroup denial and perpetuate feelings of maladjustment in the larger society (Lewin, 1948). Klapp contended that most ethnic groups oscillated between assimilation (opening) and differentiation (closing) and that the survival of a group would depend on effective opening and closing techniques. The more vitality a system has, the more alertly it opens and closes. Klapp's theoretical model of opening and closing in an open system like Canadian society has four categories – good and bad opening, and good and bad closing (Klapp, 1975). Good opening is signified by words expressing gains of information flow and implies development of growth. Bad opening implies a transgression of boundaries including information overload, noise, and lack of reinforcement. Excessive opening is characterized by a loss or lack of identity. Good closing is a reinforcing mechanism which gives the group positive identity and self-esteem. Bad closing shows loss over stressing boundaries leading to social isolation.

Comeau and Driedger substituted "vitality facilitating" for "good" and "vitality inhibiting" for "bad" in Klapp's model and contended that Klapp's terminology had moralistic connotations which were ill-fitted for understanding system analysis. They concluded that both opening and closing mechanisms were essential for the survival of cultural groups (Comeau and Driedger, 1978). On this basis Reitz found the Chinese to be the most cohesive ethnic group in Canada. Using a slightly different tack, exploring purposive and non-purposive techniques for cultural maintenance, Friesen (1988) found that though the Calgary Chinese community indicated that family ties, respect and care for the elderly were deemed to be the most important aspects of Chinese culture, most efforts to preserve the culture were spent on the continuance of customs, celebrations and traditions. Purposive techniques were defined as deliberate attempts such as endogamy, inculcation of values, preservation of language, customs, practices, traditions and artifacts. Non-purposive techniques were defined as unintentional even though they could have an indirect effect in Chinese preserving culture. It should be noted that Friesen included language, festivals, male dominance, education and gambling in the definition of customs, practices and traditions. Although he did not predict the demise of Chinese cultural identity in any directional way, he did point out that future research in Chinatown would need to identify the specific factors that would help preserve the philosophical and religious aspects of Chinese culture. It would also be useful to differentiate between purposive and non-purposive techniques in order to guarantee a higher degree of cultural perpetuity (Friesen, 1988).

Research Methodology

There were eight Chinese language schools in Calgary at the time of this study. Due to the complexity of the questionnaire, only students aged ten and above were targeted in the survey. Six of the eight Chinese schools participated in this research study. One school declined the invitation and the other had no students over the age of ten. The primary sample for this study (420 out of 555) came from the Calgary Chinese Public School located in Chinatown. In 1990, between May and June, a questionnaire survey on Chinese cultural identity was administered to the students of Chinese ancestry aged ten and above in the six Chinese schools. Of a total of 555 possible samples, 511 subjects participated, a return rate of 92 percent.

The Research Instrument

The research instrument consisted of a student questionnaire. The draft questionnaire was field tested on sixteen ethnic Chinese students outside Calgary to avoid contamination of the Calgary samples. The revised student questionnaire contained 58 questions. One hundred and forty-eight variables, either categorical, interval or ordinal were identified. Seven of which pertained to personal variables. The remaining 141 items were divided into four major categories: ethnic group identity, ethnic self-identity, intercultural sensitivity and factors influencing appreciation of Chinese culture and of other cultures.

The format and content of the student questionnaire consisting mostly of close-ended questions was divided into five parts:

- To obtain personal demographic data such as age, gender, year of residency in Canada and level of education;
- To elicit responses to questions on ethnic group identity;
- To elicit responses to questions on ethnic self-identity;
- To find out the level of intercultural sensitivity through hypothetical situations; and
- To find out the importance of various factors influencing the understanding of Chinese culture and other cultures as perceived by the respondents.

Analysis of Data

Personal Data Variables

The participants in the study ranged from age 10 to 35 with a majority (75.4%) between age 10 and 13. A steady decline in Chinese school enrollment after age 11 to 1.0% at age 18, 0.2% at age 22 and 0.4% at age 24. One mother (0.2%) aged 35, studying in the same class as her child, also participated in the survey. Of 497 participants, 3 (0.6%) did not specify their gender, 224 (45.1%) were males and 270 (54.3%) were female, a difference of 46 or 9.2%. Almost half (43.9%) were born in Canada. Sixty-one decimal eight percent (17.9%+ Canadian born: 43.9%) had been in Canada for 10 or more years, and 81% (37.1% + Canadian born 43.9%) had been in Canada for more than 5 years.

The majority of the participants (78.4%) had studied Chinese for a period of 2 to 7 years. Student enrollment seemed to have reached a plateau at ages 10 and 11. A steady decrease in enrollment was evident as the students became older. After year 7, the numbers of participants dropped drastically from 13.3% to 4.4% in year 8, 1.6% in year 9, 0.8% in year 10 and 0.4% in year 11, and participation in Chinese schools ceased after 11 years of study.

The majority of the Calgary subjects (67.6%) had received their Chinese education in Canada and their average number of years studying Chinese was 4.4 years. There was a discrepancy between the grade level of the students studied at the publicly-funded day schools and in the weekend Chinese schools where the majority of the students tended to study at a lower grade level.

Ethnic Group Identity

Five factors were considered as significant in their contributing to ethnic group identification: ecological territory, historic symbols, charismatic leadership, institutional affiliation and ethnic culture identification.

1. Ecological Territory

The majority of students (94.8%) lived outside Chinatown, 3.4% lived in Chinatown and 0.6% lived in other inner city areas. The highest concentration was in northeast Calgary (31.2%), followed by northwest (25.6%), southeast (23.1%) and southwest (14.9%). The result was consistent with Lan and Friesen's study of the settlement pattern in the Calgary Chinese community. Residential segregation was not an important factor in determining the cultural identity of Calgary's ethnic Chinese although there was a tendency for the Chinese to settle in northeast Calgary, the lower economic zone and northwest Calgary, the higher socio-economic zone. This phenomenon was attributed to the economic status of the recent arrivals and the achieved economic status after a length of time in this country.

Only 0.2% of the participants had never visited Chinatown. Forty-eight decimal seven percent of the subjects visited Chinatown frequently while 50.5% visited Chinatown occasionally. Recreation was ranked as the single most important reason for going to Chinatown. This is followed closely by Chinese school as 84% of the subjects came from two Chinese schools located in Chinatown. Religious purposes and "others" were listed as unimportant. The ecological territory of Chinatown appears to be important as a centre for socialization and Chinese schooling.

2. Historic Symbols and Ideology

The Chinese are often referred to as the people of Tang (206 B.C. to 220 A.D.) or Han (618 A.D. to 907 A.D.) because of their political and economic presence in Asia and their achievements in the arts and sciences during these two dynasties. Students were asked how they felt about being Tang or Han people, and of 301 students who had heard of these dynasties, 57.1% revealed pride in having that connection. As for feelings towards historic foreign invasion, about half of the participants (49.3%) had no opinion. For those 242 (48.7%) who expressed their opinions, 196 (81%) had a strong sense of nationalism. It appears that about two-fifths of the participants were not familiar with the history of China. For those who were acquainted with the history, there was a sense of ethnic pride and nationalism. This implication may determine the direction of future curriculum development in the Chinese heritage schools.

3. Charismatic Leadership

Six historical figures in chronological order from ancient to modern times were presented to the participants. These included the legendary Saint Emperor Yao (2000 B.C.), Confucius (624-551 B.C.), Emperor Qin (521-210 B.C.), and three 20th century revolutionaries, Dr. Sun Yat-Sen, Chiang Kai-Shek, and Mao Tse-Tung. Participants were asked to check off the names they were familiar with. The following resulted: Emperor Qin (55.3%), Mao Tse-Tung (46.7%), Dr. Sun Yat-Sen (42.9%), Chiang Kai-Shek (24.7%) and Emperor Yao (23.5%). The low scores of Emperor Yao and Chiang Kai-Shek could be explained by the fact that Emperor Yao was legendary and Chiang became obscure between two successful revolutions. In ranking the degree of admiration for historical figures, the ancient historical figures namely the Saint Emperor Yao, Confucius and Emperor Qin emerged as preferred heroes to the modern revolutionaries Sun, Chiang and Mao.

The findings showed that the subjects had more admiration for ancient figures and further confirmed the lack of historical background knowledge of China particularly the recent history. This information should provide some insight for the curriculum developer in seeking to meet the school objectives.

4. Institutional Identification

Three types of institutions were considered in institutional identification: religious, social welfare and mass media. The majority of students did not attend religious institutions. Neither Christianity nor Buddhism-Taoism, the major Chinese religions, have attracted significant worshippers. Only 32.5% attended Christian churches outside Chinatown and 12.6% in Chinatown while 15.8% attended Buddhist and Taoist temple outside Chinatown and 18.1% in Chinatown. A negligible 4.0% attended other religious institutions such as the mosque.

As for language used in religious institutions, the three Buddhist temples in Calgary all conducted their services in Chinese and Vietnamese. The usage of English in Christian church services increased outside the ecological territory of Chinatown where the host society predominates.

Welfare institutions included Chinese schools, cultural organizations, community services, clan organizations, political organizations, athletic clubs, newspaper publishers and broadcasting services. Of the 488 students who responded, 55.7% admitted belonging to at least one such organization, 35.6% belonged to two, 5.6% belonged to three, and 1.2% belonged to four organizations. All respondents went to Chinese schools. The other three organizations ranked in order from most to least memberships were religious institutions, fine arts organizations, followed by athletic clubs. The Chinese school appeared to be the single most important institution for the socialization of these youngsters.

Mass media was interpreted to include Chinese television, radio broadcasts, newspapers and publications. As many as 88% indicated that they watched Chinese television programs, 39.6% listened to Chinese radio broadcasts and 39.4% read Chinese publications. Television obviously attracted a larger clientele. A number of reasons could account for this phenomenon. For most school age children, audio-visual materials have proven to be more appealing than audio or visual materials alone. Since there are no local Chinese radio broadcasts in Calgary, news from far away may be less relevant to students' experience and hence less appealing. Other than textbooks, Chinese publications for youth were not in abundance locally. Another factor could be that newspapers and publications require a minimum vocabulary of two to three thousand Chinese characters which is beyond the level of comprehension for elementary and junior high students in Calgary Chinese schools.

5. Ethnic Cultural Identification

Ethnic cultural identification incorporated questions on language use, endogamy, choice of ingroup friends, and affinity to Chinese culture.

a. *Language use*. Questions on language use can be grouped into two categories – oral and written. For oral language, some subjects listed two native dialects since their parents or grandparents came from different parts of China. Over three-fourths (82.9%) of the subjects' indicated that their native dialect was Cantonese. Mandarin lagged far behind with 12.9% and Toishanese, Hakka and "other" totalled only 21.6%.

Dialects used in conversation closely resembled the distribution of native dialects. However, when asked which they would like to be more fluent in, the response on Mandarin increased drastically (56.1%) which was four-and-a-half times more than the native dialect (12.9%) and three-and-a-half times more than the conversational dialect (16.3%). The response on Cantonese only surpassed Mandarin by 8.7%, a drop of 18.1% from the "native dialect and 19.7% from the "conversational dialect." The growing popularity of Mandarin of Putonghua, the national dialect since the opening of China for travel and trade, may have accounted for this phenomenon. The fact that Chinese courses in universities are offered in Mandarin rather than Cantonese might have given students added incentive to be more fluent.

Communication in Chinese appeared to be restricted to use in the home. Ninety-five percent of the participants spoke Chinese at home, usually with their parents, and 98.8% of them indicated that they spoke English to "outsiders." Fifty-two-decimal-nine percent indicated that they spoke Chinese at home "frequently" while 80.3% indicated that their parents spoke to them in Chinese "frequently." Parents spoke in Chinese while their off-spring answered in English might have accounted for this discrepancy.

For reading and writing competency, almost half of the students indicated that they were uncertain about their competency in these skills – reading, 44.3% and writing 41.6%. This may have been caused by a lack of a uniform standard in curriculum and evaluation in Chinese language schools, and a shortage of suitable reading materials by which the students could evaluate their competencies. For the other half who had some idea of their competencies, nearly a third of the subjects indicated they felt competent in reading (30.0%) and writing (35.0%). A large majority of the students (72.9%) would like to be more proficient in reading and writing.

b. *Endogamy.* The criteria for endogamy were drawn from information pertaining to the practices on dating and marriage. Slightly over half (56.7%) of the subjects showed no preferences in dating while 40.4% showed no preference in marriage. Preference for Chinese partners in dating amounted to 30.4% and 49.1% in marriage. Preference for non-Chinese was 11.7% in dating and 9.1% in marriage.

It was noted that 16.3% of the subjects viewed dating and marriage with separate frames of reference. These subjects had no preference whom they dated, but had preferences whom they married. For those who had a preference, there was a strong tendency for them to prefer members of their own ethnic group. These preferences were noted three times more in dating and five times more in marrying Chinese than non-Chinese.

c. *Choice of Ingroup Friends.* Ethnic Chinese were ranked as first, second and third in terms of their desirability as close friends (51.9%, 42.% and 37.6%). This was followed by Caucasians (29.6%, 39.2% and 37.0%) and then by other Asians (11.7%, 11.7% and 12.9%). Other Asians, "Others" and Natives accounted for only a minor portion of the responses. Their small numbers in the larger society might have limited close contact with the Chinese and hence the opportunity to develop closer relationships. A contingency table analysis showed that if an individual chose a Chinese for his/her first closest friend, there would be a 50% chance of choosing a Chinese and 33% chance of choosing a Caucasian as his/her second closest friend. The same pattern held for selecting a Caucasian as the first closest friend; there was a 55% chance of choosing a Caucasian and a 36% chance of choosing a Chinese.

d. *Affinity to Chinese Culture.* An overwhelming majority of the participants (89.9%), indicated that they enjoyed Chinese culture. Among the four aspects of Chinese culture, language was ranked as the most important aspect

(79.3%), closely followed by traditional values (72.8%). Customs and practices ranked third (30.4%), while cultural artifacts ranked last (18.9%).

Almost all of the subjects consumed Chinese food (99.6%) and participated in Chinese celebrations (94.7%), and two-thirds (67.5%) practiced ancestral worship. When it came to frequency of cultural aspects practiced, 91.8% consumed Chinese food frequently, compared to 65.6% took part in Chinese celebrations and 25.6% practiced ancestral worship.

In terms of values, family loyalty came out to be the most important for the participants (84.3%), followed by love and care for the young (63.4%), care and respect for the elderly (63.2%), hard work (62.0%), obedience (43.3%), patience and non-violence (31.2%), ancestral worship (27.8%), and respect for teachers (23.5%). It is significant to note that one of the most important traditional values, respect for teachers, was last on the students' priorities.

Ethnic Self-Identity

When it came to identification by labels, a large majority of the respondents (81.1%) identified themselves as hyphenated Canadians: Chinese-Canadians (51.7%), Canadian-Chinese (29.4%), Chinese (10.3%), Canadian (3.4%) and other – Chinese-Vietnamese, Chinese-Laotian and Chinese-American (4.2%). Ethnic self-identity was further broken down into three components: "feeling" indicator of self-identity: affirmation, denial and marginality, host society acceptance, and influences on self-identity.

1. Affirmation, Denial and Marginality

The majority of the participants (71.4%) said they were proud of their Chinese ancestry: "definitely yes" (24.9%), and "yes" (46.5%). Only 2.4% were not proud (0.4% "definitely not" and 2.0% "not proud") and 25.4% were uncertain.

2. Host Society Acceptance

Almost two-thirds of the subjects (65.8%) felt that occasionally they were treated "differently" by their fellow-Canadians; 5.8% replied "frequently', and 26.8% replied "not at al." Being a "visible minority" might have contributed to this phenomenon and the feeling of being treated differently. When asked whether these experiences were positive or negative, 42.3% replied that they were neither positive nor negative, 15.5% said they were negative and 20.1% said they were positive experiences.

3. Influences on Self-Identity

When asked what the source society was for their self-identity, 15.9% said it was the host society, 11.5% said it was Chinese society, and 71.2% said that both were responsible. Family ranked as the most important influence on self-identity (90.9%). Public-funded day school came second (85.2%), followed by Chinese school(74.6%), peer group (71.8%), religious organizations or groups (28.9%), socio-cultural organizations (27.1%) and "other" (4.6%).

Intercultural Sensitivity

In exploring the degree of intercultural sensitivity, seven topical issues were presented to participants for value clarification. The issues and percentages of respondents were:

- admission of more "colored" immigrants into Canada: 59.2% agree, 30% uncertain and 9.0% disagree
- importance of keeping one's own culture and language: 39.9% agree, 38.8% uncertain and 19.9% disagree
- Sikhs wearing turbans in the Royal Canadian Mounted Police Force: 32.2% agreed, 41.6% uncertain and 24.6% disagree
- bilingual signs in the Province of Quebec: 55.1% agree, 30.2% uncertain and 13.5% disagree.
- Bilingual English and French signs in Calgary: 71.3% agree, 20.1% uncertain, and 7.6% disagree.
- non-Moslems removing footwear in Mosques: 44.1% agree, 32.6% uncertain, and 23.3% disagreed
- displaying barbecued meat at room temperature in Chinatown restaurants and stores: 39.6% agreed, 46.7% uncertain and 10.1% disagree

A high percentage of the responses favored bilingual signs in the province of Quebec. However only 39.9% agreed on the importance of keeping one's culture and language while 38.8% were uncertain. Perhaps the status of the languages (official versus minority languages) played a role in determining the responses. Admission of more "colored" immigrants was favored. In general, it appeared that the respondents had a high degree of intercultural sensitivity and cultural acceptance.

Factors Influencing Appreciation of Chinese and Other Cultures

Subjects were asked to rate eight variables which might have influenced their appreciation of Chinese culture. The variables and percentaged choices were: family (89.3%), the Chinese school (75.5%), regular day school (55.2%), peer group (49.9%), religious organizations (21.9%), socio-cultural organizations (16.0%), contact with one's own culture (40.0%), and contact with other cultures (15.4%). Clearly the most influential variables were the family and the

Chinese school although peer group, publicly-funded day school and contact with the Chinese culture were also important.

When asked their opinion on attending Chinese heritage language schools, 38.1% responded positively, 37.0% were uncertain and 23.4% indicated that they did not wish to attend. This finding is consistent with the responses received on the importance of keeping one's own language and culture. Reasons given as to the importance for such schools were: parent's wish (73.8%), future economic advantage (61.7%), interest in language (60.7%), interest in culture (54.9%) and to socialize (36.4%). In response to a question about the possible influence of the Chinese school in developing appreciation of Chinese culture, 64.8% responded positively. Forty-one percent replied that these schools also influenced their appreciation of other cultures.

On factors influencing the appreciation of other cultures, Publicly-funded day schools with 75.4% was rated first, peer group (66.4%) and family (63.8%) came next. This was followed by contact with other cultures (44.8%), Chinese school (40.5%), contact with one's own culture (20%) and socio-cultural organizations (15.6%).

Correlation between Personal Data Variables and Ethnic Self-identity

An attempt was made to correlate two sets of variables. The first set of personal data variables consisted of seven personal data variables namely age, gender, years of residency in Canada, grade level at day school, grade level in Chinese language schools, years of studying Chinese in non-Chinese speaking countries, mainly in Canada, and in countries where the official language is Chinese. The second set of variables on self-identity were: perceived nationality, proud of Chinese ancestry, influence on self-identity (host society versus the Chinese community), frequency of being treated differently and positive/negative experiences encountered.

The correlation matrix showed no significant correlation between the first and second set of variables. This could be caused by the relatively homogenous sample of the age group studied. This, together with the subjects' present developmental stage in both cultural identity and self-esteem, made correlation difficult. There is also the possibility that only superficial responses were solicited from the subjects. Differentiating experiences encountered as a result of their ethnicity or of some other reasons is also a problem for adolescents. Discussion with the subjects about their responses could perhaps shed a different light on and could clarify their responses.

Conclusions

In today's technological society where constant interaction takes place within close proximity, the maintenance of cultural boundaries among urban minorities is becoming increasingly difficult. Cultural survival depends on a multitude of complex interdependent mechanisms operating within the ethnic community and society at large centring around group identification and ethnic self-identification. In the larger society, these mechanisms are immigration, adopted ideology, societal attitude and practices. Within the ethnic community itself, they include institutional completeness, effective opening and closing strategies, and workable purposive and non-purposive techniques.

Ethnic group identification (language use, endogamy, choice of ingroup friends, and participation in religious, parochial education and ethnic voluntary organizations), depends on the ethnic community and society at large. Positive ethnic self-identification can be achieved through the empowerment of minorities. Empowerment involves deliberate attempts to improve race relationships, to promote cultural identity and multicultural education, and to provide equal access to resources in the economic, social and political spheres.

This study confirms that the Calgary Chinese community has a strong cultural identity, both group and individual, but recognizes that the Chinese culture is in almost perpetual interaction with the host society and thus is constantly being modified and transformed through this process. For example, other than family influences, this study shows that education is one of the most effective means by which to maintain cultural identity as well as to promote intercultural understanding and appreciation of other cultures. On the other hand, this study also showed no significant correlation between demographic variables and the variables on perception of self-identity and the contributing actors. The relative homogeneity of age, the nature of the questionnaire survey and the fact that all of the subjects attended Chinese schools may explain the absence of correlation.

Clearly the strong factors in identifying an allegiance towards Chinese culture on the part of the study participants would include:

- speaking the Chinese language at home, 95%
- enjoyment of Chinese culture, 89.9%
- valued family loyalty 84.3%
- strong sense of Chinese nationalism, 81.0%
- pride in their Chinese ancestry, 71.4%

To a lesser extent, these factors were evident:

- had no ethnic preference for dating, 56.7%
- belonged to at least one Chinese cultural organization, 55.7%

- selected Chinese as their first choice in friendship, 51.9%
- saw themselves first as Chinese-Canadians, 51.7%

More challenging factors were:

- attending Chinese schools was clearly parents' wish, 73.8%
- preferred Chinese partners for marriage, 49.1%
- felt concern about reading Chinese languages, 44.3%
- felt concern about writing Chinese languages, 41.6%
- preferred Chinese partners for dating, 30.4%

Perhaps the greatest impact of this study provides a national challenge, more than anything else. If Canadians are serious about multiculturalism, heritage language schools should be encouraged and supported by government and the host society. As this study demonstrates, urban Chinese culture is healthy, thanks to a strong family support. However, if support for cultural diversity is a national policy and concern, then heritage language schools, which contribute much towards cultural maintenance, should be continued and increased.

References

Allport, G. (1954). *The nature of prejudice*. Reading, Mass.: Addison-Wesley.

Baureiss, G. (1971). The City and the Subcommunity: The Chinese of Calgary. Unpublished Master's Thesis. The University of Calgary.

Baureiss, G. (1982). Institutional Completeness: Its Use and Misuse in Ethnic Relations Research. *The journal of Ethnic Studies*, 9(2), 101-110.

Beatie, B. A. (1979). *Ethnic heritage and language schools in greater Cleveland*. Cleveland State University.

Breton, R. (1964). Institutional Completeness of Ethnic Communities and the Personal Relations of Immigrants. *American Journal of Sociology*, 70(2), 193-205.

Comeau, L. R. and L Driedger. (1978). Ethnic Opening and Closing an Open Society: A Canadian Example. *Social Sorces*, 57(1-2), 600-620.

Cummins, J. (1981). *Heritage language education: issues and directions*. Proceedings of a conference organized by the Multiculturalism Directorate of the Department of the Secretary of State, Saskatoon. Toronto: Ontario Institute for the Study of Education.

Driedger, L. (1974). Doctrinal Belief: A Major Factor in Differential Perception of Social Issues. *Sociological Quarterly*, 15: 66-80.

Driedger, L. (1975). In Search of Cultural Identity Factors: A Comparison of Ethnic Students. *Canadian Review of Sociology and Anthropology*, 12(2), 150-162.

Driedger, L. (1977). Identity and Social Distance: Towards Understanding Simmel's "The Strangers." *Canadian Review of Sociology and Anthropology*, 14: 158-173.

Driedger, L. (1978). *The Canadian ethnic mosaic: a quest for identity*. Toronto: McClelland and Stewart.

Fishman, J. A., ed. (1966). *Language loyalty in the United States*. The Hague: Mouton & Co.

Friesen, B. K. (1988). The Maintenance of Culture Among Calgary's Chinese. *Multicultural education journal*, 6(1), 4-20.

Friesen, J. W. (1983). *Schools with a purpose*. Calgary: Detselig Enterprises.

Glazer, N. and D. P. Moynihan, eds. (1975). *Ethnicity, theory and experience*. Cambridge: Harvard University Press.

Greco, C. (1983). *Heritage language education in Calgary: An examination of its current status, 1982-83*. Edmonton: Cultural Heritage Branch, Alberta Culture.

Hansen, M. L. (1962). *The Third Generation in America*. Commentary, 14: 496.

Isajiw, W. W. and T, Makabe. (1982). *Socialization as a factor in ethnic retention*. Research Paper No. 134. Toronto: University of Toronto.

Joy, R. T. (1972). *Language in conflict*. Toronto: McClelland and Stewart.

Klapp, O. E. (1975). Opening and Closing in Open Systems. *Behavioral science*, 20: 251-257.

Lai, D. C.Y. (1988) *Chinatown: Towns Within Cities in Canada*. Vancouver: University of British Columbia Press.

Lan, K. S.K. (1992). Cultural Identity: A Case Study of the Chinese Heritage Language Schools in Calgary. Unpublished doctoral dissertation, The University of Calgary.

Lan, K. and J.W. Friesen. (1991). Settlement Patterns in the Calgary Chinese Community. *Multicultural Education Journal*, 9(2), 13-23.

Lewin, K. (1948). *Resolving social conflicts: selected papers on group dynamics*. New York: Harper and Brothers.

Lyman, S. (1974). *Chinese Americans*. New York: Random House.

Nahirny, V. C. and J. A. Fishman. (1965). American Immigrant Groups: Ethnic Identification and the Problem of Generations. *Sociological review,* 13: 311-326.

Newman, W. M. (1973). *American pluralism: A study of minority groups and social theory.* New York: Harper and Row.

Radecki, H. (1976). Ethnic Voluntary Organizational Dynamics in Canada: A Report. *International Journal of Comparative Sociology,* 17: 275-284.

Reitz, J. G. (1980). *The survival of ethnic groups.* Toronto: McGraw-Hill Ryerson.

Vallee, F. G. (1969). Regionalism and Ethnicity: The French-Canadian Case. *Perspectives on regions and regionalism.* B. Y. Card, ed. Edmonton: University of Alberta, 19-25.

10

The Sikh Community:

A Case Study of Cultural Persistence

Unlike most ethnocultural groups in Canada, the Sikh community has remained virtually unaffected by the traditional campaign for assimilation waged by the dominant society. Following Gordon's delineation of the seven stages towards attaining complete assimilation, Sikhs have essentially remained independent of even the first stage which suggests that members of an immigrant group have "changed their cultural patterns (including religious belief and observance) to that of dominant society" (Gordon, 1964, 70).

There are probably two reasons for this, one having to do with the success of the Sikh community in trying to maintain their own subcultural identity, and the second being dominant society's very strong opposition to Sikh ways. Some observers assume that racial and cultural acceptance may be attributed to different degrees of assimilation or inadequate socialization into the value system of the host society. Thus success or failure of a particular racial or cultural group to become assimilated is attributed to differences inherent in their transplanted cultural values (Bolaria, 1983, 160). This is definitely not the case with the Sikh community. In the first instance, Sikhs (and other Canadian immigrants from the Punjabi) have a strong link with the land of their origins. Much of their motivation towards maintaining cultural boundaries may be related to a "homeland concern" (Glazer, 1980) which focuses their attention on the Punjab and rallies their energies towards gaining its independence from the rest of India (Johnston, 1988). At the same time they also function with the framework of a very strong cultural subsystem which requires little sustenance from the dominant society.

Foremost in the campaign to thwart Sikh assimilation is public antagonism towards the Sikh "uniform," particularly the practice that loyal Sikhs are not to cut their hair (Kesh) and they are required to carry a ceremonial sword (Kirpan). Growing long hair (including beards) necessitates the wearing of headgear like the turban which was long ago adopted by the Sikhs as a means of keeping their hair in place. A great public outcry was evidenced in Canada a few years ago when the Supreme Court of Canada handed down the decision that Sikhs would be permitted to wear their form of headgear as an approved part of the uniform of the Royal Canadian Mounted Police. A similar campaign was launched against younger Sikhs who wore small versions of the ceremonial sword to school. Opponents decried the kirpan as a dangerous weapon and demanded that it be banished from classrooms and school grounds.

It is difficult to understand why the Sikhs have had to be targets of such severe forms of public disapproval when it is primarily a question of differences in costume that sets them apart from the rest of society. For the most part, Sikhs live much like other Canadians. They are employed in traditional Canadian forms of business enterprises and in the workplace. They have good market values and work hard for their livelihood. They live in standard-type homes, engage in regular forms of socializing and, like other Canadians, attend the church of their choice. Sikh temples look very little different from church buildings constructed by other faiths, and they tend to be very well maintained. Sikh organizations have contributed heavily towards Canadian national relief causes including Steve Fonyo's Miles for Millions, the Mexico Earthquake Relief, the Ethiopian Relief Fund, and the Interfaith Food bank, to name a few. Still, in a survey conducted among Sikhs in Vancouver in 1980, 52 percent said that they had virtually no contact with other Canadians and only 10 percent said they had a lot (Johnston, 1988). The evidence is clear that Sikhs are often targets of a form of racism which is virtually without any justifiable foundation. It also tends to enlarge their social distance from other Canadians. The Canadian lack of acceptance of Sikhs originates from personal insecurity, jealousy and intolerance on the part of their critics. In Canada, it seems, we are not yet free of the notion that human differences (even in costume) are always to be feared.

Sikh Origins

Essentially Sikhs are members of the culture of India. Religiously, their heritage combines both Hindu and Muslim beliefs, even though most Sikhs would object to the idea of their predecessors having deliberately tried to reconcile elements of the two world religions. Sikhism does hold common principles with both of its parent faiths, but there are also elements of both Hinduism and Islam which they reject.

The primary objections to Hinduism include belief in the caste system which, Sikhs say, projects the notion that some people are better than others. Historically, at least, Hindus believed that humans could be categorized as to their importance in the world, and members of the Brahmin class were superior to all others. At the bottom of the various levels of the system were the outcastes or untouchables. At the time of Sikh beginnings, in the early stages of the sixteenth century, about one-sixth of India's population were untouchables. A central belief of Sikh philosophy is that all religions are good, with the exception of those which regard one person as more important than another (G. Singh, 1992, 7).

It was the third Sikh leader (guru) who abolished the Hindu practice of requiring women to wear a veil in public (Purdah), and the practice of Sati which involved the self-immolation by women upon the death of their husbands. From that time on Sikhs regarded women as equal with men and were to be treated accordingly.

Relations between Hindus and Muslims in the sixteenth century were not cordial. The Muslims, in areas in which they dominated, addressed the Hindus as non-believers, and did not allow them to have access to the same opportunities as their own people. In fact, Muslims considered it a sacred act to harass and mistreat Hindus, even if by force. The Hindus, in turn, called Muslims foreigners. Into this dualism of belief systems, Guru Nanak, the originator of Sikhism, came with his message.

The Ten Gurus

When the first guru began his work he had no intention of beginning a new religion, even though he was bothered by the nuances of both Hinduism and Islam. His meetings with his followers comprised an informal fellowship of believers. These meetings gradually developed a more formal structure as the decades unfolded. Religious persecution eventually influenced a more fervent stance on the part of the membership and spurred on the formation of a militant Indian freedom movement. Although today's Sikhs see themselves purely as a religious body, they have a history of militancy which reached its full fruition at the time of their tenth and last leader (guru). Most orthodox Sikhs today try to distance themselves from acts of political extremism and violence.

Guru Nanka began the Sikh system premised on a single belief – that there is one God only. He questioned the idea of there being two Gods – one, Ram, for the Hindus and another, Allah, for the Muslims, and argued that no one should be called a nonbeliever just because he or she calls God by a different name. It was this observation, accompanied by practices which some officials conceived of as heresy, that launched the birth of the new religion known as Sikhism.

Guru Nanak was born on April 15, 1469. His father, Kalyan Chand (sometimes shortened by his biographers to "Kala"), was the revenue official for the village of Chukarkana. The family priest, who came to cast the child's horoscope, told Kala that his son would "sit under canopy, and both Hindus and Turks would pay him reverence" (H. Singh, 1983, 13). As a child, therefore, Nanak, was in favor with his neighbors, and found friends among both Hindus and Muslims. In school, at the age of seven, he surprised his teacher by writing a poem in Punjabi with the main thought, "who is truly learned?" At the age of eleven he was given the sacrificial cord which signified that he belonged to a high caste, and an appropriate ceremony was observed.

When Nanak was 27 years old, he heard the call of God. He travelled to the four corners of India and beyond, and visited the sacred places of the Hindus, Muslims and Buddhists. After holding discussions with men and women of various nations, religions and creeds, he publicly denounced the caste system and the futility of idol worship. When his ideas had incubated for twenty-four years he began to proclaim that mutual regard and respect among all peoples were the only foundation for a true religion. For him, religious pluralism was a fact of life (Neufeldt, 1987, 269). The right to life, the right to equality and the right to worship are God-given gifts to all (G. Singh, 1992, 8). The simple principles which he elaborated and which he adjured his followers to adhere to included:

1. practice love, not hollow rituals;
2. deeds alone are valued, not empty words;
3. live honestly;
4. physical renunciation is of no value; and,
5. service is the only form of true worship.

When his gospel became formalized, Guru Nanak established congregations wherever he went. A congregation (Sangat) was a formalized worship centre where singing and preaching occurred. One person was appointed to take charge of the service. These meetings were sponsored so that everyone, regardless of caste or former religious allegiance could worship together. He also initiated the practice of "Pangat" which involved the sitting together of all worshippers in a common meal. This practice continues in Sikh congregations to this day.

After visiting the high places of religion in Indian and Arabian countries, Guru Nanak spent about 18 years in a small village named Kartarpur (now in Pakistan) which he built with the help of his father-in-law and his disciples. He was revered by his followers, Muslim and Hindu alike. Before he passed away he appointed Bhai Lehna as the second Guru and re-named him Guru Angad Dev.

The *second* guru, Angad Dev (1504-1552), was the son of a shopkeeper. After hearing Guru Nanak preach he knew he had found what he wanted to do with the rest of his life. In 1532 he handed the reins of his business over to his nephew and made him head of the family. He moved to Karparpur so he could study the faith in more depth. After seven years of study he was named the second Guru and relocated to his home area at Khadur Sahib to establish a Sikh centre there. One of his major contributions was to develop and teach the Gurmukhi script in which the hymns of the faith were written. This was the beginning of the religious literature of the Sikhs. He also developed the free community kitchen, started by his predecessor, and insisted that food be furnished free of charge to all who came to worship, regardless of their caste, class or color – rich and poor alike. Through the work of Guru Angad, Sikhism became a populist movement. *Before his death he named Baba Amar Das, then aged 72, and about 25 years older than himself, to be his successor.*

The *third* guru, Guru Amardas (1479-1574), was appointed to his role at an older age and served for only twelve years. During that time, however, he added structure to the Sikh movement by establishing twenty-two preaching centres called "Manjis," assigning men or women to head them. In one instance a husband and wife team headed a Manjis (G. Singh, 1992, 9). He introduced a series of reforms in keeping with the growing crescendo of the Sikh movement, particularly elevating the position of women to equality with males. He established the concept of the common well with steps leading to the bottom of the well. He then welcomed everyone to use the water as a means of emphasizing that the equality of all those engaging in the simple act of getting water. He made Pangat (the common meal) a requirement for assembly, insisting that unless people eat together they do not bond spiritually. It was his vision that the untouchable class could not be abolished except through some direct and visible (and compulsory) means. Some high caste believers, including the emperor, objected to forced integration at worship and decided to harass the guru. After listening to the logic of his reforms, however, the emperor became convinced of the guru's wisdom and changed his ways. He then offered to allocate state funds to help finance the costs of the community kitchen but the guru refused. He believed that voluntary contributions alone should fund the service (G. Singh, 1992, 10).

Amardas' reforms effected major changes in Indian culture. Before his death he obtained a piece of land on which he envisaged the establishment of a headquarters for the Sikh movement with a temple for worship located in the centre of a pool. The temple was to be a place where God's virtues were to be preached and sung. Before his death he completed plans for the Golden Temple at Amritsar, as it is now known and named a successor, Guru Ramdas.

The *fourth* guru, Guru Ramdas (1534-1581), oversaw the establishment of the foundation of the Golden Temple at Amritsar (which means pool of Nector) in 1577, just three years after he took office. His ministry was basically taken up with the construction of the temple which was completed through volunteer labor. He also supervised the construction of nearby dwellings, which at first were built of clay and later of bricks. He envisaged that a great pool would be dug around the temple to demonstrate an openness to all people. Before his death he named his son, Arjan, as successor.

The *fifth* guru, Guru Arjan (1563-1606), saw the completion of the Golden Temple. The foundation stone of the Harimandar, the sanctum sanatorium in the centre of the pool, was laid in 1589. The temple itself was built with four doors, facing in the four directions to signify that people from all parts of the world were welcome to come and worship. As the work neared completion a famine occurred in the region and an epidemic of smallpox broke out. The guru turned his attention to caring for the sick, touring surrounding areas and offering words of encouragement and hope. When the pool around the temple ran low, volunteers dug a canal to the nearby river, Ravi, to assure a constant supply.

In summing up Guru Arjan's contributions one would have to include the completion of the temple as a central place of worship, and the assembly and formalization of the Sikh scriptures. These include the writings of holy men from all over India, including Muslim and Hindu writings, plus those of previous gurus. He was careful to include writings from individuals representing all castes as well. The criterion for including a work was simply that it seemed to be from God. The guru accepted all prevailing names for God as equally valid, and promoted the idea that all languages were valid in offering praise to God.

Guru Arjan became the first martyr of the Sikhs, and his death marked a turning point for the movement. He was tortured to death by orders of the Muslim emperor, Jahangir, on May 30, 1606, and was succeeded by his son.

The *sixth* guru, Guru Hargobind (1595-1644), led his people in a martial turn after the death of his father. Though his followers were pacifists, he began to advocate the idea that they had stand against injustice and tyranny, even if it involved military action. He took it upon himself to wear two swords which were regarded as symbols of spiritual as well as temporal vestiture. Though he did not advocate violence, he did signal the state rulers that the Sikhs would defend themselves if unjustly attacked.

The Sikh movement continued to expand with the death of Guru Arjan, and the military emphasis seemed provide an element of security in the minds of the adherents. The Muslim leader, Emperor Jahangir, had the guru arrested and placed in Gwalior, far away from the Punjab. A mass appeal to the emperor motivated him to grant release to the guru, but Hargobind refused to leave his prison unless some 52 princes, who were incarcerated with him, were also granted their freedom. The emperor recanted, and let the guru and the princes go; then he subtly arranged for an attack on the guru but the Sikh forces ably defended the life of their leader.

Guru Hargobind never returned to Amritsar after his arrest and neither did any of his four successors. Instead, he established a centre at Kiratpur, a long distance from the Muslim areas of influence, and near the Himalayas. Before his death in 1644 he appointed his grandson, Har Rai, to be his successor.

Guru Har Rai (1630-1661), was the *seventh* guru and became known as the tender-hearted guru (Pashaura Singh, n.d., 2). Although he never fought in any battles, he kept a force of 2 000 horsemen at his disposal. During his ministry the throne of Delhi was taken by Aurangzeb, who in an effort to show his military strength, executed his own brothers, arrested his father, and then turned on the various religious movements (G. Singh, 1992, 15). He began terrorizing the Sikhs in Punjab and ordered many tortures and killings. Finally, he sent for the guru, but Har Rai mistrusted Aurangzeb and instead sent his son, Ram Rai, to see the emperor. Apparently the two gained an element of rapport between them to the extent that his father, Guru Har Rai, thought that his son, Ram Rai, had misrepresented the Sikh teachings. He thus excommunicated his son and forbad his disciples to have anything to do with him. Before his death, Guru Har Rai appointed his younger son, Harkrishan to be his successor. Thus the emperor's plan to discredit Sikhism failed. (G. Singh, 1992, 1). Later on, however, Ram Rai, became the leader of a smaller sect of the Sikhs.

Guru Harkrishan (1656-1664), became the *eighth* guru, even though he was only five years old at the time. When he heard of the appointment, Emperor Aurangzeb invited the new guru to Delhi. His plan was to make the visit look like the guru was submitting to the emperor. The emperor's messenger, however, was a devoted Sikh, and intervened. Though the guru was only a young child he was made to understand the nature of the proposed visit and he acted accordingly. When he arrived at the quarters assigned him by the emperor, the guru refused to go to the palace. The emperor was naturally miffed by the refusal, but he tried to act as though nothing unusual had happened. He stated publicly that the guru, who was only a child, had come to the palace to play with his son. He then sent his son to meet the guru.

A smallpox epidemic took the life of the young guru, but on his sick-bed he uttered words which were interpreted to mean that he was appointing his grandfather's brother, Teg Bahadur, as the next leader. This appointment was delayed to frustrate Emperor Aurangzeb, and though the emperor tried to thrust Ram Rai upon the Sikhs as their next leader, the people failed to respond. In addition, several relatives of the guru tried to draw attention to themselves in such a way as to be construed as successor of Harkrishan. When their campaigns failed, Guru Teg Bahadur, took office and rallied the people. An attempted assassination on his life failed.

The *ninth* guru, Teg Bahadur (1621-1675), faced the difficult task of keeping a hostile national government at bay. He toured the eastern regions of the Indian subcontinent and preached a gospel of reconciliation. He settled his headquarters at Anandpur Sahib, married and had one son. When he heard about the emperor's campaign to convert Hindus to Islam he sent a message to the emperor suggesting that the latter concentrate on converting the leaders and the people would follow. In the meantime a delegation of Hindus approached the guru and asked for his protection against the emperor. They pointed out that their people had previously received such protection at the hands of the sixth guru and asked him to perpetuate that practice. He encouraged the people to stand firm in their faith and never to give up hope. In the meantime the emperor grew angry about the guru's suggestion about converting leaders instead of followers and ordered the arrest of the guru.

The martyrdom of Guru Teg Bahadur in 1675 was staged by the emperor as a public display of his own importance. He ordered the beheading of the guru, an event which was watched by thousands of the citizens of Delhi. Many of the guru's followers were commanded to renounce their faith and when they refused to do so, they were tortured to death. The years that followed caused a wave of intense disappointment and frustration in the Sikh community which was relieved only by the eventual defeat and death of Emperor Aurangzeb in 1707.

The *tenth and last* guru, Gobind Singh (1666-1708), was only nine years old when his father died, and he was delegated to assume the responsibilities of that office. The future of the Sikh movement was uncertain after the death of the emperor, and no one knew what the attitude of his successor might be. Some of the new guru's followers were given training in self-protection and they looked to the guru for direction against almost inevitable persecution. The guru spoke: "when all peaceful methods fail to change the mind of the wicked, it is justified to pick up the sword to save one's own honor" (G. Singh, 1992, 18).

Perhaps it was the fearless and resolving tone of the guru's words that deflected confrontation, and the guru went about his ministry among the common people. He engaged the services of 50 scholars to translate Sikh classical literature into Punjabi for the benefit of his followers.

In 1704, Anandpur Sahib was surrounded by the joint forces of the Delhi emperor, the enemy rajas and the governors of Lahore and Sirhind. After several months of failure the leaders asked the guru to leave the town and preach elsewhere. He was promised safe passage and his captors hoped that if he left they could claim at least a moral victory by it. When the guru and his men left they were attacked by the combined forces but they managed to escape. The guru placed his ceremonial plume on one of his followers who was then killed by the enemy. Thus the enemy thought they had killed the guru who really escaped (G. Singh, 1992, 21). The guru's two older sons, Ajit Singh and Jujhar Singh, and thirty Sikh soldiers were also killed. The guru's wife and two younger sons were caught by the enemy and brought to Sirhind where efforts were made to convert the two children. When these efforts failed the boys were put to death.

Eventually Emperor Aurangzeb discovered that Guru Singh had escaped. The guru sent the emperor a letter pointing out that the emperor's actions would eventually be punished, and the Sikh faith would never be stamped out. Aurangzeb apologized for his actions, but he died before he had opportunity to meet with the guru. After his death his sons fought over the throne, and the guru sided with the oldest son, Bahadur Shah, and provided him with military aid. He subsequently became the Emperor of India. The new emperor promised to punish those who had previously sought to kill the guru and eradicate Sikhism, but he failed to keep his promise. The guru therefore assigned a man named Banda Singh Bahabur to go to Punjab and punish the guilty parties. Shortly after his departure for Punjab, the guru was fatally attacked by assassins. In the meantime, having installed the holy scriptures as the official source of leadership and inspiration, there was no concern about naming a successor. He bequeathed his office to his followers in a public ceremony and named his corporate successors, Guru Khalsa Panth. The believers were now the gurus of the Sikh faith. Some observers have called this the most significant development in all of Sikh history (P. Singh, n.d., 3).

The People As Guru

Before Guru Gobind Singh died he designed and presided over a formal transfer ceremony of power from the guruship directly to his people. In 1699, at a gathering called for that purpose, he asked for a faithful volunteer to give his head for the cause, and when an individual came forward, the guru took him to a tent and returned a little later with a blood-stained sword. Many of his congregation, assuming the worst, and fearing that the guru had gone mad, fled from the scene. Without telling his people that the blood was from a slaughtered goat, and as a further test of faith, the guru asked for another volunteer and then for three more. When the fifth one had served his purpose, all five were returned alive to the people (G. Singh, 1990, 286). The guru then prepared a special drink called "Amrit," and the five were asked to participate in a show of consensus and equality. The five volunteers were named, "the five beloved ones," and were given the last name of Singh. After that all present were asked to drink the Amrit and become one with the movement and with one another. Amrit is a drink of water sweetened with sugar and blessed by stirring it with the double-edged sword. Its enactment is parallel to baptism in other religions. From that time, all formal baptized members of the Sikh faith took the last name of Singh. They agreed to abandon their previous religion and the practice of all rituals and to denounce the caste system. They have henceforth been known as Khalsa or Panth. Every Sikh has the authority to bring in new initiates by serving and presiding over their participation in Amrit.

The Five Symbols

The transfer of the office of guru to the people included a corollary requirement, namely that of the "uniform of the believer," which consists of the five "K's." Few forms of religious attire have caused as much controversy in North America. The five symbols include:

1. *Kesh* or uncut hair, represents simplicity of life, saintliness, wisdom and devotion to God. It is practiced as a symbol of purity.
2. *Kanga,* is a wooden comb designed to keep the hair tidy. This was initiated in opposition to the recluses who allowed their hair to become matted as defiance to the world. Use of the comb also implies physical and mental cleanliness. The old (hair) is weeded out and replaced with the new.

Spiritually, this means that the believer needs constantly to comb one's mind inwardly and keep it free from impurities.

3. *Kara,* is a steel bracelet which is a symbol of belonging to the Guru. It is an ethical symbol of responsibility. It acts as a handcuff to remind the believer not to misuse the hands to commit sin;

4. *Kirpan,* is the sword of knowledge and to wear it is to signify that the individual has used it to curb the root of personal ego. The sword also represents the Sovereign power of God who controls the destiny of the whole world. It is a symbol of self-respect and honor.

5. *Kachh,* is white underwear consisting of short breeches, a symbol of purity in morality, and a check against extra-marital relations (Sikh Community of Calgary, 1986).

For a century after the death of Guru Gobind Singh, the Sikhs suffered persecution from the new Indian rulers, the Mughals. At the end of the 18th century the Sikhs succeeded in establishing rule in the Punjab and began a campaign to unify the country. Maharja Ranjit Singh (1780-1839), served as the Sikh sovereign and presided over part of a forty year Sikh reign which ended with the Anglo-Sikh War of 1848-1849.

In the beginning of the 20th century Sikhs started to migrate to other parts of the world including Canada and the United States and the United Kingdom. Today there are 200 000 Sikhs in Canada.

Principles of the Sikh Faith

While many religions have at their basis a theological speculation about creation, the Sikhs have no such interpretation. The commandments of their faith are practical, and target a down-to-earth application.

Primary to being a faithful Sikh is trying to earn a livelihood through hard labor and honest means. No Sikh should be a parasite on society, and they should seek to be gainfully employed. Those who do not work obviously rely on others to feed them, and this is not acceptable. Above all, whatever kind of vocation is assumed, the underlying principle is that wages be earned through honest means, and not through exploitation or deception.

Second, Sikhs are to keep in touch with the Divine. This is primarily done through attitude and meditation. A worshipful stance implies a constant awareness that God is both Creator and companion. He provides guidance to those who seek Him. It is also a form of worship. In one's search for spiritual growth it is possible to discover the will of God for one's life. Since all of life and, in fact, the whole world is in God's hands, it behooves believers to discover the truths that pertain to their own personal journey and thus fulfill the will of God for them. In short, individuals are the executors of His will.

Meditation is not accomplished through any specific technique, and a variety of means are quite effective – reciting the scriptures. singing, sitting in a quiet place or simply thinking about one's relationship to God. Meditation, therefore, is not an art, but an attitude.

Third, is the guru's order to assume responsibility for others. This begins with wishing others well and continues to the logical projection of being willing to give one's life for the sake of others. Sikhs are to regard all people as equals. They are expected to share their homes and their food with those in need. They are to help the wounded in battle, regardless of their military affiliation.

Sikhs are commanded to share with others on the grounds that all human beings are members of a greater family. This family includes all races, religions and nations. Sharing the fruits of one's labor is a responsibility and must not be done through pride or as a means of drawing attention to oneself. To provide for others, particularly those with less means, is a "family" responsibility in the same way that a parents takes care of a young child. This implies the kinship of all people.

Fourth, is the command to moral living. Married Sikhs are to be faithful to their partners and not commit adultery. In addition, moral living has application to other facets of living as well; Sikhs are forbidden to lie, steal, cheat, or criticize others unjustly. They are not allowed to smoke, drink or use intoxicating drugs. There is some debate about meat-eating among orthodox Sikhs. Some suggest that Sikhs should be strict vegetarians and even avoid eggs. Sikhs who avoid beef but eat other meat are often influenced by the Hindu reverence for the cow. Those who do eat meat, however, usually obey the command not to partake of "Kutha" meat, that is, meat which has been slaughtered by involving Muslim religious rituals. The Muslims call the meat, "Halal" (G. Singh, 1992, 33).

Fifth and finally, Sikhs are to avoid the worship of idols or pictures and they are to be knowledgeable of the Sikh scriptures (Guru Granth Sahib). The formal regulations regarding the scriptures are as follows. First, during the day the scriptures are kept at the altar of the temple under a canopy. Before they are read, a whisk (or wand) is waved over the scriptures as an expression of respect for royalty or divinity. The temple priest is to keep the scriptures in a separate room during the night. Early in the morning the priest will remove the scriptures from the separate room and install the book under the canopy. There he will wave the whisk and arbitrarily leaf through the book in an attempt to identify a scriptural thought for the day. The passage of scripture on which he places his finger becomes his spiritual thought for the day. He will use the idea contained therein to guide his behaviors throughout the day.

There are times in the year when the scriptures are read aloud in entirety and in a continuous fashion. Individual members of the congregation will take turns in reading for a few hours at a time and will be relieved by other volunteers throughout the day.

Baptized Sikhs may choose to keep a copy of the scriptures or a portion of the scriptures in their homes. If they do so, the same rules apply. The scriptures are to be housed in a separate room (a closet will do) and they are to be put away at the end of the day and consulted early in the morning for a spiritual thought. The daily recitation of a passage of scripture will offer a spiritual context to one's thoughts and actions and remind the believer to avoid forbidden and undesirable behaviors.

When Sikhs enter the temple they take off their shoes and wear a headcovering. They show reverence to the scriptures by kneeling before the canopy under which the scriptures are located and bowing their heads to the ground. Then they take their place in the congregation. Non-Sikhs are always welcome to worship services in the temple which consist of readings and singing the hymns from the scriptures. The service is always followed by a common meal to which all are invited.

Sikhs Today

The world population of Sikhs is about 15 million. Most Sikhs (about 14 million), live in the Punjab, a province of India, and they comprise about two percent of the country's population. The Canadian population is about 200 000, and almost half of them live in British Columbia. Vancouver itself is home to about 30 000 Punjabis including Sikhs. About 8 000 Sikhs make their home in Calgary.

The first group of Sikhs came to Canada in 1897 and by 1907 a total of 2 600 had made their home in Canada. The first immigrants worked in lumber mills and on roads. Later, as they grew accustomed to Canadian ways, they made inroads into other sectors of the business world.

Internal Divisions

Like most other religious communities, Sikh have many subdivisions among them. Perhaps the most publicized division is between baptized (Khalsa) and non-baptized Sikhs (McLeod, 1989). For the Khalsa, there is only one interpretation. While they tolerate and respect other religions, their patience is thin when it comes to distinguishing among their own numbers. They vehemently take issue with the statement that whereas all Khalsa are Sikhs, not all Sikhs are Khalsa. But there *are* many other Sikh sects, like the Udasi, for example, who are the followers of the elder son of Guru Nanak, Sri Chand. This group controlled the Sikh shrines and temples in the Punjab until the 1920s (Jain, 1990).

Baptized Sikhs say that they are under obligation to wear the five "K's," but their unbaptized colleagues proffer a number of arguments to the contrary. They claim that the wearing of the five "K's" was a temporary commandment of the tenth guru, and it is no longer applicable today. Others claim that conformity to any kind of external form of appearance would be contrary to the teachings of the gurus. After all, religiosity or piousness is not measured by such temporal means. Spirituality is a condition of the heart. Still others point out that the first guru, Guru Nanak, himself questioned the usefulness of particular outward appearance from the conviction that one does not become a better person through external garb (Jain, 1990).

Towards a New Nationalism

A more serious challenge to the Sikh community than identifying or settling differences has to do with the emergence of a Sikh nationalist movement in India. The current plan of this group is to gain a separate homeland in India, known as the Khalistan. At the centre of attention is the Province of Punjab, which is divided between India and Pakistan, and a target of hostilities for more than two decades. Prime Minister Indira Gandhi made no attempt to alleviate Sikh frustrations towards obtaining a separate national identity, and instead introduced a number of economic restrictions to the Punjab in an attempt to steer investments to poorer states (Koehn, 1991). She then ordered the destruction of the Golden Temple and justified the order on the basis that it was the only option left for her to get rid of the terrorist element in the Punjab. On June 5, 1984 the Golden Temple was attacked and by the next day 554 Sikh warriors lay dead and 121 wounded by Indian forces. The army casualties numbered 92 and 300 wounded. In addition the army captured 1592 prisoners from the temple and 3 000 others from neighboring communities in the Punjab. Naval divers were employed to recover arms and dead bodies from the sacred tank, and many priceless paintings were destroyed (G. Singh, 1990, 762-763). Since the Golden Temple represents the fountainhead of the Sikh faith (Anklesaria, 1984), its being damaged spurred efforts towards achieving the development of a separate Sikh state.

Reaction of Sikhs around the world towards the destruction of the temple was one of shock and horror. Interestingly, although 10-12 percent of the Indian army were Sikhs, most of them remained faithful to the army. However, on October 31, 1984, Prime Minister Indira Gandhi was assassinated by two of her trusted Sikh bodyguards. In December of the same year, new elections were held (except in the Punjab), and Gandhi's son Rajiv was elected prime minister. After he was elected he made the situation in the Punjab a priority item and withdrew his troops in an effort to restore peace.

Since the destruction of the temple, the violent act of the state against the sacred temple has served to unify the various factions of Sikhism in the Punjab into a form of ethnic solidarity. They have also served to mobilize nationalistic dreams towards a conception of reality. Sikh patriots are now trying to mobilize against the congress of India as well as to impact their economic oppressors (Koehn, 1991). In the meantime, life in the Punjab goes on at a relatively healthy pace. The annual agricultural output has been increasing, and the Punjab per capita income is the highest in India. The province continues to provide 60-65 percent of the wheat production of the country as well as vast crops of rice. Sikh leaders say that they hope the day will come when the Punjab will separate politics from religion so that the gospel of the gurus can flourish. Perhaps when this occurs full attention can be paid to the economic distress of the underprivileged sections of society. That would be a fitting tribute to the original teachings of the gurus (G. Singh, 1990, 787).

The Canadian Experience

Sikhs in Canada are active in carving out a niche for themselves in the various sectors of society. Many operate successful businesses and their cultural organizations are thriving. New temples are being constructed and several heritage language schools (which teach the Punjabi language) are thriving. Sikhs are also entering the political scene and gaining a foothold in other areas as well. In the meantime, the Sikh community is also very much under the watchful eye of the media and the Canadian Intelligence Service. The publicity surrounding the Air India disaster in June, 1985 and the shooting of a Punjabi cabinet minister who was attending a family wedding on Vancouver Island in May, 1986 and other recent events have hurt the image of the Sikhs (Johnston, 1988).

Like other religious or ethnic communities, the Sikhs have their share of internal disagreements. A series of articles in a 1992 issue of the *World Sikh journal* are concerned with a misrepresentation of Sikh beliefs in a doctoral dissertation written by S. Pashaura Singh at the University of Toronto. Singh, a former temple priest in Calgary, wrote a thesis entitled, The "Text and Meaning of Adi Granth," which consisted of an analysis of two documents which, according to some Sikh scholars, have dubious origins (Mann, 1992, 29). Having read the manuscript, members of the national Shiromani Gurdwara Parbandhak Committee, which is dedicated to promoting Sikh scholarship, have demanded that Pashaura Singh appear before them in a hearing to defend his work. However, another writer in the same issue of the *World Sikh Journal* commendably notes that Singh is probably a well intentioned man, dedicated to defining Sikh roots. Thus the Sikh community should not seek to make an example of him: "Let this matter not become like the Salman Rushdie [affair] for that does not become us" (I. J. Singh, 1992).

On the positive side are developments in the Punjab. These happenings serve as a special source of inspiration for the Sikhs – the provision of a revered symbol (Koehn, 1991). While this contributes toward a stronger Sikh identity, it also perpetuates the uniqueness and separateness of Sikhism in Canada. Any adversity faced by the Sikhs in Canada will bolster that reality and serve to illustrate one of the polarities of Canadian multiculturalism, that of being separate but (hopefully) equal.

References

Anklesaria, Shahnaz. (1984). Fall-out of army action: A field report. *Economic and Political Weekly*, 19:30, 1186-1188.

Bolaria, B. Singh. (1983). *Racial minorities in multicultural Canada*. Toronto: Garamond.

Glazer, Nathan. (1980). Toward a sociology of small ethnic groups, A discourse and discussion. *Canadian Ethnic Studies*, XII:2, 1-16.

Gordon, Milton M. (1964). *Assimilation in American life: The role of race, religion, and national origins*. New York: Oxford University Press.

Jain, Sushil. (1990). Sikh or Kahlsa? *Canadian Ethnic Studies*, XXII:2, 111-116.

Johnston, Hugh. (1988). The Development of the Punjabi community in Vancouver since 1961. *Canadian Ethnic Studies*, XX:2, 1-19.

Koehn, Sharon D. (1991). Ethnic emergence and modernization: The Sikh Case. *Canadian Ethnic Studies*, XXIII:2, 95-116.

Mann, Kharak Singh. (1992). GNDU manuscript 1245: A post 1606 collection. *World Sikh Journal*, 12, fall/winter, 29-34.

McLeod, H. (1989). *Who is a Sikh: The problem of Sikh identity*. Oxford: Clarendon.

Neufeldt, R.W. (1987). The Sikh response. *Modern Indian responses to religious pluralism*. Harold Coward, ed. Albany, N.Y.: State University of New York Press, 269-290.

Sikh Community of Calgary. (1986). Sikhs in the Canadian Mosaic. Unpublished Paper. Calgary: Sikh Community of Calgary.

Singh, Gopal. (1990). *A history of the Sikh people, 1469-1988*. New Delhi, India: World Book Centre.

Singh, Gurbakhsh. (1992). *The Sikh faith*. Vancouver: Canadian Sikh Study and Teaching Society.

Singh, Harbans. (1983). *The heritage of the Sikhs*. New Delhi, India: South Asia Books.

Singh, I. J. (1992). The test and meaning of the Adi Granth. *World Sikh Journal*, 12, fall/winter, 8-9.

Singh, Pashaura Bhai. (n.d.). *The Sikhs*. Calgary: Guru Nanak Center, Sikh Society.

11

Postscript: Expanding Multiculturalism

"Every individual has a place to fill in this world, and is important in some respect, whether he[she] chooses to be or not."

Nathaniel Hawthorne

Multicultural developments in Canada have extensive political, sociological and educational implications. In practical terms, however, educators probably function more directly on the firing line than other professions simply because they have to work in the personal arena which frequently features a variety of forms of human interaction such as conflict, tolerance, acceptance, understanding, etc.

The first school activities designed to promote multicultural understanding featured food displays, musical festivals, films and even field trips. Gradually, universities became involved in the enterprise and now many teacher-training faculties offer courses and even degrees in the field, particularly in Native studies. Some university-related centres have produced curriculum materials, published journals and produced other useful resources for multicultural practitioners.

Possibly the most significant multicultural development in recent years has been the increased availability of funding. Monies have become available from government as well as from private sources, and this has assisted greatly in helping to enhance public awareness of and support for multiculturalism in the wider sphere. Even though multiculturalism is a relatively young academic discipline, it is apparent that its growth has evolved through a very complex series of stages.

One of the most frequently-quoted studies in the 1960s was completed by researchers within the Dakota Indian community on the Pine Ridge Reservation in the United States. Excluding the insights pertaining to local interests, many of the recommendations of the ensuing report are still relevant to contemporary situations. Some of the principles on which the final conclusions of the report are based include:

1. the involvement of Native people in the education of their children;

2. intermingling Native children with those of other backgrounds as a means of promoting truly *intercultural* education; and,

3. utilizing the services of Native experts in course-work having to do with understanding local history and culture.

Emphasizing a wide range of concerns, the Pine Ridge study also made recommendations of a more limited geographic applicability. These include:

1. amending the school day to fit local schedules;

2. inaugurating a systematic home visitation program for teachers;

3. developing a policy of hiring local personnel for school staff positions;

4. instituting a better school bussing system; and

5. restructuring the curriculum to provide for vocational education.

Many of the suggestions made by the researchers were implemented with some success, but in terms of attaining national multicultural success, it is doubtful that this kind of study had significant impact. In the meantime, the literature gradually increased.

A decade ago multicultural education came of age. No longer were studies limited to a single community, for example, Native or Black studies, but encompassed a wider scope of application and ethnicity. Innovations that proved to be at least partially effective during the 1980s included:

1. The use of teacher aides as interpreters in schools where English could be considered a second language;

2. Curriculum emendations to include local history or knowledge of specific cultures present there;

3. Interdisciplinary cooperation when seeking to establish educational needs and foci in ethnic communities;

4. Special courses for teachers planning to work in intercultural situations providing some knowledge of the culture and some instruction in methodologies that might prove to be more effective than conventional approaches;

5. Stressing cultural sensitivity to include both awareness of one's own ethnocentrism as well as seeking to understand and appreciate the nuances of a different perspective;

6. Recognizing the interference factor involved in functioning in culturally different situations, i.e. in a Native community one's task might be to educate for situations that do not exist as opportunities in that locale;

7. Seeking to develop *consistent* educational standards rather than lowering expected levels of skill in literacy on the grounds that a higher level may not be attainable in a particular cultural setting. The problem finds expression when after completing the secondary level of schooling students who wish to avail themselves of higher education opportunities may find that

functioning at a lower academic standard may not have prepared them adequately.

The principles upon which some of the foregoing approaches are based involve a concern wider than merely wanting to "help minorities to function in dominant society." Contemporary curriculum materials have been examined for elements of racism generally, for example, and for misrepresentation of or discrimination against specific groups. The concept of cultural pluralism is envisaged as promoting understanding and appreciation of diversity rather than seeking unanimity in culture and purpose. After all, some ethnic groups may prefer to live differently from the mainstream. Proposals for "urged interactions" are sometimes seen in the context of the hidden agenda of assimilation, based on the notion that interaction with dominant society is a requirement for Canadian living. In some instances it would be difficult for such cultural interactions to occur, especially in the case of geographical isolation where transportation costs would be forbidding or in the case of a Hutterite colony where such interaction might be viewed by the leaders as potentially detrimental to their concern for community endurance. A few proponents of the contemporary "new education" even go so far as to suggest that school curricula be built around a series of universal human concerns that would incorporate and facilitate the learning of humanistic modes of inquiry. Such a suggestion sounds good, but there may be at least a few corners of our pluralistic society where even such a generous approach might not be considered desirable.

Some educators of this decade are not content to work within the confines of "traditional" multiculturalism, which promotes such standby concepts as tolerance, understanding, and acceptance. Instead, they have urged that educators opt for a "stronger" method of seeking to change attitudes in the form of what has come to be called, "anti-racist education." Critics of the approach have sometimes pointed out that use of the phrase "anti" is unfortunate because of its negative connotations. After all, multicultural education represents a positive philosophy and its language and approach should reflect this.

In anti-racist education the emphasis is on confronting situations of racial discrimination when they occur in the learning context. A more direct approach, it is felt, will help students to come to grips with the hurt and frustration experienced by victims of acts of discrimination and this will motivate the students to opt for a more positive form of interaction. This approach is designed to encourage students to experience the good feeling of experiencing people living, working and creating together in a mutually-encouraging atmosphere (Simon, et. al., 1988).

Anti-racist education is a perspective that aims at permeating all subject areas and school practices. It targets the elimination of racism in all forms by equipping teachers and students with the analytic tools to critically examine the origins of racist ideas and practices and to understand the implication of our own race and our own actions in the promotion of, or struggle against racism (Lee, 1985). These exercises enable students to see that racism is learned and can therefore be unlearned. Until this objective is seriously adopted teachers face the challenge of moving students from an uncritical acceptance of the world to a questioning, quickened awareness of their world and the historical, socially-constructed role they play in it (Reed, 1992).

On the positive side, modern multiculturalism is rapidly becoming part of a greater pedagogical think-tank incorporating a broader, even world-wide perspective. Clearly the concerns of multicultural educators are linked with those of educators in every field, particularly those who rally to the emerging themes of peace education, global education, cooperative education and human rights education. Perhaps in this wider context Canadian multiculturalism will have the impact it deserves, thereby contributing significantly towards bringing about "the Canadian dream."

References

Lee, E. (1985). *Letters to Marcia.* Toronto: Cross Cultural Communications Centre.

Reed, Carole Ann. (1992). Children's literature and antiracist education: A language-planning project. *Multicultural Education Journal, 10(2), Fall, 12-19.*

Simon, Roger I, John Brown, Enid Lee & Jon Young. (1988). *Decoding discrimination: A student-based approach to anti-racist education using film.* London, Ontario: Althouse Press.

PRINTED IN CANADA